BORN TO BE BAD

BORN TO BE BAD

Talking to the greatest villains in action cinema

by Timon Singh

BearManor Media

2018

Born To Be Bad: Talking to the greatest villains in action cinema

For information, address:

BearManor Media
P. O. Box 71426
Albany, GA 31708

bearmanormedia.com

Typesetting and layout by John Teehan

Cover illustration by Ben Turner

Published in the USA by BearManor Media

ISBN — 978-1-62933-345-8

*To my parents for introducing me to the world of cinema
and not paying too much attention to what
I was watching.*

*To Helen, who has endured more action B-movies
then any wife should have to.*

Table of Contents

Foreword...xiii

Introduction 1

THE HEAVIES 5

    Sven-Ole Thorsen.. 7

    Benny 'The Jet' Urquidez 27

    Vernon Wells 41

    Derrick O'Connor.. 61

    Bob Wall.. 71

    Paul McCrane 89

    Gus Rethwisch.. 101

    Bill Duke.. 113

    Matthias Hues... 123

    Martin Kove 135

SUPERMAN II 147

    Jack O'Halloran 151

    Sarah Douglas... 167

THE TERRORISTS OF *DIE HARD*........................ 177

    Andreas Wisniewski 183

    Clarence Gilyard Jr. 197

    Dennis Hayden 207

    Al Leong 219

    Hans Buringer and the Rest 233

THE OUTSIDERS 239

    David Patrick Kelly 241

    Andrew Robinson 259

    Jeremy Bulloch 267

    William Atherton 279

    Billy Drago 289

THE FINAL BOSS 299

    David Warner 301

    Paul Freeman 315

    Ronny Cox 327

    William Sadler 343

    Julian Glover 355

    Steven Berkoff 369

    Joaquim de Almeida 381

Image Credits 393

About the Author 399

Acknowledgments 401

Index 403

"I don't play villains, I play very interesting people."
— Alan Rickman

Foreword

by Steven E. de Souza
(screenwriter of *Die Hard,*
The Running Man and *Commando*)

FROM THE DAYS OF SILENT PICTURES, movie villains have been maligned as a breed apart, but in truth, they're not so dissimilar: They pull on their nano-weave CBRN-proof ballistic trousers and jackboots one leg at a time, just like us.

They have ups and downs, good days and bad days, personal and family problems, just like us. Granted, apart from Thanksgiving gatherings, our family problems rarely include parents or siblings determined to kill us, but the main thing villains have in common with us is, *they are the heroes of their own stories,* and they're just trying to get through the day. When we writers knead that nuance into a Villain's clay on paper, on the stage it too often gets scissored out, sacrificed on the altar of Running Time to make way for another CGI sequence. Too many times, all that's left on screen is a moustache-twirling two-dimensional character that's such a paper tiger, the hero's victory seems as anti-triumphant as mounting a safari to hunt a mouse.

Villains can be categorized. Let's start with some definitions. Metaphorically speaking, a dragon the hero must slay is not always a "villain". The burning building in *The Towering Inferno*, the iceberg in *Titanic*, the shark in *Jaws*, these are challenges to overcome, but they lack the key ingredient that makes a villain: Agency. Unlike the previous examples, a villain is a thinking, planning foe, and not only does he or she not need the destructive force of a fire or a frozen sea, a good villain can present no challenge at all for the hero in physical terms – Mr. Glass in *Unbreakable* and Gollum in *Lord of the Rings* come to mind – but in their sheer cunning, long range planning and gift for dissembling, they can have us on

xiv ✝ *Born To Be Bad*

the edge of our seat in fear for our heroes, no matter what strengths they bring to the Octagon.

Next off, there is a lot of confusion about the pecking order of Villainy. For our purposes, a capital "V" Villain is, in gamer terms, the Final Boss. Often a brilliant tactician, a good Villain can kill people with autodial, let alone automatic weapons, and is best saved for a final, fatal encounter with the hero, who will have just finished working his or her way through various underlings. Just before dispatching the Villain, the hero has likely dealt with underling #1, The Heavy, who is the Villain's go-to right hand for all things nefarious. (Note: if the Villain is distant in time or space or has other mischief to deal with besides our hero, the Heavy may occupy much of both the hero's attentions and the spotlight; Darth Vader and Lucius Malfoy are prime examples of a Spotlight Heavy; Steppenwolf, more of a USDA Choice example.)

Before dispatching the Heavy, a hero will have dealt with numerous Henchmen, to wit, underlings with guns; and Minions, underlings with Gmail. Finally, there's what old Hollywood writers used to call the Dog Heavy: Whereas the Villain in a low budget Western got to feast on killing the Sheriff, and the Heavy dined out on whacking the Deputy, in the limited running time of a 65 minute B-Picture, all that was left for the Dog Heavy were scraps, like kicking a dog on the way to rob the bank, or knocking an old lady aside during the escape.

Of course, the best villains soar above these hoary stereotypes. If you've seen the films featuring the rogue's gallery of villains now in your hand, then you know that time and again these talented actors have made us scribblers look good, by breathing life into fully-formed, red-blooded adversaries audiences secretly want to root for.

So, what are you waiting for? If this were a movie, you'd be buying popcorn during the preview. Turn the page, and fall in hate all over again.

– Steven E. de Souza
Los Angeles, January 2018

Introduction

THEY SAY THAT A HERO is only as good as the villain and, for movie fans raised on 1980s action movies, we were spoilt for choice. We had Nazis, sophisticated European thieves ("Who said we were terrorists?"), former soldiers-turned-mercenaries, drug runners, martial arts killers, smugglers with diplomatic immunity, and whatever megalomaniac James Bond was facing down at that time.

Born in 1983, I was raised on a steady diet of classic movies. My parents had their own unique tastes: my mum loved musicals, Doris Day films, classic Ray Harryhausen flicks, and sci-fi; my dad was also a movie fan, but generally forgot all about them the minute the credits rolled.

As such, I was introduced to a wide range of genres – Rogers and Hammerstein classics, Hitchcock thrillers, black and white monster movies from the 1950s, big budget Spielberg blockbusters, and the staple of the decade: action movies. My heroes were Arnold Schwarzenegger, Bruce Lee, Sylvester Stallone, Jackie Chan, Bruce Willis, and Carl Weathers. If there were guns to be fired, henchmen to be punched in the face, and a world to be saved, I was on board.

It was also the era of VHS! My brothers and I would often go to the local video rental shop and look in awe at some of the amazing cover art on display. Of course, at that age, we didn't know the difference between the latest big budget offering and the direct-to-video shlock, but if the box art was gripping, we watched it! Inevitably, we ended up watching plenty of films from Cannon Studios thinking they were big budget studio movies and I was equally entertained by Indiana Jones-rip-off *King Solomon's Mines* (1985) and *American Ninja* (1985) as I was by *Commando* (1985) and *Lethal Weapon* (1987).

While 1980s action cinema may have been a time of shaggy mullets, big biceps and one-liners for the heroes, it was always the villains that stuck in our minds once the credits rolled. Whether they were kidnapping the hero's family, smuggling cocaine, unmarked Bera Bonds or Kruger-rands, or simply attempting world domination – they were always the best part of the film! Better still, they were so diverse! You had evil Russians, Jamaican drug dealing gang-bangers, the Yakuza, and multi-ethnic mercenaries all out to make a quick buck.

The more I thought about the villains, the more I realized there was also a hierarchy to them. After all, the 1980s was the age of macho action men, whose muscles were bigger than their heads. Schwarzenegger, Stallone, Willis, Van Damme and co. needed someone to go toe-to-toe against, and that meant massive, muscular henchman to provide the physical threat. There was also the loyal right-hand man, there to either hack some computer system, torture the hero, or be overly sleazy to the wife/partner/daughter that had been kidnapped. Even more dangerous was the lone wolf psychopath that followed no orders but their own and as such was unpredictable and seemingly impervious to dying.

After them, there was the man at the top: the big boss – the one pulling all the strings. Often played by a former Shakespearean actor eager to get a big, fat Hollywood paycheck, these roles came to embody Hollywood's only acceptable form of xenophobia by personifying evil as a smooth-talking, good-looking, RADA-trained British actor.

Whatever the role, what mattered was the talent and actors such as Vernon Wells (*Commando*, 1985; *Mad Max 2*, 1981), Ronny Cox (*RoboCop*, 1987; *Total Recall*, 1990), David Patrick Kelly (*The Crow*, 1994; *The Warriors*, 1979) and Steven Berkoff (*Beverly Hills Cop*, 1984; *Rambo: First Blood Part II*, 1985) created some of the most memorable bad guys of all time. This book sets out to collect interviews with them about the infamous roles they have played on the silver screen, as well as their experiences making the films, whether they felt it type-cast them at all or if it took their career in directions they could never have imagined and, most importantly, whether bad guys really do have all the fun.

Now, you will inevitably flick through this book and say, "I can't believe (insert actor's name) isn't in here! He/she totally deserves to be in this book!" and you're probably 100% correct. If you're thinking of (insert actor's name) as one of the prominent villainous actors of 1970s, 1980s and 1990s action movies, then you can almost guarantee I reached out to them for an interview. However, for whatever reason, be it scheduling, availability, or personal issues, I was unable to get an interview with them. There were at least two actors who wanted a truckload of money for a 30-minute phone interview, so, naturally, that was impossible. Interestingly, they were two actors that haven't been in a movie for at least a decade, so the idea that they could charge that amount of money was laughable. Speculate away at who they were!

Of course, there are actors that I wish I had been able to interview for this book, but who have tragically left us: Nigel Hawthorne (*Demolition Man*, 1993), Ricardo Montalban (*Star Trek II: The Wrath of Khan*, 1982), Robert Z'Dar (*Maniac Cop*, 1988; *Samurai Cop*, 1991*)*, and Powers Boothe (so many films).

Also, if you're dismayed at the lack of horror icons in here, such as Robert Englund, there is a reason for that. Growing up, horror films terrified me! It wasn't until my late teens that I watched the likes of *Halloween* (1978), *Friday the 13th* (1980) and *A Nightmare on Elm Street* (1984) for the first time. Action films were my thing, horror films were for much braver children than me. Although, there's an idea for a follow-up. Either way, sit back, put on some classic 80s rock anthems by the likes of John Parr, Joe Esposito and Stan Bush and enjoy!

The Heavies

WHILE THE PRIMARY ANTAGONIST is often intellectually superior to our hero, they don't always have the physique to go toe-to-toe with them. Instead, they opt to pull the strings from behind the curtain, sending out more physically intimidating specimens to face whatever force of righteousness is coming their way; That is why every villain needs a loyal lieutenant or chief henchmen to do their bidding.

From time immemorial, the henchman has been physically imposing, and this is no different when it comes to action cinema. Look no further than Pat Roach's massive German mechanic in *Raiders of the Lost Ark* (1981); Brion James in *Blade Runner* (1982), *Red Heat* (1988), and *Tango and Cash* (1989); or Richard Kiel as Jaws in the *The Spy Who Loved Me (1977)* – they are all hulking giants that our heroes must use their wits to outsmart if they are to survive. Tragically, these actors, each of whom personify the henchman-type so perfectly, have since passed on, but the action world is filled with actors who have played similar roles. Right-hand men are staples of the genre and, during the 1980s, they came in many different forms from muscle-bound giants to lightning-quick martial arts experts, or stoic killers. Whatever their skillset, their purpose was clear: they were expendable, to kill or be killed before the hero gets to the main villain!

Often, not much is known about the henchman. He has no fascinating backstory and no time is spent looking at his motivation. He's there, he's bad and he deserves a punch in the face. Also, if it's a Bond film, he probably has some cool quirk like a robotic hand or inability to feel pain.

While most minions of cinema are uniform and legion, action cinema likes to make henchmen physically distinguishable and diverse. Just look at the henchmen in films like *Lethal Weapon* and *Die Hard* – Asian, Black and White criminals all working together to destroy the greater good.

Growing up and watching so many action heroes go toe-to-toe with these memorable characters made tracking down the actors that played them a delight. Some are still working, some have since retired, but all had wonderful stories about making some of the greatest action films ever made.

Sven-Ole Thorsen

"You killed my snake! Thorgrim is beside himself with grief! He raised that snake from the time it was born!"
– Thulsa Doom, *Conan the Barbarian* (1982).

Select Filmography

- *Conan the Barbarian* (1982) – Thorgrim
- *Conan the Destroyer* (1984) – Togra
- *Red Sonja* (1985) – Bodyguard of Lord Brytag
- *Raw Deal* (1986) – Patrovita's Bearded Bodyguard
- *Lethal Weapon* (1987) – Mercenary
- *Predator* (1987) – Russian Officer
- *The Running Man* (1987) – Sven
- *Overboard* (1987) – Olaf
- *Red Heat* (1988) – Nikolai
- *Twins* (1988) – Sam Klane
- *The Hunt for Red October* (1990) – Russian Chief of the Boat (COB)
- *Last Action Hero* (1993) – Gunman
- *Hard Target* (1993) – Stephan
- *On Deadly Ground* (1994) – Otto
- *The Quick and the Dead* (1995) – Gutzon
- *Mallrats* (1995) – La Fours
- *Gladiator* (2000) – Tigris

After seeing his family slaughtered by the snake cult of Thulsa Doom and being sold into slavery, Conan (Arnold

Thulsa Doom (James Earl Jones (centre)) and his Riders of Doom – Rexor (Ben Davison (left)) and Thorgrim (Sven-Ole Thorsen (right)) in *Conan The Barbarian* (1982). Photo courtesy of 20th Century Fox.

Schwarzenegger) has grown up to a vicious warrior and a cunning thief. Hired by King Osric (Max von Sydow) to find his missing daughter, Conan infiltrates Doom's temple but finds himself captured and confronted by the men who killed his family decades before....

LOOKING AT SVEN-OLE THORSEN'S FILMOGRAPHY is like looking at a list of the greatest action films ever made; *Conan the Barbarian, The Running Man, Lethal Weapon, Predator, The Hunt for Red October* and *Gladiator.*

Though he is quick to say he is not an actor, Sven has played numerous infamous roles throughout the years, evolving from a stuntman to playing Tigris, the undefeated gladiator that Russell Crowe battles in Ridley Scott's *Gladiator.*

Thanks to his decades-long friendship with Arnold Schwarzenegger, he also holds the distinction of not only appearing in almost every one of The Austrian Oak's films, but has also been killed by him on-screen more than any other actor.

Originally from Denmark, where he was a champion bodybuilder and strongman (winning Denmark's Strongest Man in 1983), Sven's drive to be the best at what he does has seen him work with some of the biggest action stars and directors in Hollywood.

While I already knew Sven from films like *Conan The Barbarian, The Running Man, Predator* and *Gladiator,* it was in researching for our interview that I realized just how many of my favorite films he'd appeared in. That large German heavy that tries to kill Ben Affleck's Jack Ryan in *The Sum of All Fears* (2002)? That was Sven. The 'Would Be King' leading the rampaging army in *The 13th Warrior* (1999)? That was Sven. The Demon chasing Bruce Lee in his dreams in *Dragon: The Bruce Lee Story* (1993)? That was Sven. The list just went on and on and I was amazed at how someone so big and recognizable could disappear into so many roles.

Despite his intimidating stature, Sven is absolutely charming, and made me feel like an old friend within minutes. His quick wit, numerous hilarious anecdotes and zero tolerance for ego and bullshit made for a thoroughly entertaining conversation that could have gone on for hours. Plus, he kept calling me "boss", which was awesome.

You started off as a body builder, a dead lifter and a martial artist in Denmark – how did you end up in the movie business? Was that always the plan?

Very early on I did different sports, but in my late teenage years I found weight training and realized I wasn't dependent on teammates and I could do it any time I liked. I was tall and skinny, so I made the decision that I would spend the next ten years being the biggest and the strongest man that ever walked on earth! I had this vision that when I died one day, my friends would pick up my coffin and the bottom would go out and they'll all look down and say, 'Fuck, he was big.'

So, from 83 kg, I built myself up to 142 kg. I also got involved in martial arts. At thirty years old, I began to train with the world champion Seneka from the Japan Karate Association. Even though I was a beginner, I trained with him three times a day and after two-and-a-half years, I became a black belt and I whooped everybody's ass!

I invited Arnold [Schwarzenegger] to Denmark in the late seventies because of his movie *Pumping Iron* and shortly after that, I started the Danish Body Building Federation. By the time I was forty years old I ran the Danish Power Lifting Federation. I was running the Danish Karate Federation, I was European champion, and I was the strongest man in the world, so I went to California.

You just packed up and left? But it sounds like you were essentially the national champion of bad-assery in Denmark....

I was so busy with those sport federations, so I was in the public eye all the time and the privacy was gone. I felt I had to challenge myself. I'd become the best in those three sports and I just felt Denmark was too small. Also, the weather in Denmark sucks. I just went to California so I could lie on the beach and have a Coke!

When I arrived in Los Angeles the only person I knew was Arnold. I called him up, not to start in the movie business, but because he was the only guy I knew. I called him up and said, 'I'm in town, how about a cup of coffee?' He said, 'Come up to Bridget Park. I'm shooting a movie up here called *Commando*. Come and say hi.'

I had just left Denmark two weeks earlier and could bench press 242 kg, so I was a monster! When [the producer] Joel Silver saw me, he was so excited. He said, 'Hey Sven, how would you like to be in the movie? I will pay you $20,000, but you have to be a member of the Screen Actors Guild.'

So, I went to the Screen Actors Guild and had to prove that I'd done three American pictures outside of Denmark and then I was in "the business".

You had already worked with Arnold at this point though, hadn't you? Because you'd made *Conan The Barbarian*, *Conan The Destroyer* and *Red Sonja* – I assume those were the three American pictures you'd made outside of Denmark?

I had been in Los Angeles during the late seventies for a martial arts world championship in Long Beach and I'd hung out with Arnold. He said to me, 'I have to go and see a director who wants to do a movie called *Conan The Barbarian*. I want you to come with me.'

We went and when [director] John Milius saw me, he was really impressed by my size and that I came from Denmark. He saw me as some kind of Viking! He was writing the screenplay at the time and said, 'I need a good strong name. Give me a good strong name for a character in this picture.' I said, 'What about Thorgrim?' He loved the name and six months later he called me and said, 'Hey, Sven. I want you to play Thorgrim in Spain. Get your biggest friends. We're going to put you all in *Conan the Barbarian*.'

So, I picked ten big friends, all weightlifters, and we went down to Spain. We were called The Animals! There were ten big guys from Denmark, ten American stuntmen and ten Spanish stuntmen – thirty guys, so

A publicity still of The Riders of Doom in *Conan The Barbarian* (1982).
Photo courtesy of 20th Century Fox.

of course there was a lot of competition between us and John ended up using us for most of the stunts in *Conan the Barbarian*.

It's a hell of a film for your first movie role. It must have been an amazing experience.

I'd done a couple of small movies in Denmark as a henchman, but [*Conan*] was an experience beyond what you can imagine. It's playing cowboys and Indians all day long! Seventeen different locations around Spain, eating great food, great wine, chasing women – having so much fun!

Every day on location we were served three course meals, with fruit, cheese, and wine. And of course, there were food fights, so lunch lasted three to four hours! By the afternoon, we were all tipsy!

As Thorgrim, you were the henchman to James Earl Jones's Thulsa Doom who was, and is still, one of the best actors in the world. Was that intimidating for you?

Oh my God. He's like royalty. His voice! I remember Arnold told me that the voice on CNN was James Earl Jones. He's a Shakespearean actor and was a great help to all of us, including Arnold. It was a great experience. What a gentleman and what a skilled actor he is.

What happened to Thorgrim's hammer after the film? Did you take it with you?

The prop guys and John gave me the hammer. It was a 25 kg fucking hammer! It was so heavy, it was ridiculous. For many years I had it in my office in Santa Monica, but then a couple of years ago John got quite sick. I gave him the hammer just to encourage him because every time he saw me he said, 'You know, Sven, you're the last Viking in Hollywood and the only Viking I know with a PhD!'

I gave him the hammer and I know he used it as a doorstop in his office in New York.

You were already a champion power lifter and so you were in a great shape, but how was the transition into doing stunt work on a movie set?

Normally big guys are not so agile, but when people see me they say, 'You are a big guy, but with feet like Gene Kelly or Fred Astaire!'

It was just about combining agility and strength. Before *Conan The Barbarian*, I had never been on a horse before. I had never seen a horse. The costume weighted 50–60 kg, so with that big hammer, every time the horse saw me in the morning, he would try to hide!

Body builders are obviously very competitive. When you're doing scenes like the sword fight between you and Arnold in *Conan the Destroyer*, does it get ultra-competitive or, for safety's sake, are you both consummate professionals?

There's always competition when it comes to guys that are physical! With Arnold, we worked out together and I would teach Arnold martial arts movements. We also had a great sword fight instructor called Kiyo Yamasaki. Every day we practiced with the sword for hours and when we worked out a fight scene, it was a combination of Yamasaki's input, my input, and Arnold's input. It was all team work. We hit each other's hands several times and there was lots of cursing, but the fight came out fantastic. There were no stunt doubles, by the way.

It doesn't look like there were….

Directors fear injuring the star but John [Milius] likes to hurt Arnold, so he can feel that it's real. That's why I think the best job Arnold has ever done was *Conan the Barbarian*. He was raw, he was himself, he was natural, and he looked believable because he did it himself.

After you moved to California and Joel Silver put you in *Commando*, that must have opened a lot of doors for you as you ended up in several massive films like *Lethal Weapon* and *Predator*.

My colleagues would tease me because they just saw me as a friend of Arnold. I was a big guy, but they never really accepted me as a stuntman – but after one particular stunt, I got respect.

Was that the one in *Predator*? Where Arnold kicks in the door, says "Knock, knock" and blows you out the window?

That stunt was done the old-fashioned way! The window was facing a cliff that went down to a river. There were ten guys with a rope, and at a signal they just pulled me the fuck out! I flew out the fucking window! I never knew what happened to me, but I was out of there in one take. After that they called [me] "One Take Sven".

Is it true that Arnie got very ill on *Predator* with a kidney infection and you essentially nursed him back to health?

Yes. We shot the jungle scene in the jungles of Puerto Vallarta and stayed at a hotel just south of there. Every day, we ran from the hotel down to town and uphill again. Arnold was under a lot of stress as he had to be naked in the cold water at night in the jungle. He ended up getting diarrhea and flu, but he kept pushing himself. His kidney stopped working and he was in his bed for a whole week. I sat there reading Hans Christian Andersen trying to comfort him.

After the whole thing was over and he didn't die, Joel Silver gave me an old commando watch and said, 'You saved his life.'

As well as any stress Arnold must have been feeling, it must have been an incredibly testosterone-packed set as there you can had a very masculine cast – Carl Weathers, Sonny Landham, Bill Duke....

Jesse "The Body" Ventura.

Of course.

There's a lot of competition, but it's friendly competition. I oversaw Arnold's gym. We had a gym come down from Los Angeles that we set up in the jungle. Everybody used the gym as everybody was trying to keep up with Arnold's energy and strength. He can work twenty hours a day non-stop.

He's also a big fan of power napping, so every time there was a break, he'd sleep for five minutes and then work for five more hours. He's a bundle of energy and he motivates everybody. He's the biggest team player in Hollywood.

[Director] John McTiernan must have been impressed with you because he continued to cast you in many of his other films, such as *The Hunt for Red October* where you play the Russian COB. I must ask, as a proud Dane, you've been in lots of action films where you're

Sven reunites with Arnold Schwarzenegger in *The Running Man* (1987).
Photo courtesy of TriStar Pictures.

either a Russian or German like in *The Sum of All Fears*. Does it bother you that you're cast as like a Pan-European henchman and never a Dane?

No, it's the movies! I'm just happy to work! When I was cast in *The Hunt for Red October*, I was supposed to do *Total Recall* in Mexico, but as I was about to leave I got a phone call from John McTiernan.

He said, 'Hey Sven, I'm doing *The Hunt for Red October*, it's written by Tom Clancy and there is this part for you. We start shooting in two days.' I said, 'John, thank you very much, but I'm on my way to Mexico to do *Total Recall* with Arnold.' John said, 'Talk to fucking Arnold, I'm sure you could do both!'

So, I talked to Arnold and he said, 'Sure, no problem.' When I was in Mexico, I flew about ten times back and forth between Los Angeles, Paramount Studios, and Churubusco Studios in Mexico City on a co-worker's private jet. On one of those trips, the producer Andy Vajna, Arnold and I were flying back from Mexico and Vajna said to Arnold, 'You know, I want to do your next *Terminator* movie. What can I do to convince you I'm the right producer?' Arnold said, 'Sven, what do you think?' So, I said, 'How about Andy gives you the airplane we're sitting in?' Arnold turned to Andy and said, 'What do you say to that?' And right there and then, there was a handshake!

Arnold obviously respects your opinion if he's going to let you weigh in on negotiations about such a major movie....

I have a big brother relationship with Arnold. He would often ask me for advice. I've warned him about doing certain things, because sometimes he gets a little loose and needs somebody to say, 'No.'

Because I was bigger and wiser and a little older, he listened to me a lot. I'm always trying to encourage my friends to do their best.

You've been in more of Arnie's films than any other actor, and I think you've been killed on-screen by him more times than anyone else. Is there a particular death that sticks out in your mind?

He doesn't kill me, but there's a scene in *Red Heat*, which we filmed in a sauna. There were thirty naked women and thirty naked guys, so that was a lot of fun.

Sven (center) just before his big fight scene with Arnold Schwarzenegger in
Red Heat (1988). Photo courtesy of TriStar Pictures.

Anyway, I was supposed to fall out the window and continue the fight with Arnold in the snow. The interior shot of that scene was shot in Hungary, but there's no snow there so we went to Schladming in Austria. All the crew were making bets amongst themselves on whether I could fall out of the window and do the fight in the snow. They didn't know me except as Arnold's "hanger on".

Of course, I took all the bets and we did the fight in the snow, which was very, very cold. [Stunt Co-ordinator] Bennie E. Dobbins had a heart attack and died because of the cold. I won a lot of money in those bets. A lot of money.

I wanted to move away slightly from action films, because one role that many people recognize you for is from Kevin Smith's film *Mallrats*, where you star as the security guard LaFours.

That's a funny story, because on *Hard Target*, one of the producers, James Jacks, was talking about *Mallrats* and said that I should be in the movie.

Half a year later, I heard rumors that they were filming *Mallrats* in Minnesota, so I called up and said, 'Hey, what the fuck's going on? You promised me a job and now you're shooting the movie without me?' He said. 'Ah, shit Sven. Bring your ass out here we'll figure that out.' So, I went to Minnesota from California in my shorts and my T-shirts and you cannot believe how cold it was!

I don't say a word in the movie. I just run around and chase guys with a silly hat on, but that movie is extremely popular. People are always coming up to me with posters and *Mallrats* stuff. I sign a lot of straw hats!

Really?!

Yes. It's such a cult movie with a lot of followers. I've had couples crying that I take the time to sign their *Mallrats* posters and take pictures with them.

Would you say that *Mallrats* is the film you're recognized the most for?

I think *Gladiator.* That movie is probably the part I'm known best for.

I heard that you auditioned for over a year to get the part of Tigris. Is that true?

I heard about the movie through my friend, Lou Ferrigno, because that was originally his part. We were in Gold's Gym talking about him playing

Maximus (Russell Crowe) faces off against Tigris (Sven-Ole Thorsen) in *Gladiator* (2000). Photo courtesy of Universal Studios.

that part, so I tried to get on the movie for another cast in another role. I sent in my resume, but I never hard back.

One day, I get a phone call from Branko Lustig, the producer of *Schindler's List*. He said, 'Hey. My name is Branko Lustig. I'm doing *Gladiator*. I've heard so much about you. We need you down here in Malta right now.'

I go to Malta and they tell me they had to fire Lou because he looked too much like a body builder. In those days, there was no such a thing as body builders, just strong men and at the time, I looked more like a retired gladiator. I was still huge and muscular, but I was a little chubby.

How did Lou feel about that?

After I'd done the movie, I met Lou and he said, 'You know what, Sven. I could not have done that job, so there's no bad feelings.'

As you got the role at the last moment, did you have to throw yourself in to the fight scene training?

When I arrived, I was dead tired and Branko walked around me like I was an animal in a zoo. He said, 'Sven. Are you the right man for the job?' I said, 'Mr. Lustig, I don't know what the job is all [about], but whatever you guys want me for, I can do it.' Ridley Scott walked up smoking his Montecristo No. 2 and he looked at me and asked the same question, 'Are you the right man for the job?' He's Ridley Scott! So, I say, 'Whatever you want me to do, I can do it!' I didn't know anything about the job, so they send me back to my hotel with a storyboarded script.

I didn't know anything about the film's story, I just had that particular scene and it was pages and pages of drawings! About a hundred drawings of every move. I said to myself, 'This is too much for me, I can't do that. I'm old, fat, and I'm out of shape.' It was so tough.

Did you start rehearsing your fight with Russell Crowe straight away?

I met Russell Crowe for the first time after two weeks of rehearsing. I had been practicing my half of the fight with a stunt double. After thirty or forty moves with Russell, he screamed at me, 'What the fuck? You clumsy motherfucker!' and he threw his stuff down and he walked away!

The stunt guys said, 'Sven, you did exactly what you should have done. Take it easy. Don't get mad. Don't kill him. Yet.'

He came back an hour later and had calmed down. He said, 'Sven, let's do it my way,' even though there was no 'his way' and it was already pre-arranged. So, we did the same thing and from that day on, we had a great time. In 2000 at the Taurus Awards, which is the Oscars for stunt-men, I was fortunate to win two awards, one for the Best Fight and one for Best Work with Animals.

You're not just contending with Russell Crowe, but also the live tigers you had on set. Obviously, there were CGI tigers for certain scenes, but how dangerous was it filming with those animals?

There's a scene where Russell is running backwards and I'm chasing him with my axe and my sword. I had a tiger on each side and after the shot, the assistant director comes up to me and says, 'Come here, we want to talk to you.' In the middle of the arena, there was a tent with screens for every camera in there. We go in and he says, 'Okay, let's run camera four,' and I see one of the tigers, like a pussy cat, was pawing at my hip and shoulder. It was playing with me like I was a mouse, but I didn't feel it because I had the armor on. I also couldn't see shit, because there were only two small holes in the mask. That's why I had to rehearse for several weeks before, because it's like doing the fight blindfolded!

Everyone was looking at me wondering if I'm going to sue them, because in Hollywood people will sue anyone if their life is in danger, but I'm a Dane! I just said to Ridley, 'Mr. Scott, a Montecristo No. 2.' An hour later, on a tray, a box of twenty-five Montecristo No.2s were delivered to me!

I imagine with the heat, the dust, the tigers, and Russell Crowe, that was probably the toughest job you've ever had?

Yes, but also, at the same time, the most fulfilling as I had to use all my skills.

Didn't you already know Russell from *The Quick and The Dead* because you'd previously worked on that film?

On *The Quick and the Dead*, I had the great pleasure of working with Gene Hackman, Leonardo DiCaprio and Sharon Stone, but Russell was very subdued. He was very much into the part of playing that priest, so even when there was a break, he was still playing the part.

You have been in so many big films, such as *The 13th Warrior, Batman & Robin* (1997) and *Ghostbusters II* (1989). What projects stand out in your mind as being the most fun to work on?

The two that stand out for now and forever are *Conan the Barbarian* and *Gladiator. Conan* really made an impression on me. For that short period of time, you're a family. You bond, you cry together, you fight together, you have fun together, you work together.

With *Gladiator*, the sets were unbelievable. There were giraffes, lions, tigers, elephants. When I was there, I felt I was the character; I became the character. When I stood there in the morning, they had dressed 5,000 extras cheering for me. I got goose bumps!

When you've done big movies like that, do you feel spoiled when you work on smaller movies like *The Bad Pack* (1997) or *Abraxas: Guardian of the Universe* (1990)?

Sven (far left) appears in *Hard Target* (1993) in one of his many assorted henchmen roles. Photo courtesy of Universal Pictures.

I'm just happy. I have a job! With *Abraxas*, the director was Damian Lee and he had a company that was called *Rose and Ruby*, but in the movie business it was called *Run and Run*!

I said 'Damian, I want to work for you, but I want to be paid all my money. I want $50,000 in my bank account, and *then* I'll come out there and you can use me all day long.' Sure enough, I went out there for two-and-a-half months and he worked me for eighteen to twenty hours every day.

I'm a team player, I want everybody to be happy, I'm going to do my very best, so I never complain about the size of my trailer or the food. When you hire me, I'm going to give you my very best.

You're obviously favored by directors like John McTiernan, but are there any directors who impressed you that you would want to work with again?

Richard Donner would put up storyboards every morning, so we could see what we were supposed to shoot that day. We could always ask questions and then everybody knew exactly what they had to do. John McTiernan has a very dry sense of humor. You make jokes and then three days later, he would laugh. It takes him a while!

Then, of course, there's John Milius who's like a little boy playing with toys. He's also one of the best storytellers in the world.

You've also worked with some of the biggest stars in the world, which naturally comes with some big egos. During the Eighties, Arnie and Stallone had a very public rivalry and I read that, at one point, it almost got out of control, and you were the one that brokered some sort of truce between them. Is that true?

I set up a meeting for them in Santa Monica. In those days, I was also hanging out with Sly and he wrote a part for me in *Rambo III* (1988). I'd just done a pilot for *Captain Power* (1989) and wanted to work with Sylvester, [rather] than do a TV show in Canada, so I asked for some ridiculous things to get out of it: two cars, a massive dressing room, a penthouse, my wife on the payroll…and they said yes! So, I had to turn Sly down.

Anyway, I was quite close to Sly and Arnold at the same time and I said, 'Why don't you guys fucking meet?' So, I set up a meeting, they met, and then they both came back and said, 'That guy has too much of an ego!' But now they're best buddies!

You would have thought as you brokered a friendship between them, you'd have roles in all *The Expendables* movies….

That's not the way it works! They are best buddies now, but, in those days, they talked so much shit about each other. I've met a lot of egos. Steven Seagal, for example, there's a big ego there!

I was in an airport with a female friend and Seagal was there with Kelly LeBrock. My friend had worked with her in London, so she drags me over to say hi. I hadn't met Seagal before and when he shook my hand, he twisted my thumb. I said, 'That hurts, don't do that,' and he kept fucking doing it. I ask him not to do it again and when he continued, I pulled him in and swept his legs out from under him. Of course, my girlfriend was upset with me because I'd acted like a bully.

A week later, I'm looking for job at Warner Bros. and I found Steven Seagal's production office. I said, 'I heard that Steven Seagal is doing a film in Alaska and there's a character in it called Otto who is some kind of sidekick.' I had done my research!

Then Steven walked out of his office, and said, 'Hey Sven, what are you doing here?' I said, 'Hey Steven, I know you're shooting a movie in Alaska, so here I am.' He said, 'Are you an actor?' and I said, 'Here's my resume.' He looked at it and said 'It's called *On Deadly Ground*, but you know what Sven? I make all the decisions. I'm directing, I'm producing, and I'm starring.' I said 'Fine. When do I work?' He said, 'Let me think about it.'

That was Monday morning, and on Tuesday I was flying to Alaska for two-and-a-half months!

You guys must have patched it up if he gave you a job?

Well, here's the punch line. In the movie, I was supposed to have this big fight with Steven. He called me to set and said, 'Sven, I know you're a martial arts guy. Please kick me.' I said, 'What?' and again he said, 'Kick me.' All my stunt colleagues are standing outside and it's freezing, so I said, 'I don't want to fucking kick you.'

'Come on, Sven! Show me your skills! Kick me!' I knew it was payback time, so I did a half-assed kick, because I didn't want to hurt him as he was the star. Of course, he pulls my leg and I fall on my ass. Everyone's

Sven appears alongside Michael Caine (centre) and John C. McGinley in Steven Seagal's *On Deadly Ground* (1994). Photo courtesy of Warner Brothers.

laughing and I was pretty embarrassed. Again, Steven said, 'Okay Sven, this time, kick -' and before he could say 'me', I kicked him right in the solar plexus.

A couple of days later, when we were doing our fight scene, he hit me full blast on my neck. I took a week off, but when I came back, one of the producers saw me and said, 'What the fuck are you doing here, Sven?' I said, 'I'm here to work', but the producer said, 'Haven't you seen the dallies? When Steven hit you on your neck, he killed you. Your character's dead!' So, he conned me out of two or three weeks more work! He had a big, big ego.

I have heard that over the years. Him and Jean-Claude Van Damme seem to have clashed with a lot of people.

Oh, I have some stuff on him, too!

Jean-Claude Van Damme? From when you worked together on *Hard Target*?

He interferes in the other departments. He tells the hair people what to do, he tells the wardrobe people what to do, he tells the producers what to do. On *Hard Target*, they asked him if he was familiar with horses as there was going to be some riding. He said, 'I was born on horseback!'

In the film, he was supposed to run up to the horse, jump on it and take off. If you know horses, you know you have to let the horse know you're coming from behind. So he came up behind the horse and the horse kicked the hell out of him! He was screaming at everybody. They had to cut a lot of the scenes out. We thought he could ride a horse!

Obviously, you've been in so many films, but in many of them you are cast as the 'intimidating henchman'. Does that bother you that you've been typecast in these types of roles?

If you're a film producer, and you have a job for me where I have to wear high heels and makeup, I'm your man! I just like to work. All my ambitions have been fulfilled. I used to say, 'I've had so many second places in my life, nothing would feel like first place.'

I don't have those ambitions. I left Denmark because the fame fucked up my private life. In Hollywood, I can disappear into the crowd.

No offense Sven, but I find it hard to believe that you could disappear anywhere.

I've had big agencies behind me several times, but I'm always number four on their call list, so very often I'm my own agent. Once, I was out driving my jeep and I saw *Baywatch* (1989) was filming on the beach. So, I put my Jeep into four-wheel drive, drove down onto the beach, and stopped one meter away from David Hasselhoff. I jumped out and said, 'Hey David, I have a question for you. My name is Sven I'm from Denmark, I'm an actor/stuntman - why haven't you ever hired for Baywatch?' That's how I did two *Baywatch* episodes, and three episodes of *Baywatch Nights*!

Of course, you were in that episode of *Baywatch Nights* where David Hasselhoff fights a Viking that's been frozen in ice! You were the Viking!

Dave is a great guy. My first day on the set, I saw them all in those *Baywatch* crew jackets with their names on, so I went up to him and said, 'Hey Dave, where's my crew jacket?' and the next day I had a crew jacket with my name on it. I still have it.

Do you think it's more fun to play the bad guy?

It's just fun to work! Maybe it comes easy to me to be the bad guy, but I'm just Sven. When people call me an actor I say, 'No, but I'm that guy that can take a bullet, can take a punch and say "Ouch" the right way!'

Benny "The Jet" Urquidez

"He's too powerful. Don't panic. Just relax. Treat it like a training session."

— Thomas, *Wheels on Meals* (1984).

Select Filmography

- *Force: Five* (1981) – Billy Ortega
- *Wheels on Meals* (1984) – Mondale's Henchman
- *Dragons Forever* (1988) – Hua's Henchman
- *Road House* (1989) – Laughing Henchman
- *Tango & Cash* (1989) – Thug
- *Martial Law* (1990) – Tong Member
- *Street Fighter* (1994) – Sagat Gang Member
- *Grosse Point Blank* (1997) – Felix La PuBelle
- *Spider-Man* (2002) – Mugger

It's the final act of Wheels on Meals *(1984) and Sylvia (Lola Forner), the heir to a sizeable fortune, has been kidnapped and is being held in a castle guarded by thugs. The three heroes – played by Hong Kong superstars Jackie Chan, Sammo Hung and Yuen Biao – team up to save her, but, upon entering the castle, they come face to face with a vicious henchman who is like no opponent they've faced before….*

WITH NINE BLACK BELTS in nine different martial arts, it's fair to say that when it comes to on-screen villains, few are as physically capable as Benny "The Jet" Urquidez. During his twenty-seven year-long full-

Thomas (Jackie Chan) on facing Mondale's main thug (Benny 'The Jet' Urquidez) in *Wheels on Meals* (1984). Photo courtesy of Golden Harvest.

contact karate and kickboxing career, Urquidez won six World Titles in five different weight divisions, all while maintaining a professional record of sixty three to nil (win-loss), which included an incredible fifty-seven knockouts (although some sources say it could be more).

As well as being a martial arts champion, Urquidez found the time to become a fight choreographer in Hollywood and, from his Jet Center in north Hollywood, has trained everyone from Kurt Russell to John Cusack, the latter of whom has been a pupil of Urquidez's since 1989.

However, it is for his roles in Jackie Chan's *Wheels on Meals*, *Dragons Forever*, and the action-comedy *Grosse Pointe Blank*, where he plays a hitman, that he is best known. His lightning-quick moves and breath-taking agility make his scenes with Jackie Chan a pulse-pounding experience and it is no surprise that their two on-screen bouts frequently top polls as the most impressive martial arts fights ever put to film. In *Grosse Pointe Blank*, his brutal hand-to-hand fight with John Cusack's Martin Blank also added a level of gritty realism to the dark comedy and suddenly made Cusack a believable action star.

On-screen, Urquidez is always an intimidating presence, with a hard stare and even harder punches. His characters are also often men of few words, so it was surprising to discover that he was a fantastic storyteller, recounting his on-set experiences with delight and enthusiasm. In fact, just a few minutes into our conversation, he began recollecting how, whilst doing an exhibition fight in Hong Kong in the 1970s, he accidently accepted an invitation to take part in a *Bloodsport*-style Kumite….

So how do you 'accidently' end up in a Kumite?!

I was doing an interview in Hong Kong and somebody in the crowd yelled something in Chinese. My interpreter said, 'He says, you're not a real fighter, you're an actor,' and I laughed and said, 'I fight for a living. That's what I do. I fight for a living.' And so, he told the guy, who kept screaming and yelling, and the interpreter said, 'He's challenging you. Do you accept?' As I was getting interviewed on national TV and, if the money is right I'll fight anybody, what else could I say?

After the interview, I went back to the hotel and these two Chinese men came up to me and said, 'How much money do you want to fight this guy?' I said, 'Are you serious?' I told them, 'I want $50,000. I want this expensive mink coat for my wife, I want 20% of the TV rights and it'll take me six weeks to get in shape!' They said, 'There's no TV. And it's tomorrow.' I thought it was going to be an exhibition fight and they agreed to the $50,000!

The next day, they came back and gave me $50,000 in an envelope and the fur coat, so we start driving from Hong Kong to Kowloon. I tried to make conversation with them, asking if I was the first fight or the last, but they didn't understand me. We ended up going into the Hong Kong mountains and parking in the middle of nowhere in front of this big building.

Jesus….

I asked the guy, 'Where's all the people?' and he opened the door and inside were all these bleachers that went all the way up and around the building. The place was packed!

I asked, 'Is there a doctor?' and was told there was no doctor. I asked, 'When do I fight?' and they said, 'Now!' I put on my shorts, put in my mouth piece and I go, 'Who's going to corner me?' and this guy said, 'I'll corner you', so I went, 'Okay…where's the referee?' and the same guy went, 'I am the referee!'

On the other side of the ring is my opponent and this horn suddenly goes off! This guy turns around and yells, 'To the death!'

A publicity photo of Benny Urquidez during his kickboxing career.
Photo courtesy of Benny Urquidez.

And didn't alarm bells start ringing at this point?

Well, I heard it…but I didn't hear it. I still think I'm doing an exhibition fight! So, I go out there and I start kicking and punching and my first kick hits him right in his chin and the side of his face just swelled up! I looked at the referee and said, 'He can't go on,' but then the guy just came after me! I hit him again, right in the eye. I start showboating because I still think it's an exhibition fight, so I start doing the Muhammad Ali shuffle! I'm doing round kicks and jump kicks and putting on a show!

The round ends and my opponent's guys jump over and look at his eye, so I go to the referee and gesture for some water and he, honest to God, hands me a beer!

The horn goes again and this guy turns around and again says, 'To the death!', but this time I heard him clearly. I looked at the crowd and they were all pointing their thumbs downwards. Then, everything started moving in slow motion. I saw the guy coming at me, so I kicked him with my front leg, hit him in the eye and then kneed him in the face. He went straight down, so I stood over him, yelling at him to stay down. The guy couldn't breathe and he couldn't see! And then the crowd started throwing things at me!

The referee suddenly grabs me and says, 'Let's go! Let's go!' and they put me in the car and take me straight to the airport! They'd gone to my room and already got my luggage. I was standing in the airport with this guy's blood still on me thinking what the hell just happened?!

They rushed you out of the country for your safety?

I don't know! I came home, my wife picked me up from the airport and I told her what happened. After that, she didn't want to wear the fur jacket!

The whole thing bothered me, so six or seven months later, I told my whole family and they said, 'Why don't you tell that story and get it out of your system?' I told the story to either Black Belt magazine or Insider Kung Fu magazine, and then a year later *Bloodsport* came out with Van Damme!

You're saying that *Bloodsport* is based on your own experiences and not those of Frank Dux?

He saw the magazine and put his name to it. My brother saw that movie and said, 'Brother, you've got to come see this movie. The names are changed, but it's exactly like your story!'

There have been lots of allegations about Frank Dux over the years that insinuate he's embellished a lot of his experiences.

That's what movie magic is about. You take stories, you modify them, and Frank Dux made it his.

You know what, back when Van Damme first came from Belgium, he trained at my school. We trained for *No Retreat, No Surrender* at my gym. I was the choreographer for that and that's how he got his start.

Wasn't it *No Retreat, No Surrender* (1986) where he got into trouble for allegedly not pulling his punches during the fight scenes?

The reason for that is because he wanted the respect of the martial artists and the other kickboxers. He wanted to show he could do damage. I said to him, 'You're kicking me hard because I'm allowing you to kick me!' He went through that stage for a while. Van Damme respects strength.

One of your first films was *Force: Five*, which was directed by Robert Clouse. How did you find working with him because the on-set disagreements between him and Bruce Lee on *Enter the Dragon* (1973) are legendary and it feels like he rode the wave of that film's success for years afterwards?

To tell you the truth, he let us choreograph our own stuff for the action scenes. I thought he was very creative. Instead of him trying to create something, he would give us a scene and say, 'What would you do?'

I thought that was brilliant: as a director, that he would allow us to do what we thought would work best. For *Force: Five*, they got anyone that was big in martial arts – Joe Lewis, Richard Norton, and myself, so we all did our own choreography. In fact, I trained Richard Norton when he came here from Australia.

Was that the film that brought you to the attention of Jackie Chan and Sammo Hung? Is that how you ended up in *Wheels on Meals*?

At that point, my career was really taking off, and Jackie and Sammo heard that not only was I an actual fighter, but I was also making a living from it. They didn't know exactly how good of an actor I was, but they knew I could do movies and in terms of fighting. I was doing things that nobody else was doing. They wanted to know how good this American was, so when I got there Jackie looked me up and down. One of his guys got a power shield, and another stuntman who spoke a bit of English said, 'Kick it'. I asked, 'How hard?' and Jackie pushed his thumbs up. So, I kicked it, and I dropped this guy through the kicking shield with a spinning back kick. Jackie just looked at me and put his thumbs up.

As a full contact karate and kickboxing champion, when you first started making films, did you find you had to rein yourself in? After all, real fighting and movie fighting are two very different things.

When I was young, we used to go out to the malls to do demonstrations. My brother would put a cigarette in his mouth and I'd do a spinning back kick to knock it out without touching him. When it comes to doing movies, because of my experience doing martial arts exhibitions, that stuff is easy!

So how did you guys choreograph your fight?

At first, Jackie would do some moves, like a spinning wheel kick, and then put up his hand as if to go, 'Ok, your turn.' I went out there and did stuff he's never seen – jump spinning crushing kicks, dragon sweeps, rolling flip-flopping and he would just look at me with his thumbs up.

His interpreter would say to me, 'OK, Jackie does this' and Jackie did a move and then he'd ask, 'What would you do?' I would say, 'This, this and this,' and demonstrate, and we started choreographing our fight. I watched what Jackie would do and then he'd watch what I would do.

It sounds like it was a really collaborative relationship.

When, we went to Spain we had a blast! Jackie wanted to learn how to speak English, so he'd sit right next to me and put his arm around me. At the time, I was really uncomfortable with that! He kept looking like he wanted to sit on my lap! He'd always want to sit next to me to practice his English. Finally, six weeks into the movie, I got comfortable with it, because that's just who he is. Once we'd finish lunch, we'd play soccer and I would teach him how to speak English. We even slept together on the set. Everyone would go home and the two of us would sleep on the set!

In his biography, Jackie says the fight between you two in *Wheels on Meals* is probably the best fight scene he's ever done. He says all the way through his book that during the filming, he'd try and goad you into a real fight.

That's what he kept on saying. He told me, 'One day, we are going to fight,' and I'd look at him and say, 'For real?' and he'd put his thumbs up.

When we were in Spain, he'd have everyone on the set betting on a fight between us! After a few weeks, I'd ask him, 'When are we going to fight?' He kept saying, 'Soon.' One week before the end of production, I looked Jackie in the eye and said, 'Jackie, you're never going to fight me, are you?' and he just laughed and smiled and put his thumbs up like 'You're right, I'm not going to fight you!'

It's such an energetic fight scene, but how was it for you as you have the added challenge of wearing braces?

Yeah, and Jackie was hitting me hard with these golf gloves! Whenever I kicked him into the boxes, he winded himself, but he'd simply put his thumbs up and put more pads under his shirt! We had such fun. When I look at someone I see a diamond in the rough. I see their shine, even if they can't see it. I saw that in Jackie. I saw it in his ability and that's why our fights were injury-free. I had the best of him and he had the best of me.

Then you came back in *Dragons Forever,* where you start off doing that flying kick into Yuen Biao.

Jackie Chan and Benny Urquidez reunite in *Dragons Forever* (1988).
Photo courtesy of Golden Harvest.

By then, we knew each other very well. After *Wheels on Meals*, we all knew what to expect, and we were prepared for it.

What do you think makes you an intimidating villain on screen and why do you think people are drawn to you as a villain?

Have you ever seen those blowfish when they inflate themselves? My energy blows up so big that it's believable that I can hurt someone like Johnny [Cusack]. I can take him out and kill him. That's the reason why I make a great villain – I can be very scary!

How, then, did you go from kickboxing to choreographing and training actors in Hollywood?

When I wasn't defending my title, I would do a movie, and then after I would go back to kickboxing. I turned down a five-picture deal, because I was getting ready to defend my title. The studio said, 'You would turn down a five-picture deal?' and I said, 'My fighting comes first!' I worked hard for my titles, and ended up turning a lot of movies down. There was a time when I was blackballed for a while.

Is that why you would show up in films like *Tango and Cash* in a tiny part, as you'd be off training for a title bout?

Exactly.

I want to talk about *Road House (1989)*, because you trained Patrick Swayze for that film. There's behind the scenes footage that shows you training Swayze to music to get his timing better. How did that come about?

I trained everybody on that film, but, with fight choreography, it has a certain rhythm. Patrick was getting frustrated, because he kept tripping over himself. He was going, 'What's wrong with me?! I'm a dancer. Why can't I get this rhythm?' After a few days, I could see he was taking it hard, so I started choreographing all the fights to music.

I went on set the next day and said, 'Patrick, I want you to watch me.' I put on the music, and I started first with my hands, and then my body, and finally my legs. I started doing the technique like a dance movement.

He watched me and started getting into the beat. Then he got up and he started moving with the beat. I would do some dance moves and he would do some dance moves and we had a blast! We started dancing, doing different moves and mimicking each other. So, I said to him, 'That's how I'm going to choreograph you!' and he was so happy. Every time we went onto the set, he brought music and it was a party. We danced and partied through the whole film! It was awesome. I couldn't believe I was getting paid for that!

Tell me it wasn't you that taught him how to rip out people's throats!

When Patrick walked, it reminded me of a bobcat, like he was stalking his prey. Once, he was walking on the set and he had no shirt on, and every time he would take a step, his muscles would move in motion like a bobcat, and that's how I choreographed him – like he was a bobcat striking his prey! With Sam Elliot, he moved like a bear! For him, it was just power moves! Nothing fancy!

Is that how you ended up training the cast of *Street Fighter*? Because you recognized what style would work for a certain type of actor?

The director, Steven E. de Souza, would say to me, 'I visualize this character being a military fighter and this character being a traditional martial artist,' so I would take each actor and train them each differently.

I have nine black belts in nine different systems including my own system called Ukidokan. I would take each character and train them in a different type of fighting. Not one of the actors learned the same move! I didn't put in random fancy moves because I don't care about fancy moves, I care about the character! That's how I became a fight choreographer, and then a second unit director, and then a stunt coordinator – so that all the hits are seen on camera!

One thing I want to discuss is your long-standing relationship with John Cusack. Even in *Say Anything... (1989)*, he namedrops you as the face of professional kickboxing. How long have you guys been training together?

He's been my student since 1988. He was just 17 when Don 'The Dragon' Wilson brought him along to The Jet Centre!

The aftermath of John Cusack and Benny Urquidez's fight scene in *Grosse Point Blank* (1997). Photo courtesy of Buena Vista Pictures.

He put you in *Grosse Point Blank* in the prominent role of the hitman, Felix La PuBelle, that's tries to kill him at the school reunion. The two of you have this great fight in the school corridor – how did he pitch that to you?

He had a story in his head and said, 'I would love for you to play this character,' and I said, 'Sure, but John, how real do you want this?' He said, 'I want it real, Sensei!' and I said, 'Then that's exactly what we'll do!'

The first time he kicked me, he kicked me in the chest! He's 6' 4", so I said, 'Kick me a little lower,' and the next time he kicked me, he kicked me into the lockers! I didn't have pads on and my back went into the combination lock so hard, I had the numbers printed on my back!

The director said, 'Why is he hitting you like that?' and I said, 'Because he knows he can!' That's why John wanted me, because he knew he didn't have to worry about kicking me, or throwing me onto cement. That fight scene was easy with John. Normally, it would take three to five days to shoot, but we did it in six hours.

Was it your idea to be stabbed in the neck with the pen?

When John stabbed me in the neck the first time, he went, 'Oh, I'm sorry, Sensei!' but I said, 'Johnny, I'd rather you do it hard, right the first time, than so-so ten times!' He didn't mess around! It marked my neck, but it was awesome!

Do you go with John on most of his films to help with fight scenes? You're listed as doing stunt work on the likes of *Con Air* (1997) and *1408* (2007).

Most of them, except when he's doing a lot of dialogue. When it's action, I go with him!

Did you go with him to China for *Dragon Blade* (2015) and have a re-union with Jackie?

I did! I choreographed their fight. They asked me if I wanted a cameo, but I said I was good behind the camera. I was just there to choreograph the fight between the two of them.

You've also worked with some of the biggest names in action cinema - Stallone, Russell, Chan and Van Damme - apart from John Cusack, who you've obviously trained over decades, who stands out as being the most fun to work with or train?

Morgan Freeman. He was seventy-years-old when I worked with him on *The Contract* (2006), but he is so fun! Brian Dennehy – I took 42 lbs. off him on *Gladiators* (1992). He was so into the training that he dropped 42 lbs. and I loved him for it. Shannon Lee! Oh my God, I did a scene with her and I had pads on, and when she kicked she side kicked me, she hit me so hard. When I looked at her, it was like looking at her father, and her brother at the same time. Man, it was unbelievable.

I can't say enough about the actors that I work with because the first week, they all seem to hesitate, a lot will resist me until I gain their trust. I can push them right to the edge, but they must have faith that I won't let them fall. When it comes to these stars, and brand name actors, I've been very blessed to work with so many of them.

Are there any action films that you've seen recently that you're im-pressed by?

For me, most of the action films these days are doing a lot of acrobatics, and for me, that's not reality. I look for people who can do fights without wires and trampolines. I admire warriors that can fight with just their own body strength. My wife doesn't like to go with me to the movies – I get too technical, but we don't go that often.

Not even to all of John's?

I go to a lot of romantic movies because of my wife!

Do you think it's more fun to play villains than to be cast as the hero?

Let me just put it this way: the only two people in a film that really count are the good Good Guy and the bad Bad Guy. In between, everyone else gets lost in the shuffle – unless they're a really good actor, but without a good Bad Guy, you can't have a Good Guy. You need a really bad guy to make the Good Guy look good. You need the ying and yang. You need the balance. You need a good Bad Guy – it's important!

Vernon Wells

"Ever since you had me thrown out of your unit, I've waited to pay you back. Do you know what today is, Matrix? Pay day!"
— Bennett, Commando (1985)

Select Filmography

- *Mad Max 2: The Road Warrior* (1981) – Wez
- *Weird Science* (1985) – Lord General
- *Commando* (1985) – Bennett
- *Innerspace* (1987) – Mr. Igoe
- *Last Man Standing* (1987) – Roo Marcus
- *Fortress* (1992) – Maddox

John Matrix – a retired Delta Force operative – has found out that someone has been targeting members of his former unit. After an attack at his home in the mountains, Matrix's daughter, Jenny (Alyssa Milano), is kidnapped and he is captured by a group of mercenaries. He is shocked to learn that the man behind his daughter's kidnapping is Bennett (Vernon Wells), one of his former soldiers, who was discharged due to his love of excessive violence, and who now has revenge on his mind....

WHEN I FIRST CONCEIVED OF WRITING this book, and was jotting down the names of actors I wanted to interview, Vernon Wells's name was high up on the list.

41

Bennett (Vernon Wells) and John Matrix (Arnold Schwarzenegger) settle old scores in *Commando* (1985). Photo courtesy of 20th Century Fox.

When it comes to some of the most memorable villains of action cinema, many people go straight to Vernon Wells. The Australian actor achieved worldwide recognition after playing Wez, the psychotic biker in *Mad Max 2* (or *The Road Warrior*, as it is known to our American cousins). However, for many, he'll be best remembered as Bennett in *Commando*.

I was first introduced to Vernon Wells at the tender age of ten-years-old, at a sleepover at a friend's house. I'd never seen either *Mad Max 2* or *Commando* before, but my friend convinced me that they were "the best films ever made." He was right. They were everything a ten-year-old could ask of cinema! Of course, it took us years to realize that Wez and Bennett were played by the same actor. It's not like there was an Internet Movie Database (IMDb) around in 1993 and, to be fair to our ten-year-old selves, Wez looks nothing like Bennett, who must be one of the most unique villains to ever grace the screen.

With his porn star moustache, leather trousers, fingerless gloves and fanatical desire to kill Schwarzenegger's John Matrix, Bennett has long been a fascinating character for film fans. Many have theories about Wells's take on the character – why does he look like "Freddie Mercury on steroids"? Is Bennett secretly in love with Matrix? Why does Bennett wear chainmail? This was why it was imperative that I talked with Vernon for this book.

With the characters of Wez, Bennett, and *Innerspace*'s Mr. Igoe at the forefront of my mind, I had no idea what to expect when I called Vernon. He was incredibly gracious with his time, especially as he was about to go to Sedona for Wolf Week, a large convention dedicated to the conservation of wolves.

Warm, hilarious, an animal lover (Liam Neeson's film *The Grey* (2011) was apparently "total wank" for its portrayal of wolves), and dedicated to his fans, Vernon Wells is nothing like the characters he's best known for portraying onscreen. Better yet, he was happy to answer every stupid question this writer had.

How often does this happen? Someone like me calling you up to discuss the famous roles in your career. Is it a frequent occurrence for you?

No, not really. There's a lot of stories done on me that I really have nothing to do with. They just did one the other week – "Iconic bad guys of the Eighties: where are they now?" They led off with me, and all the characters I have done, saying, 'He's the grandfather of bad guys, who just does the occasional convention, and that's basically it.' All my friends rang me and said, 'Have you seen this shit?'

I was going to say, looking at your filmography, you're a non-stop worker! You've got seven films coming out this year (2017) alone.

I'm doing films back-to-back. Where do these writers get their frigging information? Don't they ever go to IMDb, or do they do it to get a rise out of everybody? Empire Magazine did a wonderful thing where they voted on who they thought were the Top Ten Villains over the last twenty years. I came in number two!

I had a guy ring me up who wanted to do a story on me, but all he wanted was dirt on Mel Gibson, so I just hung up.

Does a day go by when someone doesn't yell, "Let off some steam, Bennett!" at you?

[Laughs] Not so much. You know what the fun part about being me is?

Go on...

I don't get recognized. Hardly ever. [People] will recognize me from *The Road Warrior* and they will walk up to me in the strangest places. I remember one night, I went to see a film with my wife and I was waiting for her to come out of the toilet. Suddenly, this voice in my ear went, 'You can run, but you can't hide.' I just about had a heart attack right there. I just froze, and this lady walked over and she said, 'I'm so sorry, sweetheart. He watches that film religiously, and he as soon as he saw you he was beside himself.'

I turned around and there was this guy in his thirties, and he looked like a five-year-old kid. He was so excited. He was jumping up and down on the spot. I went, 'How did you recognize me?' because I've now got a beard and long hair and he said, 'Your eyes and your voice, dude, you can't disguise them!'

People do the funniest things. I remember being in Las Vegas, and I was in an elevator with my wife. We were coming down from the twenty-

Wez (Vernon Wells) goes on the rampage in *Mad Max 2* (1981).
Photo courtesy of Vernon Wells.

second floor and this guy got on a couple of floors below us. He was just standing there, and I was talking, and all of a sudden, he went, 'Oh my god, you're the guy from *The Road Warrior!*' I went, 'Yes.' He said, 'That is so amazing.' I said, 'Thank you,' shook his hand, and he just stood there with his mouth open looking at me until the elevator got to the bottom.

I guess that's the weird thing about fan interactions. You probably have one of two situations: people know who you are, and probably ask you the same three or four questions; or, people just stand there, and it gets weird very quickly.

Totally weird. Sometimes I just stand there looking at these people going, 'Say something,' but that comes with the territory.

With Wez being the role that you're most associated with, how did you end up getting cast in *Mad Max 2*?

I'd done three or four TV shows, but never as an actor. I was a country boy – I rode horses, I drove everything that had wheels, I could handle guns and things like that. If I had a line, I hated it. The truth is, I never wanted to be an actor, it didn't appeal to me. I was the lead singer in a couple of very successful bands, and my mother had been a country and western songwriter. I followed in her footsteps and that's where I saw my-self. Acting was the furthest thing from my mind, until I was involved in a car accident.

I fractured two vertebrae in my back and couldn't move or work. While I was recovering, I was a total pain to our manager, who went around every agent in Melbourne trying to get me a job. Finally, one of them said, 'Look, we're looking for a guy that can ride horses for a series of cigarette commercials. Can you send him in?' I went in and they went, 'You're perfect,' and I got it.

I did these five commercials for this new cigarette brand which, by the way, never went on the market, it was all a tax write-off, and they started sending me out as an extra on different shows. I was making a damn good living. People would see me standing in the crowd and say, 'Hey you! Big and ugly! Get your ass up here!' but when they asked me to say something, I would be terrified.

What I loved was the mechanics of being involved in a production. I got behind the camera and I started learning everything I could. I started directing TV commercials and opened a company with some friends of mine who were directors. Of course, that didn't last either.

I was then asked to do a stage play called *Hosanna* (1973) by Michel Tremblay, a French-Canadian writer. It's a two-hander, which means there's only two actors in the play. For two-and-a-half hours! I said no for about five months, but finally my brother convinced me to do it. It turned out to be a big hit and ran for four-and-a-half months to full houses. While it was playing, George Miller's girlfriend, Sandy Gore, happened to see me on stage and said to George, 'I found Wez.' She said I was one of the bravest actors she'd seen in a long time. 'He has no fear of what he does. He just gets out there and lays it all on the line.'

How did George describe the role to you?

George came down to Melbourne and we had a cup of coffee, talked, and told each other stupid jokes. He left and I had no idea why he needed to come down, because I wasn't interested in that side of the equation. I figured the stage play was it. That was my fifteen minutes of fame and I didn't need anymore.

Three months later, my manager rang me and said, 'You have to fly to Sydney for wardrobe and makeup test.' I went, 'For what?' and she said, 'For this new film, *Mad Max 2*.' I'd never seen the first one, so I had no idea what the second one was.

I thought the first *Mad Max* (1979) had been a massive hit in Australia?

It was. I just hadn't seen it, so I really didn't know what it was about. I read the script and I was like, 'No, I can't do this. This is way above my pay scale.' I just said no, but George had so much faith in me. He saw this something inside me that I couldn't see, that I was afraid of, in a way.

What was it in the original script that concerned you about playing the role?

I didn't think I was good enough. I was a non-actor and the character had to be real. That was the point.

Three years ago, I was in Japan for the opening of *Mad Max: Fury Road* [2015]. George was there and we went out and had dinner, and I asked him, 'Why did you choose me, George?' He said, 'I needed to hire someone who, when I said to them, 'I need you to jump off that building,' would jump. I needed someone that wasn't jaded by the whole system, someone that was so enthusiastic to do it and get involved! I also needed someone that when the women looked at him, they would just go, 'Anywhere else, I would fuck him to death!"

I went, 'You got two out of three,' and he just laughed. That's what he was looking for and, apparently, I had all those things, and he brought them out of me. I think that's why whenever the film's mentioned, everybody thinks of my character. It was never planned that way.

Well, Max is a man of very few words and Mel underplays the role a lot. Whereas Wez and your performance is larger than life. You're right in both Max and the audiences' faces, literally in some cases.

It caused a bit of a rift between us. I adore Mel, and I think he's one of the best actors of his generation. He's also an amazing director. Mel has directed five amazing fucking movies. He and George can stand toe-to-toe. I have nothing but all the praise in the world for him. I loved working with him. He gave me everything I needed to make that character work, and at no time on that set in the freezing cold did we ever have a cross word. Never.

He can't have been that upset about you overshadowing him because *Mad Max 2* propelled him straight to Hollywood, so it must have been a very temporary rift that the two of you had.

I think it was more the way the press went after it. They just kept blowing it up bigger than it was. Today, I would work with Mel in a heartbeat. If Mel walked through the door of my office and said, 'I'm doing a film. I want you in it. I've got $5. Will you do it?' I'd give him $5!

I've always thought that, as a villain, Wez is very progressive. He has a boyfriend, and when he's killed, that's what drives Wez's obsession to go after the Feral Kid and Max. I was wondering what the backstory was for that.

Everybody thought he was my boyfriend, but I didn't. There's a scene that's not in the film, but is in the script that explains this.

A publicity shot of Wez (Vernon Wells) and Jerry O'Sullivan as Golden Youth
in *Mad Max 2* (1982). Photo courtesy of Vernon Wells.

We had an opening scene where all these marauders go to this farmhouse and rape and kill everyone. I ride up and just watch what they're doing. Then, this little blonde kid comes running out and one of the marauders grabs him by his hair. He's about to cut his throat when I stop him. I put him on the back of my bike and he becomes my surrogate. I never saw him as my lover, but everybody else did. I saw him as this young kid that I saved and that I was bringing up as my son, the person who will take over when I die. That was how I looked at it, but people looked at it the other way, and I used to get really bent out of shape about it.

However, I soon realized that that was stupid because people looked at the film the way they wanted to see it. I think it's because George created an ambiguous world. A world where sexuality has no defining line. Male and female roles are totally blurred. I think it's the reason that the *Mad Max* films are so successful, because George blurs that line, and you accept it.

Obviously, George did that in *Fury Road* to massive critical acclaim and box office success. With *Mad Max 2*, where the budget was probably a fraction of *Fury Road*'s, did you end up doing a lot of your own stunt work due to the limited size of the production?

I did a lot of it, but as George would tell you, he had to tie me down occasionally, because if I got killed or I broke something, they wouldn't have me for the rest of the film. Jumping on and off trucks and doing all that stuff just came naturally, but there were things like the flip off the fort's boardwalk, when I grab the guy and smash his head in, I didn't do that. I couldn't have done that. I would have broken every bone in my body. The costume was so cumbersome and heavy. You had to know what you're doing.

There was another stunt where I was transferring between the motorbike and the truck that didn't have the back on it. George wouldn't let me do that because he was afraid that if I hit one of those wheels I would go under. I agreed. We all did most of our stunts, but we had an amazing stunt crew.

The stunt director Max Aspen fractured his back in a stunt he did with the car when he gets bitten by the snakes. That was basically it. Nobody was seriously wounded. George is safety-conscious to a fault. Everything has got to be so safe, because- you think about the final chase scene: there's probably twenty motorbikes and ten vehicles driving at full power, just one false move, and you're on the road, being run over by a semi, and probably twenty other vehicles! I got my elbow chipped from a boomerang when the kid threw it, and that's it.

After *Mad Max 2*, Hollywood obviously came calling and you semi-reprised your role of Wez as the Lord General in *Weird Science*. Was it (producer) Joel Silver or (director) John Hughes that was a fan of *Mad Max 2*?

Joel Silver. Once again, I didn't want to do it.

Really?

Because it was just repeating the role. I was like, 'I've done that. I don't really want to go there again.'

I also didn't want to come to America. America terrified me. But eventually, of course, I got brought over to do the film. I think one of the

Bennett (Vernon Wells) in his distinctive outfit in *Commando* (1985).
Photo courtesy of Vernon Wells.

selling points was John Hughes, because I knew what he'd done - *Sixteen Candles* [1984], *The Breakfast Club* [1985], *Ferris Bueller's Day Off* [1986]. When somebody like that is directing you, you should go and do it for a bit of fun.

If you look at Lord General, he's nothing like Wez. He's a lot more fun. He's got this twinkle in his eyes. Wez wouldn't have done that. Wez would have come through the door, screamed, and started shooting the shit out of everybody. There were two different attitudes to the same character.

Then Joel Silver put you in *Commando*.

While I was there, Joel took me to meet the director of *Commando* (Mark L. Lester), but he didn't want me. When I finished doing *Weird Science*, I left, and I went back to Australia to, once again, direct commercials.

Joel Silver tracked me down, and at that point they were probably three weeks into filming. He said, 'There's a ticket for you at the airport. Get your ass on a plane tomorrow.' I had twelve hours to put my life in order.

You weren't the first pick for Bennett and you ended up replacing an actor. Do you know what happened there?

What I heard, and I can't tell you if it's true or not, was that the actor was two inches taller than me, but a lot slimmer, and Arnold was very worried about the fight scenes. He thought it would not look authentic that this guy could stand a chance against him. I think it became a little bit of a problem, but I also heard he was a method actor, which apparently drove Arnold mad. I think the first one's probably closer to the truth. I loved my costume, but it was very tight.

We should talk about the costume. Was that already designed for the previous actor, and you literally had to step into his shoes, or did they change the costume for you?

No, it was exactly the way he had it. I flew to the States and they didn't have time to make a new costume.

It was always going to be the chain mail vest, the fingerless gloves, and the leather trousers? Just on someone a lot slimmer and shorter?

It's called a stoker's vest, which people wore when they were putting the coal into the furnaces of ships. They made it up to look like it was chain mail, but if it had been real chain mail, it would have weighed about 45 lbs. There's no way I'd have been dancing around if I were wearing that. I'd have been crawling around the floors. Also, I don't know a lot of chain mail where the pipe would have gone all the way through so easily.

To me, the costume was what it was, and what it should have been for the character. It made the character. Making me look like Freddy Mercury was not intentional, but it kind of happened.

I think it made you stand out.

I think so. They brought out an issue of Mad Magazine after the film was released, and it had a scene where I'm talking to Arnold, and across the chainmail, it's got printed, 'I am not Freddy Mercury on steroids.' That's when I decided I had to accept it.

What was the character Bennett like in the script? You infuse him with a sort of exuberance and slight craziness that I can't imagine was there on paper.

We didn't have a lot of time to sit around and discuss it, so a lot of what you saw, was me. [Bennett] always felt that he was better than Matrix, and that he should have been the team leader. The whole thing for him was payback. He wants to destroy Matrix to show everybody that he's the better man. He enjoyed what he did. He had a twinkle in his eye that showed he liked kidnapping little girls, and blowing people up!

I always enjoyed playing Bennett because he had an agenda, and he was going to see it through to the end. I think that's why the fight scene at the end worked so well. There was no, 'If you kick my ass, I'm going to walk away and crawl into a corner and cry.' It was, 'I was going to go out there to kill him,' and that was the end of it.

You guys really do look like you're going at it in the final fight. You're fighting in a furnace, Arnie looks like he's sweating buckets, and you're wearing thick layers. What was it like to film?

We shot it over three days, and it was very intense, and extremely mind-numbing. You got exhausted so quickly because of the heat. There were

Behind the scenes with Arnold Schwarzenegger on *Commando* (1985).
Photo courtesy of Vernon Wells.

live burners going so it was hot as hell. We were always sweaty.

Arnie and I went at it. We're big boys. There was no, 'I'm just going to tap you on the shoulder and you pretend I've hurt you.' We were in there doing it to make it look as real as possible.

Considering the actor that you replaced was allegedly a method actor, and you seem much more laid back, how did Arnie react to you coming in three weeks into the production? Was he welcoming?

He's a total joker, but he wasn't welcoming because he thought that I was a little too laid back. He told Joel that he really needed a man, not a pussy! The first scene we did together was where he's tied to the table and I put the knife to his throat. It was the first thing we did together, and I didn't know who he was. I couldn't even pronounce his name, for God's sake.

After we did the actual scene, Joel walked out to Arnold and said, 'Do you want me to recast?' and he said, 'We'll keep him, but never give him a real knife!' The minute we did the scene, Arnold realized that I was deadly serious. From that moment on, we were the best of friends. All he did was

On set with Alyssa Milano in *Commando* (1985). Photo courtesy of Vernon Wells.

play jokes on me through the whole shoot. He'd pull my trailer apart and do horrible things to me.

Hang on. Arnie pulled your trailer apart?!

Arnold is like a big kid. That was fun to be around.

There's almost an entire subculture based around Bennett, so I would be right in thinking, that of all your fans, *Commando* fans are the most intense?

Oh God, yes. The fans for *Commando* are really intense. There's a whole group over in England that each year all dress up as Bennett.

I took a long time to get used to it, as I was always afraid of celebrity, as I never grew up with it. I grew up in a totally different culture where being a movie star was not the end-all and be-all of everything. Even now, I hate it when people go, 'Man, you are such a big star,' I say, 'No, I'm just a very lucky actor.'

To me, the film works when everybody works really hard to make it work, not when you've got one person who thinks the world revolves around them.

After *Commando*, did you find you had lots of new opportunities or did you feel that pressure to "be a star"?

Strangely enough there wasn't a lot of pressure, because once again I went home to Australia. The pressure came after I did *Innerspace* with Steven Spielberg. For some reason, because that film was a hit, I was invited to be in everything. However, it quickly died down because it wasn't a massive hit. Now it's become this cult classic and everybody wants to talk to me about it now!

In *Innerspace*, as Mr. Igoe, you're essentially a mute Terminator. How did Joe Dante end up casting you in that film?

I was leaving America to go home to Australia again and my manager called and said I had an audition with Joe Dante for his new film. I went and met Joe and he told me there was no dialogue, but the character could put all kinds of weapons on his fake hand. I thought it was really cool.

We were sat at this round table with a glass surface held on top of it, and as I got up to leave and catch my plane, I leant on the edge of the table and the whole top lifted up and I just went flat on my ass! Joe just looked at me and said, 'That's one of the noblest ways I've ever seen somebody try to get a movie.'

Well, it got you the role!

I flew home and when I arrived in Australia there was a guy standing in the terminal holding a card with my name on it. He said, 'I have a telegram for you, sir.' I thought something had happened to my mother, but it was from the casting director. It also had a ticket to fly back to Los Angeles immediately! I was in Australia for two or three hours! I saw my family in the terminal, walked over and said, 'Hey, it's been really cool to see you guys. Bye!'

During *Innerspace*, Spielberg was at the top of his game and Dante had made *Gremlins* (1984) and *Explorers* (1985). What was it like working with some of the biggest names in the business at that time?

When we started, Joe said, 'Steven wanted you to do this because he loves *Mad Max* and he loved your character. However, he knows you use your eyes, you use your voice, and you use your hands, so you're going to have a fake arm, you're going to wear sunglasses, and you're not saying a word! He wants to see if you can really act!' I just stood there stunned. For an actor that is like saying, 'I'm going to break both your legs and now I want you to run around and jump on a horse!'

During filming, Joe always used to say to me, 'Smaller'. His reasoning was that I'm so big that even when I don't speak, I could still be imposing so that's how I played it.

Steven came to the set which I thought was wonderful and, of course, I did what everybody on the planet hopes they never do when they get introduced to Steven Spielberg. I just stood there and went, 'I really loved *E.T.* [the Extra-Terrestrial, 1982]!'

I love Joe, I did three films for him. He's the nicest man to work with and Steven's the same. I run into him all the time at the grocery store.

Are you serious? I can't imagine for a moment that Steven Spielberg does his own shopping?

He does! I was at 39 Flavors (an American ice cream parlor) with my wife, and Steven Spielberg, his wife, and two of his kids came in. I said, 'There's Steven Spielberg, I've got to go and say hi,' and my wife went, 'Don't you dare. He won't have a clue who you are. You will just make a fool out of yourself. I won't stand here and be embarrassed by you.' So, we just walked out, but about two weeks later, we were going to the local supermarket and Steven and his son walked out of it. I went 'Steven!' and he turned to his son and said, 'This is the guy I told you about who did that wonderful film *The Road Warrior* and who did *Innerspace* for us!' His son asked me loads of questions and I said, 'This is my wife Grace who doesn't believe you'd remember me!' and he just cracked up.

I have to ask you about the vibrator hand attachment in *Innerspace*....

Oh my god, few people pick up on that! That was done as a joke. Steven was in England producing *Batteries Not Included* [1987], so what they would do was that they'd send the dallies over to him. Joe, being Joe, every so often did a scene that was just a little bit off-kilter just for laughs.

That scene with the vibrator was done as a joke, but Steven loved it so much, it was left in the film. The funny thing is, most people don't get it, but I love all that shit. We all take ourselves so seriously. I love that film, I really do. Everybody in it was so wonderful and I just had the greatest time doing it.

You're also familiar to a whole new generation thanks to roles in shows like *Power Rangers*.

The funny thing is, now, that I'm hired more by kids in their thirties than by my own generation! There's a whole new generation that were raised on stuff like *Mad Max*.

Do you think your roles in films like *Commando* and *Innerspace* helped your career or do you feel you got typecast as a villain after that?

When you play the villain you're like the flavor of the week, but what people don't realize is when you do a major film and you're playing the villain, you're not on the same pay scale as the guy playing the hero!

The thing is, if you say, 'I want more money,' they just show you the door and bring someone else in. I think I was fortunate in some ways,

Vernon terrifying a whole new generation of viewers as Ransik in *Power Rangers Time Force* (2001). Photo courtesy of Vernon Wells.

because I managed to do three iconic movies, one after the other, which doesn't really happen a lot, but people had no idea who I was, and that played against me. I didn't have a recognizable face, I didn't go out to all the Hollywood premieres, I wasn't a junkie, I didn't drink, which I also think played against me!

I was also my own worst enemy as well, because I didn't want to do what I was doing. I was sick of playing the villain after a while, so I tried to get out of it and I screwed things up. Then I met my wife and suddenly things changed, virtually overnight. I was going to auditions and walking out the door with the contract in my hand. Now I've got to a point when I don't even to go auditions. Directors and producers just ring me and offer me roles. I think if I had gone along the path I was on, I'd have gone from being the villain to the hero's friend. Now, I'm a character actor. I got dragged into this kicking and screaming, but now I've won and I'm happy.

In your eyes, what do you think makes a good villain? Do you feel that of all the roles you've done, playing a bad guy was more fun?

The villain is always more fun, because the villain has no parameters. The more villainous the villain is, the more people love him! To me, it's very simple: I was told once upon a time, very early in my career, 'A villain is a good guy who considers a good guy to be the villain.'

That's how you play it. You never play a villain as a villain. You play the villain as the good guy trying to do what he wants and you see the good guy as a villain trying to stop you. You give him a multi-dimensional layer which gives you more places to go. I think that the villain is always the best role in a movie, and I'll never ever turn one down. It's just too much fun playing them.

Derrick O'Connor

"I'm the guy that changed the course of your life, man..."
– Pieter Vorstedt, *Lethal Weapon 2* (1989).

Select Filmography

- *Hawk the Slayer* (1980) - Ralf
- *Time Bandits* (1981) – Robber Leader
- *Brazil* (1985) – Dowser
- *Lethal Weapon 2* (1989) – Pieter Vorstedt
- *Deep Rising* (1998) – Captain Atherton
- *End of Days* (1999) – Thomas Aquinas
- *Daredevil* (2003) – Father Everett

Detectives Riggs and Murtaugh have been investigating the South African consul-general Arjun Rudd (Joss Ackland) who has been operating a smuggling ring and hiding behind diplomatic immunity to get away with his crimes. However, that hasn't stopped the two gung-ho police officers from harassing him at every turn. Fed up with their persistence, Rudd orders his right-hand man, Pieter Vorstedt, to kill the police officers pursuing them. Vorstedt captures Riggs and reveals he had been hired to kill him several years ago, but accidently ended up killing Rigg's wife. With several of his friends dead at the hands of the South Africans and this new revelation, the stage is set for Riggs to enact vengeance upon those who have wronged him and his partner.

Pieter Vorstedt (Derrick O'Connor (right)) protects Arjen Rudd (Joss Ackland)
from the investigations of Riggs and Murtaugh in *Lethal Weapon 2* (1989).
Photo courtesy of Warner Brothers.

LETHAL WEAPON 2 IS HEADED BY two wonderful and distinctly non-South African actors, Joss Ackland, and Derrick O'Connor. Cast in the role of Arjen Rudd, Ackland came to represent, for many action film fans, the face of South Africa's ruthless apartheid government, forever remembered for his infamous line "Diplomatic immunity!" However, it was Vorstedt, Rudd's right-hand man, who shocked audiences. It was Vorstedt who killed off key supporting characters including; the consulate's naïve secretary, Rika van den Haas (Patsy Kensit); and a few of Riggs and Murtaugh's fellow police officers, played by the likes of Dean Norris (*Total Recall*, 1990; *Starship Troopers*, 1997) and Jeanette Goldstein (*Aliens*, 1986).

Naturally while writing this book, I did reach out to Joss Ackland to talk about the villainous role of Arjen Rudd in Lethal Weapon 2 and his other roles in films like *The Hunt for Red October* (1990), *Bill and Ted's Bogus Journey* (1991) (which he apparently hated) and even *Miracle on 34th Street* (1994)! Tragically, at the time of writing, Mr. Ackland was battling a serious illness and was unable to take part. Luckily, we still have his many wonderful performances to remember him by.

Despite appearing in big-budget films like *End of Days*, *Daredevil*, and *Pirates of the Caribbean: Dead Man's Chest* (2006), O'Connor only occasionally appears on the big screen these days, choosing instead to live in San Francisco with his wife. If you were to look at Derrick O'Connor's filmography, the role of Pieter Vorstedt would be an anomaly. For years, the Irish-born actor, who was a member of the Royal Shakespeare Company (RSC), was a regular on British TV, appearing in shows such as *Z Cars* (1962) and *Crown Court* (1972) before appearing on the big screen in genre films like *Hawk the Slayer* and *Time Bandits*. He was more than happy to discuss his time working on *Lethal Weapon 2*, and certainly didn't pull any punches when discussing some of his more famous co-stars over the year.

How's your South African accent these days? Can you still pull it out the bag?

Pretty much. It's easy to do and my first wife's mother lived in South Africa, so I was quite familiar with it. That role was more fun to play than straighter roles I've played. In the UK, I'd been in *The Sweeney* (1975) and stuff like that, and I'd played Ralf the Bowman in *Hawk the Slayer*, which was good fun!

How did you, an Irish-born, RSC trained actor, end up in Hollywood?

I was getting married and we were on our way to Hawaii. My wife is from San Francisco and, as we were getting ready to go, my agent suggested I pop into Warner Brothers on the way. So, I went in, and they told me all about the part, and asked if I could hang around for a few weeks. I told them that I was planning on going to Hawaii, so they said, 'Oh… you better meet the producer then.'

Hang on. You just dropped into Warner Brothers and they offered you the role straight away? Didn't you have to audition at all?

I had to read for it, but they gave it to me straight away, which is very unusual for Hollywood. They kept asking me to hang around, and introduced me to the producer [Joel Silver], and he also asked me to stick around. I kept saying, 'No, I'm going to Hawaii,' but then I met the director [Richard Donner] and Mel Gibson, and they said, 'Right, you've got the part.' They gave me a script and that was it! I hadn't heard of anything like that happening before.

Do you think your ability to nail the South African accent helped?

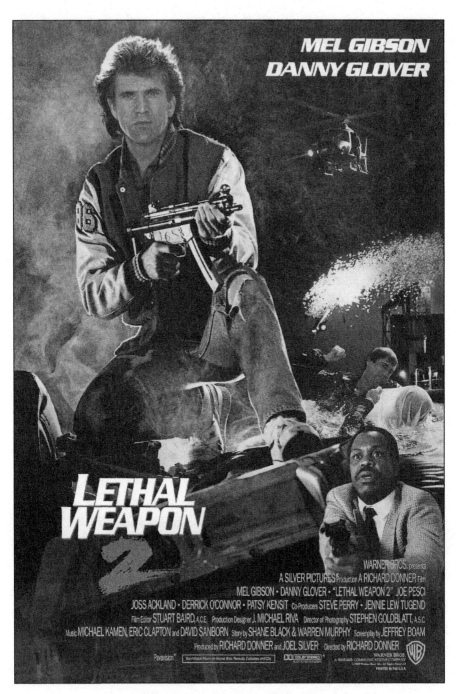

The theatrical poster for *Lethal Weapon 2* (1989).
Photo courtesy of Warner Brothers.

Yeah, I guess it did. I've got a pretty good ear for accents, so that wasn't really a big deal for me. It was a bit of a fluke. It was all a bit strange really.

The first *Lethal Weapon* had been a massive hit. At the time, did you know you were reading for the sequel?

I had no idea what it was. I hadn't seen the first film, I hadn't heard of it. I didn't know anything.

The script for *Lethal Weapon 2* reportedly went through a lot of re-writes. In the first draft by Shane Black, the character of Pieter Vor-stedt was apparently called 'Benedict' and was written as Riggs's arch-nemesis. Did you ever see this earlier version?

I never saw a different script, so it was always Pieter Vorstedt for me. It stayed the same all the way through.

With the South African apartheid government still in power at the time, did you have any reservations about taking the role, or were you happy to stick it to the regime?

No, I hated the fucking regime. I hated everything about it, and so it was quite good to nail the bastards. It was quite a treat to do that, but there were things we did that were cut out of the final film.

When Danny Glover goes to the embassy to get a South African passport, in one version, he got up on the desk and took all his clothes off and started acting like an ape on the table. Unfortunately, they cut it out, but it was quite the social commentary, in a funny kind of way.

In your scenes with Danny Glover, you have to use certain racial slurs towards him. I imagine that must have been awkward?

It was all very professional. You've got to do it right. You can't mess about with it. I mean, you do it right or not at all. There's no pussy-footing with it really.

Usually Hollywood studios are wary of insulting territories where they can potentially sell such a big movie, but they seem very forthright

about sticking it to South Africa. Were there ever any conversations about changing the ethnicity of the bad guys?

Always South African. No, Warner Brothers were committed to it, and it never changed, which was good because normally they're changing scripts like this all the time, but there was none of that going on.

How were your scenes with Mel? Most of your scenes are together and you have that big fight scene at the end.

It was fine. I mean he's had a lot of bad press, but I haven't spoken to him since the film. When we were working together, he was perfect, and he was always on time. I can't say anything bad about him at the time, but I haven't seen him since.

Did you already have a background in martial arts or did you have to train for your final fight with Mel?

We learnt a French fighting style called Savate. It was a technique that French sailors picked up on trips from Marseilles to Singapore. When they got to Singapore, they'd learn some martial arts, and then adapt it on the way home, when the ship would be rolling around, so they ended up developing this new style of fighting. It was good fun and very interesting to learn.

Do you still keep it up?

No, that was it really. I'm not a big gym fanatic.

You had a spectacular death! Being crushed by a cargo crate is a good way to go.

I know! I think the old 'crate on the head' is a good one. They had to build a model of me for that. They built this fucking automaton that must have cost a fortune.

I thought they just dropped a hollow crate over you.

No fucking way! It was a real crate! The thing they dropped it on was an automaton with a working head that could move. It was quite an intricate piece of work, but it must have cost them $10-20,000!

You said your first wife was South African. Once the film was released, did you go back there? Do you know how the film, or how your character was received?

Never. I never went back. I hate the place.

Once the film came out and was a big box office success, you seemed to avoid the trap that many actors falls into, which is to get cast in similar roles. You didn't get cast as a villain again after *Lethal Weapon 2*, so was that a conscious effort on your part?

You go for what's available and what's being offered. I never liked being typecast, but I never thought I'd end up in America anyway. I thought I'd do *Lethal Weapon 2* and then I'd return to England. I never foresaw a career here at all.

I went back and did stuff for the BBC, and then I went to Australia and filmed *Centrepoint* (1990). That was a fun part to do, but then (Margaret) Thatcher pissed me off. She's a fucking monster. So, I thought I'd do a couple of films a year in the U.S. and make it work as my wife lived in San Francisco.

You did seem to end up being typecast as a priest in a couple of films – *End of Days* and *Daredevil*. How did that happen?

I've no idea. I gave up the Catholic faith when I was twelve, but they're very straight-forward in the U.S. when it comes to casting.

In *End of Days*, you had the role of Thomas Aquinas. What was it like doing a big budget film with Arnold Schwarzenegger?

Ah, the big Austrian Plank. He'd flirt with women all over the set, and he's so rude. I would try and speak some German to him and he wasn't interested. He's just a rude fucker, that's all.

That's a shame, because you two had a lot of scenes together.

He'd be there with his big, fat cigar. He's a big fucking oak tree of a person! He's alright, I guess. Someone must love him. Something in his favor is his arguments with Trump. I was impressed when he did that. I thought, 'Good for you, Arnie. You've got some guts.' Affleck's a lot brighter! But we didn't really talk much as he had a busy schedule.

I was going to ask about your relationship with Terry Gilliam as you've been in several of his films.

The first time was when I played a flying Hogfish salesman in *Jabberwocky* (1977), and then I was in *Time Bandits* as one of the Merry Men, and that was great fun. Cleese was great fun and we changed the script a lot because Terry gave us the freedom to do that.

Originally there was a scene between me and Cleese and I thought, 'Wouldn't it be funnier to have a guy to come in to translate what I was saying because I was so stupid and thick?' He'd ask me a question, and I'd say gibberish, and someone would have to translate what I'd said. That worked out quite well.

O'Connor appears in the cult monster movie *Deep Rising* (1999) as Captain Atherton. Photo courtesy of Buena Vista Pictures.

With all these films you've been in, are you recognized on the street at all?

No, I keep well away from all that. Someone did recognize me in Macy's once. I think that was it! I'm not very recognizable I guess.

You are also in one of my favorite guilty pleasure films, *Deep Rising*, where you play the ill-fated Captain Atherton.

(Laughs) *Deep Rising*?! That was the worst experience I've ever had in my life. It was terrible! It was fucking awful! It was nothing of a part; there was nothing there, but it was the most money I'd ever made. I was just bored fucking senseless. It was unbelievably boring. We had to do these shots with the monster and it was all very complicated with the green screen and all that. We had to follow a yellow balloon with our eyes!

With all the roles you've done, do you think playing bad guys is more fun?

Absolutely, yes. It is the best thing you can do and it takes you out of playing moral compass-leading men parts, which are a bit boring. As a bad guy, you get to do things you wouldn't normally get to do and that is more fun!

Robert Wall

"Boards don't hit back!"

– Lee, *Enter the Dragon* (1973)

Select Filmography

- *The Way of the Dragon* (1972) – Bob
- *Enter the Dragon* (1973) – O'Hara
- *Black Belt Jones* (1974) – Mob Henchman
- *Game of Death* (1978) – Carl Miller
- *Enter the Ninja* (1981) – Thug
- *Code of Silence* (1985) – Thug
- *Invasion U.S.A.* (1985) – Vince
- *Firewalker* (1986) – Jose
- *Hero and the Terror* (1988) – Wall
- *Blood and Bone* (2009) – O'Hara

Notorious crime lord Han (Shih Lee) is hosting a martial art tournament on his mysterious island attracting fighters from all around the world. British intelligence has dispatched Lee (Bruce Lee), a skilled Shaolin warrior, to infiltrate the island to find evidence of Han's involvement in drug trafficking and prostitution. However, Lee is also going for his own reasons – O'Hara, Han's trusted bodyguard, was responsible for his sister's death several years earlier.

Lee (Bruce Lee) is unimpressed by O'Hara's display of strength and intimidation as they square off in *Enter the Dragon* (1973). Photo courtesy of Bob Wall.

I REMEMBER THE FIRST TIME I saw *Enter the Dragon*. I was eleven or twelve and had just discovered Jackie Chan films, thanks to Channel 4 screening the likes of *Project A* (1983) and *Police Story* (1985) late at night. My uncle told me that if I loved those movies, I'd definitely have to check out Bruce Lee's.

Of course, I knew who Bruce Lee was, but I had never seen any of his films, so my uncle lent me his VHS tape of *Enter the Dragon* whilst doing some terrible, and now that I think about it, racist impressions of Bruce Lee's 'Don't concentrate on the finger or you'll miss all the heavenly glory,' speech. He never got the VHS back.

I watched it constantly, and a year later, all of Bruce Lee's other films were re-released on VHS, too. Sure, they were dubbed, and all the nun-chuck scenes had been removed but, up until then, acquiring the likes of *The Big Boss* (1971), *Fist of Fury* (alternatively titled, The Chinese Connection, 1972), *Way of the Dragon* (1972), and *Game of Death* (1978) had been impossible. It wouldn't be until Hong Kong Legends re-released the films on DVD that I would see them uncut and in their original language, but at the time I didn't care. I became obsessed with Bruce Lee, reading every book I could find on him, and watching every film and documentary ever released. I even watched a bunch of Bruceploitation films like *Game of Death 2* (1981) and *Re-Enter the Dragon* (1979), starring a bunch of look-alikes with similar sounding names (Bruce Li! Bruce Le! Bruce Lai! Bronson Lee!) to get my fix. It was nothing compared to the real thing.

Bruce Lee was one of a kind and the fact that he died a decade before I was even born, and still had such an impact on my life, speaks to his legacy. He has inspired millions of people around the world, brought martial arts to the mainstream, and is one of the most enduring icons of the twentieth century. Naturally, for this book, I had to track down someone who had worked with him, on some of his iconic films, and my first thought was Robert "Bob" Wall.

In the 1970s, Robert Wall was already a karate champion and one of the most prominent names in the sport, alongside Joe Lewis and Chuck Norris. It was no surprise, then, that his and Bruce Lee's paths would cross and, recognizing his talents, Lee would put him in two of his films – *Way of the Dragon* and *Enter the Dragon*.

Aged seventy-nine, when we spoke, Robert Wall had just finished his morning workout and was more than happy to talk about his times with Bruce Lee, as well as his long-lasting friendship with Chuck Norris, and the many rumors and conspiracy theories that still, to this day, surround the making of *Enter the Dragon*. However, where we started was in discussing how he and Chuck helped Arnold Schwarzenegger move into his first apartment....

How do you know Arnold?

When he first got here in sixty-nine, he looked Chuck Norris and I up. We spent a lot of time with him, and were with him the first day he got his first apartment. He was very excited. He had a little one-bedroom apartment in Santa Monica, and had this gigantic oak bed with double mail slots over the headboard, which I thought was interesting. I pulled out one of the pamphlets that went in there, and it said, "How to Develop the Outer Head of the Tricep by Arnold Schwarzenegger, $2.95." I put it away and pulled out another one. It said, "How to Develop the Inner Head of the Tricep."

He had all the body parts there. He hadn't been in the country six months at that point and was already making thousands a month. Chuck and I used to go to his birthday every year, but everyone was smoking cigars, and a lot of other things, so after a few years we just didn't want to go back. We don't do drugs and we don't smoke, so after a while we floated away.

Clean living has obviously paid off for you. You've just finished your morning workout and you're a ninth-degree black belt in several martial arts.

Yes, but the degree doesn't mean anything. I've met black belts that claim to be seventeenth degree, so I'm kind of down on degrees. One of my first instructors was Gene LeBell, who started MMA [Mixed Martial Arts]. I consider him the toughest man on earth. He was the greatest martial artist ever. He did the first MMA fight in 1962 and he took out a guy who was a rated boxer – Milo Savage – a light heavyweight from Salt Lake City. Gene choked him out.

Savage made a mistake of saying he had knocked out several drunks in bars, that had claimed to be black belts. He foolishly put out a challenge of $5,000 to fight any martial artist. At that time, there was no way to make money in the martial arts other than teaching, so Gene, who would strangle his grandmother for $100, took up the challenge.

Milo studied up who Gene was and came into the ring all oiled up, so that Gene couldn't get hold of him. It took Gene to the end of third round before he got him. He picked him up and body slammed him. I thought he killed him!

Jesus.

[laughs] Savage was unconscious for 20 minutes. That was the first MMA pro fight! For $5,000! Gene always said, 'Wear the rank you can defend on the mat' People will tell you they're a seventeenth degree, twelfth degree, tenth degree or whatever. 99.9% of them can't fight. Those who can fight don't talk about their ranks.

Obviously, you're a martial arts legend – you're the CEO and co-founder of World Black Belt, you were a member of the world professional team, you've fought and trained with the best in the world – but how

did you get into martial arts in the first place? Obviously in the fifties, it wasn't as well known or established as it is now.

When I was a freshman in high school, I was five feet tall and 93 lbs., so I got beat up a lot, and I didn't like it. When I was in the eighth grade, the biggest kid in school, who was 250 lbs., wrecked my bike and beat me up. He went to the bathroom, and when he walked out, I picked up a brick and smashed him in the face. It took him out of school for a year. It crushed his cheek bones, knocked out his teeth, and broke his nose. It completely changed his look forever. I told him and everybody else in school, 'If you ever start with me again, I'm going to take a rock, tree, club to you. Nobody's going to beat me up again.'

That reputation worked for me in the eighth grade, but when I went to high school, nobody knew who I was. I decided to take up the only martial arts available which, in those days, was wrestling. I got the hell beat out of me for the first year, so I started working out with the biggest guys in school and, by my third year, I was undefeated. Wrestling got me a scholarship to college, and when I got there Judo was just taking off. I didn't know what Judo was, so I started and, of course, got the heck beat out of me for the next year!

Then I heard about Gene LeBell. Gene had won the two-time AAU Judo nationals of 1954 and 1955 in San Francisco. I became one of his early black belts. I studied Thai boxing, Jiu Jitsu, Shorin-ryu Okinawan style, Taekwondo. We were always training.

I have concluded over the years that Thai boxing, American boxing, Jiu Jitsu and wrestling are the four you really want to put your time in. That's where I put my time in.

In the fifties and sixties, you'd meet a lot of wise guys – guys in the street, body builders, airborne rangers – and they'd also say, 'How can a guy like you beat a big guy like me?' so we'd do spinning legs and flatten them.

It sounds like you did a lot of working out by picking fights on the street with a lot bigger guys. I'm sure that was very satisfying for someone who was bullied as a younger kid.

Yes, I enjoyed beating up big guys. With martial arts, most of the traditional karate instructors punched and kicked air and never got hit, so they didn't have a way to really determine what worked and what didn't work.

When you're getting into street fights, and having tough guys try to beat you up, it gave Gene and me an opportunity to test our techniques.

You then became a member of the world professional team with Chuck Norris, Joe Lewis, Mike Stone and Skipper Mullins. In my mind, you guys must have been like the "Rat Pack of martial arts". What was it like, in that period of your career, where essentially you guys were the "best of the best"?

They're all terrific guys: terrific fighters, terrific athletes, and we all trained together. Skipper Mullins was from Texas, so he couldn't train as consistently with us. Mike Stone, Chuck Norris and Joe Lewis – the four of us worked out a lot. The best of the best always wanted to train.

Skipper Mullins was a Lightweight, Chuck Norris was the Middleweight, and Mike Stone was the Light Heavyweight. I was the Heavyweight. Joe Lewis a Super Heavyweight. Of course, Mike Stone was the best fighter in 1963-64. He won everything that there was to win, and retired. Then Joe Lewis and Chuck Norris came on the scene in 1965 and they started winning everything.

We always wanted to train with the best, it just happened that we were also friends. We wanted to dignify the martial arts and create a profession, so Chuck and I built training schools which became very financially successful.

With all that success, how did you get into acting? Obviously, you were and still are a martial artist, but how did you and Chuck make the move from being professional fighters in the ring and putting that on screen?

Chuck and I always wanted the world to know about martial arts and how great it was. We started the most successful martial arts school in the world and, at that time, we were the first people to teach women and children. That wasn't done in those days. We felt that woman had more sexual crimes committed on them and would need to protect themselves, and that children needed more training than men, so we really specialized in that.

Chuck and I also taught private lessons in those days. We taught Jack Palance, Paul Newman, Steve McQueen, Freddie Prinze (Snr.) – we taught them all. Freddie Prinze (Snr.) and Steve McQueen were my two personal

Bob Wall in training. Photo courtesy of Bob Wall.

favorite students. They became phenomenal. We wanted to spread the word and then we met Bruce in 1962.

I always assumed that you and Chuck probably met Bruce at the 1964 Internationals, where he did his infamous demonstrations like the one-inch punch and the two-finger push up?

No, we met him way earlier. He came to train with our whole team: he trained with Gene, he trained with Chuck, he trained with Joe, he trained with Mike, he trained with me.

I met Bruce at a restaurant in 1962 at a Kung Fu demonstration. Bruce was just one of us. We all loved Bruce. He was very bright. He was very funny. He was very smart. He was a brilliant athlete and trained like a world champion. The thing that separated Joe Lewis, Mike Stone, Chuck Norris, Skipper Mullins and Bruce Lee from everyone else was how they trained. Champions always train harder and longer and study a variety of things to get better and better and better.

Bruce left the U.S. and went off to Hong Kong after *The Green Hornet* (1966-67) was cancelled and became a massive star with *The Big Boss* and *Fist of Fury*. At what point did he get in touch with you and Chuck and ask you to come out for *Way of the Dragon*?

Here in the U.S., *Fist of Fury* was called *The Chinese Connection* and, with those first two films, Bruce had no say, he was just the star actor. The director Lo Wei had his own ideas about how the fights should be – and they were pathetic. People could jump 800 feet into the air, have lunch on an airplane, and land. It just didn't appeal to us. We wanted the reality of martial arts on screen.

Bruce loved Chuck. I believe that Chuck was his favorite martial artist of all time, because he's not only a brilliant martial artist, but he's a brilliant man. He's kind, he's bright, he's mellow, but he's very intense. Bruce and he were quite a bit alike, except Bruce was very open, and Chuck was very shy, and couldn't talk to three people in a room!

One day, Chuck and I had just finished working out when he got a call from Bruce Lee. When Chuck hung up, he said, 'I'm going to Rome and then Hong Kong. I'm going to do a film with Bruce,' and I said, 'You're not doing it without me. We're 50-50 partners!'

You forced your way into *Way of the Dragon*? That's very canny of you!

Bruce couldn't afford the whole budget for *Way of the Dragon*. It was $250,000 and he was going out of the country which just wasn't done at the time. For *Way of the Dragon*, Bruce formed his own production company, so he had the decision about where and how he'd make his films and do the fight scenes.

We flew out there in coach and Chuck said, 'Bruce says he's going to have the camera there when the plane lands. When we get there, we've got to go to First Class and ask the flight attendants if they can the hold people back. Bruce wants us to step out, look left and right and he's going to be filming it!'

So, Chuck walked out, Bruce filmed him and then I let everyone in first class out. They were very kind and everybody was very generous to us, considering nobody knew who we were at that point; we were just two strangers asking if they'd wait a minute. When Bruce saw it, he said to me, 'You're a hero and you're in the film!' So, when you see that scene in the movie with the plane landing, that's really us landing and getting off the plane.

Your character is called, I'm assuming intentionally, Bob, and you're very much the strong and silent type. Was there any kind of backstory that Bruce told you about your character?

The backstory was that the bad guys wanted me to get Chuck Norris over there so he could beat up Bruce! That was the backstory!

When we got there, Bruce said that he wanted to shoot the fight in The Colosseum, but it was closed. My wife's Sicilian, so she made a few phone calls and arranged to get us in there! That was one of Bruce's fantasies, to shoot a fight scene there.

How did you find working with a Chinese film crew as you and Chuck must have felt like outsiders at the time?

After we finished filming in Rome, we went to Hong Kong and Chuck was challenged to a fight by a guy who we'll call 'Wang Bang Lo'. They didn't know I was coming, so they didn't challenge me, but they were obsessed with Chuck.

Bruce told him not to do it because, 'If you beat up one, there's two. You beat up two, and there's four more!' Chuck is one of the nicest people on Earth, but he's also one of the toughest. He's way tougher than people believe, but he's so good he has no need to tell you, but he's very competitive. I could tell he was agitated, but he didn't want to do anything about it, so I said I'd handle it.

I went to the press and said, 'Wang Bang Lo wants to fight Chuck Norris, but as I'm his student, I'll fight him. We're going to be in a show called *Enjoy Yourself Tonight*, a week from tonight. Have [Wang Bang Lo] come down, and bring on his friends. I'm going to kill him on live TV. I want to do it on live TV, because we want to make sure nobody can say I used a club, or I cheated or had four guys helping me!'

Christ, Bob!

'It's going to be a death match! It's gonna be Wang Bang Lo's last fight! So, come on down!' A week later, we go down there and there were thousands of people on the street. Of course, Wang Bang Lo didn't show up because it's one thing to put out a challenge, but it's quite another when it's going to be for real. The producer of the TV show was obviously upset and asked us to put on a demonstration. He said, 'I want to see a real fight. I want you people to get up and do real fighting.'

So Chuck and I did a demonstration: he just literally beat the crap out of me. The last thing he did was a jump-spinning back kick that hit me in the stomach. I went flying. After that, we didn't get any more challenges!

With Bruce overseeing the whole production on *Way of the Dragon*, how did you find him as a director?

We shot our fight scene out near Kowloon. It was a very dirty, dusty field, so Bruce and I both wore eye contacts. It was a nightmare and I had to take mine out after the second day. Bruce had this eyewash called Darling and that saved us for the first two days, as we were constantly cleaning our eyes with it.

After we shot the fight scene, I was at the airport to fly home and, suddenly, there was this huge crowd as if Elvis was there. It was Bruce and he just came walking through customs with a case of Darling eye wash for me. It was such an act of kindness, but he and Linda [Lee] were both amazing people.

Bruce obviously trusted you enough to invite you back for *Enter the Dragon* to star as O'Hara. Again, you play a man of intimidating stature and few words. From an acting point of view, did you ever want more lines or were you happy to just be the physical threat?

I never wanted to be an actor. I had a certain talent for it and even got offered a three picture from Warner Brothers, but my wife and I chose not to accept it because it wasn't the lifestyle for us. When you're making a film, you go away for months and there's going to be drugs and women, and it's not like you're going to be celibate, so you have to make a decision. All the actors I taught, from Elvis to Steve McQueen, every one of them got divorced. I'm in love with my wife and that's what I wanted.

I always did the parts that my friends asked me to do. When Bruce asked me, I did it, no matter what the character was. When we did *Way of*

Bob Wall as the villainous O'Hara in *Enter The Dragon* (1973).
Photo courtesy of Bob Wall.

the Dragon, Chuck and I didn't see ourselves as bad guys, but those were the parts that were offered, so we did it.

There are so many stories surrounding the production of *Enter the Dragon*, namely about Bruce and the director Robert Clouse not getting along.

Robert Clouse, the world's worst director, fought with Bruce all the time. He didn't like Bruce and I because, in his eyes, we weren't actors. We were only martial artists and he never appreciated our skill or our talent. He had no respect for us. He would shoot John Saxon and Ahna Capri forty-two times, but he would want to shoot us once and be gone.

Bruce was a perfectionist, so it's going to be his way or the highway, and so they had a lot of fights.

Was it anything specific or was it just a clash of styles?

It was lots of little things. When I got there, my character's name was a Japanese name. It was Okasa and I said, 'I don't look like an Okasa. I'm Irish. It's got to be O'Hara,' so I changed the name. But, Robert Clouse also had a bunch of names in there that Bruce couldn't say because of the Rs…

Like "Mr. Braithwaite".

Yes. He took them all out except Braithwaite, which he left in.

Then there were the fight scenes. With Bruce, you never shoot a fight scene less than five or six times, because he wanted all the angles. He wanted to shoot it low, shoot it high, and have it totally covered. Even if we did it perfect the first time, Bruce would want to shoot it five or six more times.

Bruce finally just ran Clouse off. He did all the fight scenes except the ones with John Saxon on the golf course scene. I did those after we came back from Hong Kong because John wanted his scenes to be spiced up a bit. I went up to Griffith Park and I took a bunch of my black-belts up there, but Bruce was the fight co-ordinator for the rest of the film's fights.

The character of O'Hara is portrayed as someone who is, let's face it, a bit of a bastard. He's responsible for Bruce's sister's death in the film and when he's defeated, tries to stab him with a bottle. Did you ever try

and add any sort of layers to the character or were you happy to have him unredeemable and just have him beaten up by Bruce?

Obviously, as a professional fighter I didn't want to get my ass kicked! I was a world professional champion, so I don't take defeat easily, but it's what the character must do so I separated it.

In my mind, O'Hara was an egotistical bully, so I would try to add layers to the character, but Clouse was forever changing and taking my dialogue [out].

Is it true Robert Clouse also cut a bunch of your scenes?

He was always cutting scenes because he didn't like me and I didn't like him. What was cut were establishing scenes. There was one where I was a bodyguard for a general and five or six guys attack the general with ice picks, but I kill them all.

However, Bruce didn't like the way it was shot. When we got back to Los Angeles, he said, 'Let's shoot a bunch of fight demos,' so I had him break boards over my arms, my legs, and my stomach. It was the same with the fight scenes between me and Bruce. Clouse didn't like us and wanted us to get hurt.

Bruce and I were really close. I loved him, and I did that film for him. I was making $10-12,000 a week at that time, and the film was only paying me $500 a week. I did it because I loved Bruce. When we were doing our fight scene, before each take Bruce would say to me, 'I'm going to try and break something!' All through the movie, he was trying to break my ribs, rupture my spleen, whatever. He was always trying to hurt me, and we would just laugh about it, because I can take a terrific whack! That's what separates the men from the boys. When they hit you with their best shot and you're smiling, they realize you're [in] a different league.

Does it annoy you that there are so many false rumors about the fight scene between the two of you, where people claim you deliberately tried to stab him?

When we first did the fight scene, it was just too fast. You couldn't see what we were doing. People wonder if they sped Bruce up, but he was like lightning.

When I was holding the bottles, he said to me, 'Bob, I want you to try to stab me in my right pec. If you can stab me in my right pec, stab me, because that way it'll look real.' As it was coming from the back hand, it was slower, so he had more time to see it. We shot it five or six times perfectly and, as Bruce and I worked out so much, we knew each other inside out.

When he kicked the bottle and hit my arm, the bottle was meant to fly out of my hand so that when he spins around, it's not there. The seventh time, he hit behind the elbow, so when he tried to spin, the bottle was still there, and he jammed his fist into it. That's how he cut himself.

Two days later, [producer] Freddie Weintraub came to me and said, 'You got to leave town.' I said, 'Why?' He said, 'Well, Bruce is going to kill you.' I said, 'That was bullshit. We're best friends.' So, we went to Bruce's house, got there, and Freddie explained to him there was a rumor that he was going to kill me, because I'd apparently cut him intentionally. Bruce got on the phone and called five or six people to find out where the rumor was coming from. It was coming from Robert Clouse.

The three of us got in the car and went to his hotel. When he opened the door, I slapped Clouse on the top of his head and he fell on the ground. I stood on his hand and said, 'These rumors are going to stop. If not, I'm going to put you in the hospital,' that stopped the bullshit and, of course, a week later, Bruce came back, and he hit me exactly where he was going to hit me.

Nobody had a clue how hard Bruce was hitting me, but he would unload on me. I had extras in front of the chairs to keep me from falling into them, because I could have gotten seriously hurt. One time, the extras were goofing around and, when I got hit, I flew into them. One got his arm trapped under a chair, and my 205 lbs. slammed down and snapped his arm!

As well as Bruce, Enter the Dragon had several talented martial artists working on it like Jim Kelly, Yuen Biao, Sammo Hung, Jackie Chan and Bolo Yeung. Did you know any of them before you started working on the film?

I hired Jim Kelly for the film. Another actor was signed to do it, but called in sick a couple of days before. Bruce called me and said, 'Get me a tall, handsome, well-built black man who's an actor and a martial artist.'

It was a lot of pressure because in the fifties, if a black person walked into a martial arts school, they wouldn't be taught. The Chinese would only teach Chinese. If you're a *gwai lo* – a foreign devil – they wouldn't teach you. However, Bruce's first student was black and his best friend was Japanese. Bruce himself was one-eighth German. I got on the phone and started calling everybody, and I picked Jim Kelly.

I didn't know Sammo. Bruce hired him. Sammo and Bolo were local guys. Bolo, of course, was a terrific guy. He was the Hong Kong body building champion, and was hired for his build and size. He was called the Chinese Hercules back then.

It's a tragedy that Bruce never got to see the success of *Enter the Dragon*, but it's even more unfortunate that his legacy goes hand in hand with various assorted conspiracies that surround his death? Even your own documentary is called *Curse of the Dragon*.

That was tongue-in-cheek, because there were so many bullshit stories that he was killed by the mob, or that he was poisoned, or it was some deadly kung fu killer. It was all bullshit, and a lot of it started because Bruce was popular with the ladies. People would write stories about him and many were not true, so Bruce would have harsh words with those guys. Once he died, they could publish whatever they wanted. Anything about Bruce sold.

Bruce Lee died a decade before I was even born, yet I grew up on his films. Does it still amaze you that decades after he died, he still has such an impact on the world?

It really doesn't, because Bruce was brilliant, handsome, and beautifully built. He was the first person to marry ballet with martial arts. He had an on-screen presence like nobody else, and the tragedy of his death at thirty-two fuels the mystery. Although, it really is no mystery, as I have his autopsy report. Brandon [Lee] was also a brilliant kid, who tragically passed away very young.

At the time were you ever invited to appear in any Bruceploitation films - those cheap knockoffs with actors that looked like Bruce Lee?

Yes. I turned them down. I didn't want to do anything that would take away from Bruce.

Didn't Bruce plan to have you in his next film, where he'd play a secret agent tracking terrorists, and you'd be his CIA contact – a Felix Leiter to his James Bond?

He was going to play an international agent whose responsibility was to wipe out a big drug ring. I was going to [be] an American CIA [agent], come from America, who would get killed . . . but not by Bruce!

After *Enter the Dragon*, you had a few minor roles in *Black Belt Jones* and *Enter the Ninja*, where you played henchman-type characters. Was it mainly because of your wife that you didn't pursue any bigger roles?

I did favors for Fred Weintraub, whom I loved and adored. He was the producer on *Black Belt Jones*, and I did it because Freddy and Jim wanted me to do it. I trained everybody in that film. Most of the bad guys in there are my students!

Is it the same with Chuck? You've appeared in a bunch of his films such as, *Invasion USA*, *Firewalker*, *Code of Silence* and several *Walker Texas Ranger* (1994-2001) appearances. Were they all favors, too?

I did them because Chuck asked me, but more importantly, I did them to stay in the Screen Actors Guild. You have to work so many days a year! With Chuck, I did eight of his films, and twenty-six episodes of *Walker*. I don't have to work anymore after so many years, but at the time, that's why I did it.

I know mutual respect is very important to you, and during the writing of this book one name has repeatedly cropped up whenever ego is mentioned – Steven Seagal. I believe you've also had issues with him in the past. What is it about that man that seems to upset so many people?

He's just not a nice person, he can't help himself. He's very insecure, and he's not much of a martial artist. He used to make up stories, like he was the first Caucasian to have an Aikido school in Japan. It wasn't his school, it was his father-in-law's school. He used to say things like 'No man dares face me,' and I put up with it for years until, in 1986, he made some nasty comments about me and I had a little chat with him then.

I've rolled with the toughest people on earth – boxers, wrestlers, and martial artists – and they are also the nicest, and most respectful. But I have three phrases of wisdom: don't grab their wife's toosh, don't threaten their children, and don't urinate on their dog - then you're going to see a side of them that will give you nightmares, if you live.

Please don't tell me that Steven Seagal did all three of those things to you?

Steven Seagal was just always saying nasty things about people, from Bruce Lee to Chuck Norris, and so on. One day, Gene LeBell was on [the] set of Steven's second movie . . . Steven wasn't smart enough to know who Gene was. Steven was hurting all the stuntmen intentionally, so some of them decided to set him up.

Seagal always said he was the world's toughest man, so one of them said, 'You're not really the world's toughest man. That bald, fat guy over there is the world's toughest man.' So Seagal walked over to Gene and said, 'Put me in any holds you want, I'll get out of it.' Gene wound up chocking Seagal out. Not once, but twice. Steven did the only manly thing he could do, he fired Gene and threatened to sue him.

I'm obviously a big fan of martial arts films and, a few years ago, I was watching Michael Jai White's *Blood and Bone* and you crop up at the end as O'Hara. Do you watch martial arts films today, and are there any fighters that impress you?

I have a lot of respect for Michael Jai White. He is an excellent martial artist, and he asked me and Gene LeBell to come out and do a couple days shoot as a favor, so we did. I don't really care for most martial arts films, and I don't watch most of them. I love Jackie Chan, who was in *Enter the Dragon*. I have a lot of respect for him, but when they started doing this wire stuff like in *Crouching Tiger, Hidden Dragon* [2000], I turned it off.

I watched about half of it and I said, 'Oh my God. This is just pathetic.' I'm a fighter. I respect fighters.

You should check out *The Raid* (2011) and *The Raid 2* (2014) with Iko Uwais, I think you would appreciate them.

Ok, I will. I have great respect for great fighters, but as soon as I hear about a martial arts film with the traditional chopsocky stuff, it doesn't thrill me!

How did you end up moving away from acting and getting into real estate brokering? It's seems like a very different career path from where you started.

When Chuck decided to become an actor, we sold our training schools, and made more money on the real estate than we did on the schools. Seventy percent of the earth's wealth is held in real estate, and there's so much money to be made.

I'd love to get a bunch of these young MMA guys making a bunch of money and get them into real estate because athletic careers don't last forever. I don't care what kind of martial artist you are, but being a martial artist at twenty is a lot different than being a martial artist at ninety!

Paul McCrane

"*I know you. You're dead! We killed you! WE KILLED YOU!*"

– Emil, *RoboCop* (1987).

Select Filmography

- *Fame (1980)* – Montgomery
- *Purple Hearts (1984)* - Brenner
- *RoboCop (1987)* – Emil M. Antonowsky
- *The Blob (1988)* – Deputy Bill Briggs
- *The Shawshank Redemption (1994)* – Guard Trout
- *ER (1997-2008)* – Robert Romano
- *24 (2006-2007)* – Graem Bauer

After being gunned down by Clarence Boddicker's ruthless gang, police officer, Alex Murphy (Peter Weller), has been reborn as the cyborg RoboCop. Created to clean up the streets of Detroit, it isn't long before RoboCop comes face to face with one of his killers who is attempting to rob a gas station: Emil M. Antonowsky.

DICK JONES (RONNY COX) MAY HOLD ALL the power in Detroit as the number two guy at Omni Consumer Products (OCP), but when it comes to dirty work, he calls Clarence Boddicker (Kurtwood Smith). Boddicker's band of thugs are a diverse bunch; Leon Nash (Ray Wise)

Paul McCrane stars as Emil in *RoboCop* (1987). Photo courtesy of MGM Pictures.

likes fancy clothes and hitting the night clubs, Joe P. Cox (Jesse D. Goins) is a hyper-active ball of energy who has no qualms about throwing a police officer to her (supposed) death, and then there's Emil (Paul Mc-Crane), the team's young driver who is willing to do anything Clarence orders, including murder.

Naturally, all of Boddicker's men come to a brutal end, but none of them get it as bad as Emil, who crashes his truck into a vat of toxic waste, and horrifically melts – until he's hit by a car and explodes. It's shocking, brutally violent, and hilarious.

With a career spanning three decades, Paul McCrane has been a constant presence on TV screens around the world, but is probably best known for his role in *ER* as Robert Romano. Unfortunately, as probably one of four people in the world who never watched the infamous medical drama, I had no idea his character was considered one of the show's antagonists and, instead, focused primarily on *RoboCop*, and the film's mini-reunion in *24*, where Paul appeared as Jack Bauer's brother, alongside Ray Wise and Peter Weller.

Paul was an absolute delight to talk to and was even apologetic for having to delay our interview many times. As the man is constantly working, I completely understood that speaking to a jobbing film writer was lower on his list of priorities! I assuaged his guilt by saying he was no-where near as hard to track down as his *RoboCop* co-star Ronny Cox.

I've been chasing Ronny Cox for four months! He's touring the world with his folk music.

I'm thrilled to hear that Ronny's still playing music. He started doing that about fifteen years ago, maybe more. I didn't know if he was still doing it. Ronny and I also worked on the infamous *Cop Rock* (1990) together. It was shortly after that, that he got a recording contract, as I recall.

You both appeared in *RoboCop*, but, whereas Ronny Cox went on to play a host of evil corporate or stern military types, you seemed to deliberately avoid prominent villainous roles by appearing in TV series like *Under Suspicion* (1994-1995), *Champs* (1996) and *From the Earth to the Moon* (1998). Is that something you deliberately wanted to do?

In terms of my own career, we have to go back a little further when I first started out. I started acting professionally when I was sixteen-years-old, and in my very late teens I did *Fame*. For some years after that, in terms of typecasting, I was invited to audition for every fragile teenage or young adult character that came down the pipe. I made a decision in my mid-twenties that I didn't want to do that anymore. I was trying to fight that typecasting and I intentionally told my reps – who thought I was out of my freaking mind – that I wasn't going to go up for those roles anymore. I wanted to go up for bad guys. They thought I was nuts.

    RoboCop was actually a bit of a departure for me at that point. It was one of the first sort of villains that I played. Then, of course, afterwards, I was thought of as a villain, because that's the nature of this business. It's understandable that when a role comes up, if you've been memorable in one kind of thing, that would pop into people's minds.

    I would say I'm more known as a villainous character actor now than anything else. The character in *ER*, while he had some complexity, was definitely the antagonist in the show, most definitely. Even on *24*, that was, you could say, a sort of villainous character. It's a little bit unavoid-able, but I certainly have tried to pursue, and tried to encourage my reps, and everybody in the business, to think of me as not being a stock villain character.

After *RoboCop*, I would say I probably avoided taking character roles that were very, very similar to that, for the exact reasons that you say. I do think it's very challenging, but it's much less so in the theatre where you can play a wide variety of characters.

After appearing in *Fame*, you said you wanted to go up for the role of Emil in *RoboCop*, and your agent was against that. How did you manage to persuade Paul Verhoeven and the producers, and even your agent, that you were the right person for the job?

It was mostly about convincing my reps. When an audition came up for a part that was a sensitive, fragile character, I would just decline to go on it. When they really found out that I was serious, then they, to their credit, would actually start pursuing roles that I was interested in. When it came to *RoboCop*, I had an audition and I didn't do terribly. Paul [Verhoeven] liked what I did and we were off to the races. We had a ball.

Can you remember what you had to do for your audition? Was it any of the scenes from the final film?

Murphy (Peter Weller) comes face to face with Clarence Boddicker (Kurtwood Smith (left)) and his gang, including Emil (Paul McCrane (centre)) in *RoboCop* (1987). Photo courtesy of MGM Pictures.

Yes, it most certainly was. I don't remember specifically what ones, to be honest. It was probably the gas station scene.

When you first read the script, Clarence Boddicker and his gang of misfits are probably the most reprehensible bunch of villains seen on screen. They're all rapists, killers, and murderers. When you're playing a character who's that unredeemable in a film, are you ever tempted to go over the top in your performance or do you still play it with a certain nuance?

There are films or material where, by design, it requires a more in-depth examination of the character. In a film like *RoboCop*, first it comes down to: what's the intended film? What's the tone of the film? What's the style of the film? What's the style of the storytelling? Paul, very consciously and articulately, was doing a film that intentionally exaggerated violence. To be frank, when I first heard the title, I thought, 'What kind of piece of crap is this?'

I read the script though, and I loved it. It was a very conscious, smart, and intellectual – frankly, design – to talk about the dehumaniza-tion of society and people, which is what the metaphor of *RoboCop* is really about.

Paul wasn't looking for a rich, nuanced examination of the psychol-ogy of a sociopath. He was looking for broad strokes. That was why a lot of the choices that I made, and that he asked for, were done.

Can you remember what the character of Emil was like in the script? Was it all there on the page or were you able to bring your own unique bearing to the role?

I think it was largely on the page. I tried to bring as much as I could to what I understood to be on the page. Paul was very articulate about what he wanted in a way that made a lot of sense. I wouldn't say I invented the character, but there's some things that happened that were serendipitous, such as the 'I like it!' scene.

That moment became a bit iconic. As we were shooting that scene, I think it was either the boom operator, or the sound mixer, made a refer-ence to a different film. I can't even remember what it was! That's why I did the reading that I did, because he and I were joking around about it. I'd love to claim credit for when I've come up with something great!

One thing I can say, that I can take credit for, was the beard design, which I did on my own, but bottom line is that the character was largely on the page.

In the film, you spend most of your scenes with Kurtwood Smith, Ray Wise and Jesse Goins. Did you guys all get on? Did you hang out together off set during filming?

Yes, a great deal. We had a lot of fun and hung out a lot socially while we were making *RoboCop*. None of them are assholes, they're all really good guys.

Kurtwood and I stayed the most in touch. The other guys, when we run into each other, I'm always happy to see them, but life leads us all in different directions. Fortunately, we had a good chemistry on screen, in part because we all really liked each other, and had a lot of fun together.

The film is famed for its excessive violence and one of the first scenes where that is evident is when you guys execute Alex Murphy. What was it like filming that scene? It's very shocking, but it's a very over-the-top. Was it serious on set, or were you guys having fun with it simply because of the gratuitous levels of violence?

I must be honest, I don't really remember filming that scene as much. Frankly, it was all in a day's work at that point. Obviously, all the firing of the weapons was done separately from the shots of Peter and his stunt double being squibbed. Paul wanted to show a dehumanized glee in all that activity, and I think we all did our best to exemplify that.

In terms of technical ability, you also had Rob Bottin on set who did the special effects in *The Thing* and who was responsible for your melting man make up. Researching that scene, I read that the MPAA wanted to cut it, but it elicited such a reaction from test audiences that they kept it in. Can you think why that is? Because of all the characters in Boddicker's gang, you arguably get the most gruesome and spectacular death.

[laughs] Yes, it's pretty spectacular. I'm not so sure that it was a sense of justice that the audience feels, if a truly vicious character gets what's coming to him, or if it was just a result of the spectacular nature of what happens! There are ways that each of these characters stood out, in little,

Emil comes to a sticky end during the finale of *RoboCop* (1987).
Photo courtesy of MGM Pictures.

special ways, and the glee that my character takes in the violence worked. I think that's what people were honestly responding to – seeing this character get dumped into the toxic waste thing, and then the effect of Rob's make-up. Do you know what a RUD is?

No.

It stands for Rapid Unplanned Disassembly, such as when a rocket explodes! When this character literally disintegrates on impact, I think the audience reacted as much to that effect as anything else. It could have honestly been any one of the characters who the audience is rooting to get theirs, and I lucked out as it's my character that got it!

Can you remember how you found the make-up process, because it looks like it was really heavy?

It was extraordinarily tedious. We shot that scene over the course of two days and it was a full upper body prosthetic, from my torso upwards. The first day it took six-and-a-half hours just to put the makeup on, and two hours to remove [it]. The second day, they got it down to about four hours, but it was sitting in a chair, with this giant latex appliance being put on me, with a dot of glue every square inch!

Rob Bottin and his special effects crew work on the 'melting man' effect
in *RoboCop* (1987). Photo courtesy of MGM Pictures.

It was exceedingly tedious, but I'm glad to have done it. That scene is
really a model for Rob's work, which I was thrilled to do, because he really
was quite extraordinary in what he does.

What does the car hit that causes that spectacularly gooey explosion?

I wasn't there when they shot the impact moment. You see me in the fore-
ground as the car's approaching and you see me through the windshield,
but there's an intercut at the moment of impact. I think it was watermel-
ons and garbage. I don't remember what it was that got splattered onto the
windshield, but it wasn't me, so that's good!

**You also appear to be pretty involved in a lot of the stunt work that
goes on in the film. You're driving the truck at the beginning and, during the exploding petrol station scene, you seem to be very close on
your bike. What was it like shooting those action scenes, coming from
something like *Fame,* which was, comparatively, stunt-free?**

I didn't do every bit of the stunts, but I did some. I rode up on the motorcycle, and I was there for part of the gas station explosion, but I'm not an

idiot, and neither was Paul! There are people who are trained to do these stunts, and they absolutely did them.

I didn't roll out of the toxic waste vat, that was a stuntman in a modified version of the makeup. I just emerged from the pool of sludge. I was an athletic guy, but if there was anything that got seriously dangerous, I didn't do it. Stuntmen were used very judiciously, and very appropriately, as well they should.

With your long and varied career, you've been in things like the *The Shawshank Redemption* and you were Rocket Romano for eleven years, what role do people most recognize you for? Is it *ER*, or do you get thirty-something-year-old men coming up to you in the streets saying, 'Dead or alive, you're coming with me'?

[laughs] I must say, it's very, very surprising to me that I am recognized for a variety of things. A lot of people, to this day, remember *RoboCop*, and a surprising amount of people remember *Fame*, which is nice because I had hair then! Of course, a lot of people know me from *ER* and *24*. I'd say it's probably *RoboCop*, *Fame*, *ER* and *24* are the most frequent things I'm recognized for.

That fifth season of *24* is like a mini *RoboCop* reunion, as Peter Weller and Ray Wise both appeared in it as well.

I think they very consciously did that because they were fans of the film, so they tried to bring several cast members into it.

How did you end up getting cast as Graem Bauer, Jack's brother?

At that time, I'd started directing, and I was spending most of my time directing television, and I just got a phone call as me to appear in the show. It was simple as that. I don't think they had even planned that I was going to be Jack's brother. They wrote me in as a character and then, as they were developing their story, they decided to reveal the whole family aspect with James Cromwell as our father.

I often wondered how they wrote that show, and you've confirmed what I always thought – they're making it up as they go!

There are times where people have an architecture for a season in mind, and there are other times when they really don't, and they're entirely winging it. This is the interesting thing about television. As you're shooting, and as the episodes are airing, people are observing what the chemistry is, as opposed to what they imagine – sometimes for better, sometimes for worse - there's a somewhat improvisatory response that the writers should take advantage of.

My assumption is that they may have had thoughts that this character might go somewhere else, but there was certainly no indication when I first took the job on *24* that the character was going to be revealed to be Jack's brother!

I must ask you very briefly about your role as Guard Trout in *The Shawshank Redemption*. The legacy of that film is incredible considering that it was a flop on release.

Really? Did the numbers say it was a flop?

I think, when it came out, it was one of those films that didn't do as well as was hoped, but once it was on VHS, it found its audience.

Paul McCrane stars as Graem Bauer in the fifth season of *24*.
Photo courtesy of 20th Century Fox.

I have to tell you, at that time in my life, I paid no attention to the box office numbers, so I didn't know that. It's just a film that from the first time I read it, worked on it, and saw it, I thought it was an extraordinarily good film. Frank Darabont did an extraordinary job, and I am frankly not surprised that it's endured as much as it has. I didn't have much to do in it, but I'm thrilled to have been a part of it.

You also share your scenes with one of the most terrifying characters seen on screen, Byron Hadley, played by, by all accounts, the couldn't-be-nicer Clancy Brown.

Clancy is a terrific actor. He's the nicest guy you'd ever want to meet. Bob [Gunton] is great as the warden, but there's something about Clancy's performance that is more subtly sinister.

At this point in your career, what are the roles that your agent brings to you? Is it mainly villainous roles?

At this point, I spend almost all my time directing, which I enjoy a great deal. In terms of acting, there's no role at this point that I would turn down, but I'm looking for something that's interesting to play. If it's an interesting character, even for just one scene, then I want to do it. I don't care if it's a good guy, bad guy, villain, hero – but I'm interested in some complexity and nuance. If I get an opportunity to do that, then I'm happy.

Gus Rethwisch

"I love this saw! It's a part of me... now I'm gonna make it part of YOU!"

— Buzzsaw, The Running Man (1987).

Select Filmography

- *The Concorde . . . Airport '79* (1979) – Gregori
- *House II: The Second Story* (1987) – Arnold The Barbarian
- *The Running Man* (1987) – Buzzsaw
- *Twins* (1988) – Dave Klane
- *Fist Fighter* (1989) – The Beast
- *The Scorpion King* (2002) – Barbarian Guy

After being falsely accused for shooting civilians during a food riot, helicopter pilot, Ben Richards (Arnold Schwarzenegger), is imprisoned for life. He escapes, but is quickly captured by the authorities in the totalitarian police state that America has become, in 2017. Forced to compete in the TV show The Running Man, *where criminals are forced to battle modern day gladiators, called Stalkers, Richards soon finds himself being hunted by the current champion Buzzsaw (Gus Rethwisch).*

CASTING AGENTS IN THE 1980S must have faced a constant battle to find actors that were physically imposing enough to stand up to Arnold Schwarzenegger on screen. Luckily for them, Schwarzenegger's stardom

Ben Richards (Arnold Schwarzenegger) finds himself hunted by the chainsaw-
wielding Buzzsaw (Gus Rethwisch) in *The Running Man* (1987).
Photo courtesy of TriStar Pictures.

had seen numerous body builders, power lifters and wrestlers come to
Hollywood to seek their fortune.

Standing at 6' 5", power-lifting champion, Gus Rethwisch, fit the bill
perfectly. After starting off in assorted TV roles, where he played heavies or henchman, Rethwisch was eventually cast as the memorable Buzzsaw in the Schwarzenegger-starring, dystopian classic *The Running Man
(1987)*. Whether he was head-butting his own fans, hurling his motorbike, or threatening to castrate Arnie's character, Ben Richards, there was
something about him that you couldn't take your eyes off.

It also helped that when Buzzsaw was eventually dispatched by Richards – his own chainsaw is jammed upwards between his legs – Schwarzenegger delivers the best deadpan, one-liner of his career, "He had to
split."

Even with the UK's ITV channel heavily editing eighties action films
for violence and swearing, *The Running Man* was a firm favorite of mine.
When I first saw it, I was deep into my *Gladiators* fandom. Saturday nights
in our house generally consisted of back-to-back watching of *Baywatch*
(1989-2001), *Gladiators* (1992-2000), and then *Blind Date* (1985-2017) -
for mum.

To discover that Arnold Schwarzenegger had made an ultra-violent
version of my favorite TV show was, at the time, like finding the Ark of

the Covenant. Sure, most of the satire went over my head (and has now become strangely prescient in 2017, the year in which the film was set!), and it was missing female Gladiators like Jet (the object of my adolescent adoration), but, it was essential viewing!

Trying to track down the rest of the Stalkers proved difficult. Jim Brown (Fireball), the famous American football player, is still acting; Jesse Ventura (Captain Freedom), like Schwarzenegger, is a former US governor; and, tragically, Erland van Lidth (Dynamo) and Professor Toru Tanaka (Sub Zero) died in 1987 and 2000, respectively. However, I did locate Buzzsaw!

There were rumors that Rethwisch lived in Germany, others said he lived in the US, but it turned out that, today, Gus is the president of the World Association of Benchers and Dead Lifters and is often travelling around the world, appearing at conventions and competitions. After weeks of sending emails to any potential leads, my phone rang, and it was the man himself!

How does one of the world's strongest men, and a champion power-lifter, end up getting into acting?

It started with a Tom Selleck pilot that never made it to series. It was a TV movie called *Boston and Killbride* [1978] before *Magnum P.I.*, which I think started in 1980. The studio was out looking for someone for the pilot, and a casting director was sent down to the gym, and found me working out. That's how it started.

I remember that, for that part, I was meant to be wearing a tuxedo. However, at that time, I was wearing a size sixty-six. That meant I had 23.5" arms, a 65" chest, and a 44" waist. They couldn't find a tuxedo anywhere in California or Hawaii that would fit me! They decided to put me in shorts in the shallow end of a pool with a gun strapped around my shoulder. I just stood there and had my hand on the butt on my pistol and that was my role. The costume director said he had worked with Raymond Burr and Lou Ferrigno, but that I was the biggest man he'd ever fitted!

After that, I did a couple of episodes of *Hawaii Five-0* [1968-1980], where I played a strongman for the Japanese Yakuza. That was a bit weird, but I had a couple of lines in it, and I was the main bad guy!

After your TV roles in *Magnum P.I.* and *Hawaii Five-0*, you got your first film role in *The Concorde . . . Airport '79 (1979)*.

It wasn't a super-big role, but it was filming in Hawaii and they put me up in the Sheridan Hotel for a whole month!

I got the role because the costume director from *Boston and Killbride* told the producer that I was the biggest guy he'd ever seen. I played a Russian weightlifter and, apparently, lots of Russian weight lifters and pro wrestlers tried out for the part, but I got it, just from what the costume director had told people.

It was all set to be a much bigger role, but by the time other actors had got involved, and their agents had lobbied for bigger roles, I got pushed to the background.

There were agents all over the production, and I met Dino De Laurentis, who was the main producer, and that was exciting. I also got to meet Robert Wagner, George Kennedy and Mercedes McCambridge. Do you know what Mercedes McCambridge's most famous role was? It was only her voice?

I don't think so.

She was the voice of the Devil in *The Exorcist* [1973].

Oh, really?

Buzzsaw is featured prominently on promotional posters for *The Running Man* (1987). Photo courtesy of TriStar Pictures.

Yes – we talked about that a lot. She said during filming, everyone was laughing at the scene where Linda Blair was throwing up and levitating, and then, suddenly, the set got real weird. The last three days, the lightbulbs in the studio – thirty lightbulbs – all just exploded in a row! Boom, boom, boom! Whenever they tried to fix them or replace them, it would be good for a couple of hours, and then they'd explode again, all in succession. They finally had to switch studios. It was like that particular one was haunted, and no matter what they did, they couldn't stop these lightbulbs from exploding.

You then went on to *House II: The Second Story* where you played the character Arnold The Barbarian, who I assume is a deliberate reference to Arnold Schwarzenegger's *Conan The Barbarian*. Did you know Arnold at that point via the weight-lifting circuit?

I'd put on a big power lifting tournament in 1978 and Arnold had been a guest speaker. I think that was the first time I met him. He tried to get me a part in his film *Conan The Destroyer*, but Will Chamberlain was a little bit bigger than I was at the time and he beat me out.

I assume as you knew Arnold, he didn't mind you riffing on his role? Or did he find it quite amusing?

We never really talked about it too much. I don't know why they called me Arnold The Barbarian, but on both *Twins* and *The Running Man*, we used to joke around a lot. I used to offer him one of my gym's T-shirts and I'd ask, 'Are you a medium or a large?', and he'd go, 'I'm a 2XL at least!' I'd say, 'No, on your best days you're an XL!'

I got the part of Buzzsaw because I was at the Expo eighty-six in Vancouver. I was walking around all the different exhibits, and the security people were looking, and staring at me. I said to my wife, 'Maybe I could go down to California, stay with your aunt, and see what jobs I can get out of this.'

I got lots of small parts; regional commercials, and I was working out at this gym, squatting with over 800 lbs., and this stunt coordinator for *House II* came up to me and said, 'We've already cast this guy from Hawaii who weighs 250 lbs., to play Arnold The Barbarian, but you make this guy look small. I think you've got the perfect look.'

I went to the director's office and as soon as he saw me, he got on the phone and said, 'Tell the guy from Hawaii we're going to go with somebody else.' That's how I got that part! Interestingly, I ended up auditioning for *House II* and *The Running Man* forty-five minutes apart.

That's quite a difference in productions! One was quite a low budget horror sequel and the other was a major Hollywood production. How did you find going between the two productions?

It wasn't that different to be honest. Both films did most of their filming in California. *The Running Man*'s budget was $20 million which, at the time, was quite big, but *House II*'s was around $1.5 million.

On the set, I met a guy named Royal Dano, who I knew because my wife and I watch a lot of old Westerns and this guy was in everything! I got to read with him, and I never realized at the time how big he was. He was probably one of the biggest character actors ever. I'm interested in actors like that because they do so much work and they appear in everything. He had over 100 film credits to his name.

Was that what you were aspiring to at that point in your acting career - or, as you were just starting out, were you just taking notes?

I was taking notes. The problem is you have guys like Schwarzenegger who is 210-230 lbs., and Dolph Lundgren who is 6' 6" and probably weights 250-260 lbs.; I was just too big to be the hero. I trained with Dolph in a gym in Hawaii, and he had trouble doing a 315 lbs. bench for 3-4 reps.

Now you're making me feel inadequate.

In 1982, I'd just done a weightlifting tournament in Tennessee called The Power Cup, and I won it. At the time, I weighed about 340 lbs., but it wasn't fat, believe me! I was doing 500 kg for three reps! If I got down to 275-280 lbs., it might have been a good transition, but I was more concerned about being the Strongest Man in the World.

Most of the lifters these days have the big faces, the tattoos, the ear rings, and they're loaded on steroids. I'm not going to say that we weren't taking steroids, but we weren't taking nearly as much as they are today! Today, they're just killing themselves. I'm still doing good at 70, but I only weight about 260 lbs. now.

Gus Rethwisch stars as Arnold The Barbarian in *House II: The Second Story* (1987). Photo courtesy of New World Pictures.

What was the process for getting cast in *The Running Man*? Did you have to bulk up at all? Learn how to wield chainsaws?

I didn't do well in the audition, and so they said, 'Here's the deal: you're a Stalker, you're broke, you're blood-thirsty. You like to kill people. You haven't killed anyone in a long time. You don't have any money, so come up with some dialogue that you're going to exchange with the director.'

I got up, put my head against the wall, thought for a second, got into a crazy mode as if I wanted to kill every sonofabitch that was in my path. I went over to the director and just went off on him. I got a standing ovation and that's how I got the part.

Initially my part was called The Toolman, and I was meant to have this crazy vest with all these tools hanging off it – screwdrivers, wrenches but they decided to simplify it and just give me a chainsaw. The hardest thing was that I had to ride a motorcycle. I'd never ridden one in my life. I had to take a lot of riding lessons to learn how to ride one!

I don't think The Toolman would have been as memorable.

I think Buzzsaw is a much better name. I'd already done some logging before, so I knew how to handle a chainsaw. When we first did the chainsaw, we didn't have a blade, but it didn't sound right, as it didn't have the teeth. So, the director asked both Schwarzenegger and me if we could do it with the real thing, to make it more realistic. We agreed, so in the end we were basically fighting with each other, with a real chainsaw.

Jesus Christ.

We had a signal that we'd do [with] our eyes if we felt the chainsaw was getting too close to our necks. One time I signaled and he didn't respond, so we got into a fight. He was pretty strong, and he only weighed about 210-220 lbs., but we were probably only three or four inches away from cutting each other's heads off!

I'm surprised they let you use a real one, considering how competitive body builders and power lifters are by nature. Adding a real chainsaw into that mix seems to just be a recipe for disaster, or decapitation.

Yeah, well, there was a company that changed all the safety regulations in stunt work. I think it was after a helicopter accident with Doug McClure, which happened around that time. Otherwise I don't think they would have let us do it!

Is it true that the producers of *The Running Man* dubbed you in the final film?

Yeah, during the part where they were cutting my balls off. That had to be dubbed, because my voice wasn't that high! They dubbed it to make it more high-pitched.

The line, 'I love this saw. This saw is part of me and I'm going to make it part of you!' - that was my line. I told Paul Michael Glazer about it and he said, 'Yeah, that works pretty well,' and he said to Schwarzenegger, 'What's your retort?' and he said, 'Keep it.' And that's how that scene happened!

I imagine it's the film from which most people recognize you from. Have you ever had to deal with any crazy fans asking you to punch them in the face like in the film?

No, but I've signed a lot of chainsaws. I was in the hospital a few days ago with an irregular heartbeat, and the emergency room surgeon, and four nurses even asked me for autographs!

I had a small legal problem a few years ago as I was accused of supposedly assaulting someone in a bar. Some young guy came up to me, and heard I was Buzzsaw, and wanted to arm wrestle me! I said, 'Look, I'm too old for this stuff,' because I used to get it all the time, so I don't go to bars anymore! Anyway, after it was over, the lawyer who was prosecuting me, the lawyer that was defending me, and the judge all wanted autographs! I said, 'It was a good thing you didn't put me in jail, otherwise you wouldn't have gotten jack out of me!'

You seem to have pretty much stopped acting these days, but I did notice your last role was in *The Scorpion King* (2002) with The Rock.

In that movie, the part had already been shot. Arnold's old lifting buddy, Sven-Ole Thorsen, had already got the part, and shot it. A make-up guy I knew from *The Running Man* and *Twins* told me that temp audiences didn't like Sven, so they were reshooting the scene.

I went back down to Los Angeles on a Sunday and, in what I think is one of my biggest accomplishments, they spent $600,000 reshooting that opening scene, and a couple of other scenes with The Rock, myself, and the full crew, 100 miles north of Reno.

I just had to hit my mark and growl, but when I started to walk off stage, I torn up this wall that separated the different sets. I just tore it up and I think that's what impressed them. I just destroyed it. I thought either they're either going to send me a bill or I'm going to get the part!

I did the same thing with *Magnum P.I.* One of the episodes I did, I had to slam my head against a locker door. They had about thirty people lined up to audition for the part of a crazy football player that was trying to kill Magnum. I walked into the audition office, turned around and slammed my head against the wall four times. I had blood coming down my forehead and I looked at the casting director, the director, and the producer, and I said, 'I want this f-ing part and I want it f-ing now!'

Jesus, Gus.

That can backfire on you.

I bet! I'd have called the police!

There was still about twenty people left to interview, but the casting director came out and said, 'Right, the rest of you guys can go home.' And that's
how I got it.

**There is one more film I want to ask you about: *Fist Fighter*. Not many
people have seen it, but you're unrecognizable in it as The Beast, who
kills the prisoners for the General's amusement. How did you get that
role, and how was filming that? It's got quite a cult following these
days.**

I'd done a national commercial for Miller High Life, and I had the same
agent as Matthias Hues, who had done a lot of B-movies, and who was
also in the film.

They had to do four hours' worth of make-up on me every morning.
It was filmed in a sixteenth century monastery, but all the monks had
ended up getting tuberculosis, so they shut it down. It was at the top of
a very big mountain. I remember a really long, winding road, probably
about 10,000 feet up. It was interesting to film in a place like that, but I
got very sick. You know that artificial smoke they use? It really affected
me, so I lost another part that Tex Cobb got on *Raising Arizona* (1987)
with Nicholas Cage. I had to audition with a lady where I was meant to be
sexually aggressive. I know I nailed the line, but my voice was messed up,
and it went to Tex Cobb.

When we flew down to Mexico City, they were filming a James Bond
movie, and I was sat in first class, and ending up talking to a guy who was
a producer on the Bond movie. We talked about putting me in a film, but
I think they went with someone else. Probably the guy who played Jaws
[Richard Kiel].

**Although you've been somewhat typecast in the role of the 'imposing
henchman', do you think playing a villain or a bad guy is more fun that
playing the hero?**

Yes, playing the bad guy is definitely more interesting, and a lot more fun
than playing the hero. You get to really flex your acting muscles. John
Wayne, for example, apparently once said to Michael Caine that if you
want to survive in this business as a leading man, 'You don't want to say
too much. Walk slow and speak slower.' How many times did you ever
see John Wayne really lose his temper? They all have to be the cool lead-

ing man. It's like Rock Hudson said, 'I'm not an actor,' and they said, 'You don't have to be an actor, you're a star!'

You gave up in acting in 2002, was that because, as you previously mentioned, your health problems, or were you tired of the business?

When I was in Los Angeles, I would stay in a YMCA. I'd go there for three or four months at a time, and while I got a lot of commercials, I wasn't really getting any big parts.

Probably the thing that stopped me becoming a bigger character actor was the death of my agent Herman Zimmerman. He died shortly after *The Running Man*, and that affected me. He was a damn good agent, and he really liked me. I called him up when I was starting out and he said, 'We have a guy already who's 6' 4" and 250 lbs.' I said, 'I'm 6' 4" and 350 lbs.!'

I was going back to Hawaii, so I went to his building and walked through the door of this tiny office in North Hollywood. The door was probably no more than six feet high, and wasn't very wide. I went through the door sideways, went up to his desk and slammed both of my fists down. He was already 70–80 years-old then, but he looked up at me and said, 'I'm glad you came!'

Bill Duke

"You scared, motherfucker? Well, you should be, because this Green Beret is going to kick your big ass!"
— Cooke, *Commando* (1985).

Select Filmography

- *American Gigolo* (1980) – Leon
- *Commando* (1985) – Cooke
- *Predator* (1987) – Mac
- *Action Jackson* (1988) – Capt. Earl Armbruster
- *Bird on a Wire* (1990) – Albert Diggs
- *Menace II Society* (1993) – Detective
- *Payback* (1999) – Det. Hicks
- *X-Men: The Last Stand* (2006) – Trask

After letting Sully go, John Matrix (Arnold Schwarzenegger) is looking for the next person that can help him find his missing daughter. Cooke (Bill Duke), another one of Bennett's mercenaries, is set to meet Sully at a nearby motel. Then Matrix, and Cindy (Rae Dawn Chong), an air stewardess who has been caught up in the chaos, head there to find him.

WHILE MOST ACTION FILM AFICIONADOS will know Bill Duke from his acting roles in the likes of *Commando*, *Predator* and *Action Jackson*, few will be aware of his accomplishments as a writer, producer, and director. In

Cooke (Bill Duke) gets up to some "macho bullshit" in *Commando* (1985).
Photo courtesy of 20th Century Fox.

fact, Bill Duke has directed over sixty films and TV shows, from episodes of *Hill Streets Blues* (1983-1984), *Miami Vice* (1988) and *The Twilight Zone* (1987) to feature films like *A Rage in Harlem* (1991), *Deep Cover* (1992) and, surprisingly to many, *Sister Act 2: Back in the Habit* (1993).

As head of the Duke Media Foundation, Bill Duke is working on a host of media projects that are designed to prepare adolescents for the future with a host of media and financial literacy tools. Using his knowledge of the entertainment industry, Duke has developed a wide range of apps, games and virtual world experiences that he hopes will benefit the next generation. He's also a flag-bearer for black actors and film-makers hosting a media camp that teaches everything from screenwriting to producing, and directing. And you just knew him as Mac in *Predator*....

It's not surprising that Duke has been appointed to the National Endowment of Humanities by former President Bill Clinton, and has been honored by the Directors Guild of America with a Lifetime Achievement Tribute.

When we spoke, he was getting ready to travel to Los Angeles for a special thirty-fifth anniversary screening of *Predator*, where he would be reuniting with some of the cast, including Arnold Schwarzenegger, so I asked him how he got started in the business that had clearly failed to pigeonhole him, and the challenges that black actors and filmmakers face in the film industry.

You are unique among the people I've interviewed for this book, as you're not just a working actor, but also a director. Do you primarily think of yourself as an actor or a director, or has that changed over time?

It's hard to say, but these days I would say I'm more of a director, because there are things that I want to say through film, and directing allows you to do that.

I started out as a theatre actor, but I was also a writer so I wrote my own plays and directed some of them. When I found directing, I discovered that I loved working with actors. I was lucky enough to go to some good schools and was also able to teach acting. That's what started my career, in terms of being an actor, but at the same time I was always writing and directing. It's what got me [in]to the industry.

In your early film roles, you played a wide range of characters, such as a young, black Muslim in *Car Wash* (1976), a gay pimp in *American Gigolo*, before appearing in several action films as either a henchman or as a cop. Was this a conscious decision by you to avoid being stereotyped in the industry, or where you accepting any and all roles at that time?

I did not want to get stereotyped, and there were certain projects that I didn't want to be attached to because of the things that I believe in. I tried my best, but sometimes I took jobs because they paid well, but there were certain things that I didn't want to do, so I didn't do them.

As a 6' 4" black man, there must have been certain types of roles that casting agents and producers would try and put you in that you felt were right for you?

Anything mean, black, dangerous, and criminal! I played some bad guys, but I also wanted to expand my ability to explore my potential as an actor on many levels. That was always a challenge and continues to be for many actors, but we're fortunate enough to be in the business that we want to be in, and doing things we want to do, so that's the good part. It is competitive, and it is difficult, but that's the price you pay.

"I played some bad guys, but I also wanted to expand my ability to explore my potential as an actor on many levels." - Bill Duke. Photo courtesy of 20th Century Fox.

Hollywood can be problematic when it comes to stereotyping, and I imagine for black actors it's an even greater challenge. How did you walk that line between sticking to your ethical beliefs, and having to work?

It's a big challenge, because I have bills to pay like everybody else, and so you can't be too choosy. If you're offered a selection of roles, then you have the privilege of being able to choose what you do, and I've tried my best to do that.

Do you feel the industry has gotten better in terms of the roles on offer to young black actors?

[long pause] I think it has to a certain degree, but we have a long way to go. It's better than it was in the sense that there is greater diversity in terms of light and dark-skinned faces on screen, and the stories being told.

Our founding fathers, Paul Robeson, Sidney Poitier, and Harry Belafonte set the ground, but Sidney Poitier was the greatest of all, and is our leader. He was so diverse and was one of the first actors to take their acting experience and leverage it into directing and producing. They're pioneers.

Today, it's better, but we still need a larger ratio of films featuring blacks, Hispanics and other minorities. I think the Internet has given us a greater platform and ability to do that, and I always encourage people [to] discover themselves through the opportunities online, rather than waiting to be discovered. If you're always waiting, that opportunity may not come. It's hard, and when I first started out, there was no internet, no cell phones; there was nothing. Today it's different, and I applaud that.

The first big film I made was *Car Wash* and Michael Schultz was a director. That received a lot of recognition because it featured Richard Pryor, The Pointer Sisters, George Carlin and Danny DeVito. A lot of names were in that film, and so everyone got a lot of attention. That really put me on the map.

In the eighties, I obviously grew up watching you in big action films like *Commando*, *Predator*, and *Action Jackson*. How did you come to the attention of producer Joel Silver, and how did you get into the group of actors that he regularly cast in his films?

Joel Silver hired me for *Commando* and then, after that, he bought me back for *Predator* and *Action Jackson*. I auditioned for *Commando* and Joel had seen my work, so he cast me in the film. Working on that film was great because it was like one big family. Arnold has no big ego, and works well with everybody. He wants to see a positive experience on the set, so he's a leader. Between him and Joel, that's how it works.

Joel liked my work and we hit it off as people. In those days, Joel was ahead of his time. There was no film like *Predator* before Joel Silver came along. He was a visionary. On *Commando*, and later on *Predator,* we were under really wild conditions, up in the jungle in Puerto Vallarta. When I say jungle, I'm talking about snakes that, if they bite you, can kill you, just crawling around in front of us! During the first week for *Predator*, there were so many challenges. The craft service guy had to put netting around the tent because of the bugs. Every time we went to get some food, there were bugs everywhere! The first week we complained and refused to eat the food, but that was all the food there was, so, by the second week, the bugs were called protein! I think everybody is surprised at how the film is regarded as an action classic today.

With the success of *Predator*, do you find that you were given more opportunities or did producers no longer consider you for more unique characters like Leon in *American Gigolo*?

It's difficult because Hollywood is so political, and the climate changes from day to day. I think a lot of things that I would have gotten disap-

Behind the scenes on *Commando* (1985) with David Patrick Kelly (left),
Charles Meshack (second left), and Arnold Schwarzenegger.
Photo courtesy of 20th Century Fox.

Bill Duke reunites with Arnold Schwarzenegger in *Predator* (1987).
Photo courtesy of 20th Century Fox.

peared, because if they see [you] in a big role, they'll often see you as the character instead of the actor.

I primarily think of you as your more villainous roles, in films like *Commando* and *Bird on a Wire,* but then you shifted into playing a large number of law enforcement characters like in *Action Jackson.* Was that important for you – to see a black man in a positive position of authority - or, post-*Predator*, were those the roles that were offered to you?

It was both: an opportunity and a conscious decision. Many times, tall black men are cast as villains, so I didn't want to just be seen as a stereotypical, dangerous, horrific human being, I wanted to have an impact, and have my humanity seen.

In this business, if you're perceived in a certain way, you're cast in a certain way, especially in roles where your humanity is not needed. It's getting better, but more needs to be done.

Do you think you were successful? What is the role that most people associate you with?

Bill Duke goes toe-to-toe with his *Predator* co-star Carl Weathers in *Action Jackson* (1988). Photo courtesy of Warner Brothers.

You're not going to believe this, but the character that I'm most remembered for is from *Menace II Society*. Do you remember my line? 'You know you done fucked up, right?' I get that daily! Daily! Older people, young people, kids, they all come up to me and said, 'You know you done fucked up, right?' [laughs]

In your directing career, you've helmed numerous films from *Hoodlum* to *Sister Act 2: Back in the Habit*. Is there a particular genre that you like to direct or do you like to mix it up whenever you can?

I'm driven by scripts. I read a script and if really touches me, I try and get the project off the ground. I'm not trying to sound elitist, but there's not a lot of great writing out there anymore, but I'm attracted to great writing. I know that the action and the franchise potential is important, but I just love great writers, man. Great writing touches you and when you read a script as a director, things just come to you. The story explodes of the page because of the writing and that's what I'm interested by.

In terms of feature films, there's a paradigm shift going on. Action films are still really popular, but studios are understanding the competition that they face from the likes from Netflix, Amazon, Hulu and Crackle. For independent film-makers, it's not easy because smaller films with great scripts don't make as much money as *Spiderman, Batman, Superman,* but Netflix is doing some great stuff, and some of their films are now up for awards. The same for HBO with *Game of Thrones.* Their shows are well written and very well put together. There's an attempt within studios to try and change the paradigm, but it's hard if you've been in the system for a while, and you're used to having certain kind of scripts and projects.

If I find a great script and it'll cost $5 million to make, studios are reluctant because if it costs $5 million and only make $15 million, that's no big deal to them, but if they spend $150 million and the film makes $2 billion, that makes more sense!

You've done your share of big budget films, but in terms of working, do you mainly stick to directing these days, as opposed to acting?

Yes, I guess. I'm still acting and have some new films coming out next year, but mostly I focus on projects that I want to get done as a director.

Looking back at your career, are there any roles that you're particularly proud of?

I did this television show called *Palmerstown, U.S.A* (1980-1981), about segregation, that Norman Lear and Alex Haley came together to do in the eighties. I really enjoyed that because I played a father in a segregated community. In the show, my son and a young white boy became friends, forcing their fathers to become friends too. It was about the humanity of both sides, not always about race and mental conflict, but about humanity. I think that kind of message is probably more important now than it's ever been, especially with everything that's going currently on in the United States.

Matthias Hues

"I come in peace."
– Talec, *Dark Angel* (1990).

Select Filmography

- *No Retreat, No Surrender 2: Raging Thunder* (1987) – Yuri
- *Fist Fighter* (1989) – Rhino
- *Dark Angel* (*I Come in Peace*, 1990) – Talec
- *Star Trek VI: The Undiscovered Country* (1991) – Klingon General
- *Kickboxer 2: The Way Back* (1991) – Neil Vargas
- *Mission of Justice* (1992) – Titus Larkin
- *TC 2000* (1993) – Bigalow
- *Death Match* (1994) – Mark Vanik
- *Black Rose* (2014) – Black Mask Killer
- *Showdown in Manila* (2016) – Dorn

Houston cop, Jack Caine (Dolph Lundgren), has a problem. A series of murders, all over the city, featuring weaponry that no-one has ever seen before, has both the police force and local drug gangs on edge. They have every reason to be nervous, because the person responsible for these deaths is actually an alien. The imposing Talec (Matthias Hues) shoots his victims full of synthetic heroin in order to extract endorphins from their brains. This is then used to create a new drug called Barsi, that is in demand all over the galaxy. If Caine doesn't stop Talec, then Earth could soon become a target for alien drug lords seeking to harvest the finest in intergalactic narcotics!

Extraterrestrial drug dealer, Talec (Matthias Hues), lies about his intentions in the sci-fi actioner, *Dark Angel* (1990). Photo courtesy of Vision International.

STANDING 6' 5" WITH HIS MUSCULAR PHYSIQUE and signature long blonde hair, Matthias Hues has been a familiar face in action films since the late 1980s, when he replaced Jean-Claude Van Damme as the villain in *No Retreat, No Surrender 2: Raging Thunder.*

Originally born in Germany, Hues grew up as a track and field athlete before excelling at martial arts. Despite being proficient in kickboxing, Hues worked in hotel and health spa management before moving to Los Angles to seek his fortune.

While training at the infamous Gold's Gym, in Venice, where Arnold Schwarzenegger and Lou Ferrigno used to work out, Hues was asked to screentest for *No Retreat, No Surrender 2*, despite having no previous acting experience. The moderate success of the film led Hues on a career of playing intimidating fighters and henchmen, most famously as the alien drug dealer battling Dolph Lundgren in *Dark Angel* (1990).

When I spoke to Matthias Hues, the non-stop working actor had just finished filming in eastern Europe, and was only too eager to talk about his wide-ranging career that saw him; move from spas to the silver screen, share scenes with some of the most famous names in action cinema, including Cynthia Rothrock, Don "The Dragon" Wilson, and Mark Dacascos, and bravely shoot in Cambodia for *No Retreat, No Surrender 2.*

Your career has taken a unique path. How does someone go from opening health clubs in Paris to shooting action films on the streets of Los Angeles?

When I was young, I attended a special restaurant business school that takes four years to complete, if you want to work in hotel management. I loved everything that had to do with hotels, and I figured it would be a great way to see the world and meet interesting people, because sooner or later everyone shows up in a hotel! Everyone has their own stories and their own history, so I was very attracted to the hotel business. It felt very glamorous. Once I had graduated, I had to go to the army because everyone in Germany must join the military, but after fifteen months, I moved to Paris.

If you live in Europe, London and Paris are the hip places that you dream of visiting. I'd read so many books about Paris, and I was intrigued by the bohemian lifestyle, and meeting so many artists and musicians. I wanted to be part of it and thought that the hotel business was the best way to do it.

Paris is so cosmopolitan, and I worked in pretty much every high-end hotel you can imagine. Then there was a gym next to my hotel on the Champs Elysees and it was where all the celebrities worked out. I worked there, and I felt like I was like these celebrities, even though you're not, because they were such an eclectic group of dancers and singers. And then Jane Fonda and all these American aerobic trainers came along, and my mind started going towards Hollywood, as everything seemed to come from there. I went back to my hometown and opened a Jane Fonda aerobic gym called California Fitness Studio. I bought myself an American Jeep and lived a Baywatch-type lifestyle! And then I saw *Rocky IV* and this big, tall Swedish guy [Dolph Lundgren] and thought, 'Hollywood! That's my next step!'

Have you always been into physical fitness or was it something that you developed an interest in while you were in Paris?

I was always a track and field athlete. It was always something I really enjoyed, and I was pretty good at it. I always told my parents that I wasn't going to make money from my physicality, which you can't in Germany, unless you're a professional athlete. I had done German and European championships, but I wasn't a professional. It wasn't a job, but I figured it might come in handy one day.

Matthias Hues is no stranger to the gym in this publicity photo.
Photo courtesy of Ron Derhacopian.

When I decided to go to the United States, I knew I could make an impact if I was bigger, better, faster, or anything larger! You know Americans and how they feel about size! I really understood that concept and in the eighties, everyone was ambitious. There was no internet, not many television stations, so you really had to stand out.

It was also the time of the muscular action hero as well, so it was a perfect time to move to Hollywood.

Yes, it's all timing. It was the same for Arnold [Schwarzenegger], because that look wasn't trendy when he made it in Hollywood. The time was right. He became *Conan* and that physicality became appealing. With that, Stallone, and all the other copycat action heroes- the world was open for anyone who wanted to come over. It didn't matter what country you came from, as long as you were muscled! You just had to stick out and believe that you were special. If you believe it, other people will believe it. People came from all around the world. I wasn't the only one, and we all went to Gold's Gym in Venice.

The one thing that separates you and Dolph Lundgren from the other big muscular action heroes of the time, is that the two of you are proficient in martial arts. Was that something you grew up doing?

Not really. I was doing Taekwondo, but I wasn't pursuing it like Dolph. It was just something that came easily to me, but I never paid attention to it. I did when I realised that people liked it, because Arnold and some of the other action stars weren't really into [it], so neither was I until I replaced Jean-Claude Van Damme in *No Retreat, No Surrender 2*!

At that point, were you trying to replicate or emulate any other actor's career path, or were you trying to forge your own?

I think that's a really good question because I think the biggest mistake you can make is to try and be the next Arnold, the next Van Damme, or the next Seagal. You must be the next you because there is already an Arnold, a Van Damme, or whatever. You must come up with your own something. When I got to Los Angeles, I looked up Dolph Lundgren to ask for a job. I met him a couple of times and I thought, 'Okay, you're now the competition.'

Also, as a group of actors, we all knew each other. Dolph, Van Damme, Seagal – everyone knows each other. We all hung around together, and it was very competitive. That's what fuelled the industry. It was an amazing time.

Your first film role saw you replace Jean-Claude Van Damme on *No Retreat, No Surrender 2: Raging Thunder*, because he and Kurt McKinney refused to go to Cambodia to film it. How did you suddenly end up shooting in south-east Asia on a sequel to a hit film, with no acting experience?

The writers and producers didn't know what to do, so they literally opened a phone book, when to the gym section, and called the first gym and asked for anyone from Europe who could do martial arts! I think I had literally joined Gold's Gym that month, and the manager knew I wanted to be an actor, so he called me up to his office when the call came in and sent me off to the producers to audition. I got the job and then I was suddenly in Thailand!

It was an amazing adventure and was incredibly beautiful, but it was a crazy shoot as we were in the jungle on the Thailand-Cambodian border. We crossed over the border a few times and there were some near misses, fights, and all kinds of crazy shit, but it was amazing. I thought life couldn't get any better.

You were working with Cynthia Rothrock and Corey Yuen, who were established martial arts legends. How did you find your first experience with on-screen fighting? Did it come easily or was there quite a large learning curve?

It didn't come easily, and there was a point when I really had to have a talk with myself about whether I really wanted it, because I wasn't used to the Chinese fighting style. Their coordination and endurance were amazing, and all the stunt guys were on a much higher level than I was. I had to make a decision, and I decided that I'd rather die in Thailand than give in.

You do a lot of your own stunts in the film and, of course, have that incredible death scene, involving being dragged along by a jeep and falling into an alligator pit. How did you find that physically?

It wasn't so bad, but nothing is bad when you're twenty-six years old and on a movie set! Nothing is bad! It was easy, and I could still do it today. It was fun, like being on a playground. I wanted to really please these people, because they don't take prisoners. No one knew me, no one liked me – I was just a white guy with no experience! I'd never done anything like this in my life, [and] that was a pretty shock for everyone. I had to really earn it, but by the end, there was not one person who didn't respect me, because I earned it.

Cynthia, of course, is an amazing fighter. She's incredibly tough, and we still hang out. She's never in a bad mood! I love her because most actors are sissies, but she isn't. This is not a business for sensitive people. You must be tough, especially in our genre. You must be prepared to go to shitty locations and work long hours.

How did Jean-Claude Van Damme feel about you stepping into his shoes?

He didn't know me at that time, but after he knew who I was, he was very nice to me. After he saw *Dark Angel*, his agent signed me, and he gave me

In recent years, Matthias Hues has shaved off his trademark long hair.
Photo courtesy of Ron Derhacopian.

all kinds of tips about what not to do in Hollywood. He was the first one in Hollywood that came up to me and said, 'I just saw your movie. Now you're one of us.'

After *No Retreat, No Surrender 2: Raging Thunder*, you did a lot of films where you played big henchmen-type roles, such as in *Kickboxer 2* and *Fist Fighter*. Was it something you tried to fight, or were you happy to take whatever work came your way?

I fell into it. I liked it. It gave me a certain identity, and I liked the challenge of those fights. It's brutal to do and you work long hours. What we do is very physical, and you get injured all the time. It's not for everyone, but I liked it.

After I filmed *No Retreat, No Surrender 2*, the movie didn't come out for over a year, so I had no job, nor any money. I was doing all these stupid little jobs to survive. When the movie came out, the phone rang the next day offering me a job, but for a whole year nothing happened. I also couldn't speak English very well. I auditioned for *Rambo III* [1988] and *Over the Top* [1987], but they just laughed at me because my English was so bad.

You also stood out from other actors because of your distinctive long blonde hair. Did you grow it for that reason, or did you just like the look?

Well, it was eighties at the time, but it is all about being different. I was the big guy with the long hair, and then that became like my look. It was a bit of a mistake, because I turned down a lot of movies where they asked me to cut my hair, and I didn't out of fear. I thought I was sticking to my guns, but I lost a lot of movies as a result.

Okay, but then you got cast in *Dark Angel*, which is probably your biggest role. How did that role come about? Did you audition, or did Dolph Lundgren recommend you?

I auditioned. I got a call saying that the producers were looking for a basketball player, or track and field champion. I was track and field, so I walked into the production office and saw all these massive basketball players and professional athletes.

I walked in to meet the director, Craig R. Baxley, and he took one look at me and said, 'This is your job, but you're going to have to do everything I say. You're going to have to be willing to die for it. You'll have to do every stunt because I want to see your face. That's why we need an athlete, because we need someone that can actually do what the character can do.' I said, 'No worries! I'll do anything!'

The poster for *Dark Angel* (1990) featuring Dolph Lundgren and Matthias Hues. Photo courtesy of Vision International.

Did Dolph remember you at all from when you first moved to Los Angeles?

He was the first person in Hollywood that I walked up to and asked for a job. At the time, he just made fun of me and put me down, but I was just one of the many people who come up to him every day, so he didn't take me seriously.

Was there any on-set payback?

I didn't have to say anything, because Dolph came up to the director and said he wanted to take his shirt off in the final fight scene with me. The director said, 'No Dolph. If anyone's taking their shirt off, it's Matthias, not you!' [laughs]

Are you amazed at how many people remember you from that role? You only have one line that you repeat throughout, but I'm willing to bet people come up to you all the time and say, 'I come in peace.'

Yes, still to this day. It's unreal. This film didn't really hit until the late nineties. Then, any country I went to, I was mobbed. I couldn't believe it. I was not a movie star, but everyone in the world suddenly knew me. It was so weird. I'd be in a nightclub, and the DJ would suddenly say, 'I come in peace' and people would buy me champagne! I would land in airports and I wouldn't have to go through customs. I would get a police escort! It was beyond anything I've ever experienced in my life.

The film wasn't a massive hit at the time, but your next role was *in Star Trek VI: The Undiscovered Country*, where you played a Klingon General.

The whole process was fantastic. I got a call from Paramount asking me to audition for the film's director. I was very nervous, but I got the job and I couldn't believe it. They sent me to school to learn Klingon! It wasn't easy, and I've forgotten most of it now. The next thing I knew, I was on the sound stage, and I was walking around the U.S.S. Enterprise. There was Spock! Captain Kirk! And Christopher Plummer – what a storyteller! I only worked on the film for three weeks and wished I'd had a bigger role, but I was just grateful to be part of it.

After that, you must have thought that your career was on the rise?

It's weird to explain. On the last day of *Dark Angel*, I met Jake Bloom, who is a massive Hollywood agent and lawyer. He said, 'I represent Arnold, Sly, Dolph and Bruce Willis. I've watched ten minutes of this film's footage, and you're my next action star. You're going to be the biggest thing ever. I'll offer you a three-picture deal at any studio you want. One-million-dollar salary. You have to sign with me tonight.'

I couldn't believe it, so I signed with him the next day. I went to his agency, and there was a massive conference room with food and champagne, and all these people pitched me possible roles. Then *Dark Angel* came out and the film didn't make any money, so they dropped me. Bloom called me to his office and said, 'I'm going to drop you, but I'm dropping everyone! Arnold! Stallone! Things have changed! It's all about Keanu Reeves and Brad Pitt – they're taking over the action market. You guys are all out!' So, my shot was gone, and it was the same for Arnold and Sly. They disappeared for several years.

That wasn't until the mid-nineties, though. If this was in 1991, Arnie was just about to make *Terminator 2: Judgement Day*.

Right, but they strung me along for about a couple years. Nothing ever happened. They didn't know what to do with me. There was no market and my last film hadn't made any money, and it didn't come out till 1993! Before I knew it, two years were over, and it was a complete bust.

I grabbed whatever I could get. I got a call from John Daly, one of the producers of *The Terminator*, and he offered me a film called *Highway to Hell* [1991], but I later found out that they wanted me to wear a mask, so I walked away from the project. A lawyer called me and said, 'If you don't do the movie, you will never work in Hollywood again!' I said, 'I don't think it's good for my career, because you don't see my face and you never told me about the mask!'

I don't know if these people can ruin your career, but for a couple of years, again, I didn't work. A lot of times when you're young, you turn down movies. I turned down *Cyborg* [1989], I turned down being Hulk Hogan's nemesis, because Van Damme always said, 'You have to do what you think is right for you. Everyone is going to push you into something.'

When you were taking whatever jobs you could find, did you end up doing any projects you weren't particularly proud of?

Most films are fun, so I have never regretted one, even if it's the silliest B-movie. They are so much fun because the crew are making something for no money, and put so much love and effort into it. It's such a great community, and they are committed filmmakers. They just don't have much money.

When you're in a business, it's best to learn and work your way up to the big time. You must start with nothing. Look at Roger Corman. He really knows how to make movies, and is excited about coming to work.

Is that why you work repeatedly with actors like Don "The Dragon" Wilson, because he's passionate about his projects?

Absolutely. Don is a gentleman, who has a fantastic and friendly personality, and isn't driven by ego. These are the kind of people you want to work with.

Have you ever thought about directing?

Yes, of course, I'd love to, but it's not that easy because it's also a financial struggle. You need to find someone that is willing to risk their money.

Would you have liked to have played the hero or are you still happy to play heavies?

Now I'm older, I could play the Liam Neeson roles very easily. The father that kicks some ass! I cut my hair recently because people kept saying I was limiting myself.

Looking back at your career, is there anything you wish you'd done differently - perhaps chosen a different path as a fighter-choreographer, or does your passion lie with acting?

I would have done everything the same, except I would have taken every job they offered me. Any job – no matter what! Mask, no mask; long hair, no hair. Like all actors I'm quite insecure, but I love watching people and analysing everything. You've got to be willing to die for your craft. There's a lot of ups and downs, but that is what it's like to be an actor.

Martin Kove

"We do not train to be merciful here. Mercy is for the weak. Here, in the streets, in competition: A man confronts you, he is the enemy. An enemy deserves no mercy."
            – John Kreese, *The Karate Kid* (1984).

Select Filmography

* *Cagney & Lacey* (1981-1988) – Victor Isbecki
* *The Karate Kid* (1984) – John Kreese
* *Rambo: First Blood Part II* (1985) – Ericson
* *The Karate Kid Part II* (1986) – John Kreese
* *Steele Justice (1987)* – John Steele
* *The Karate Kid Part III* (1989) – John Kreese
* *Wyatt Earp* (1994) – Ed Ross
* *Death Match* (1994) – Paul Landis
* *Extreme Honor* (2001) - Packard
* *Crocodile 2: Death Swamp* (2002) – Roland

Moving from New Jersey to California hasn't been easy for Daniel (Ralph Macchio). Luckily though, his football skills have caught the eye of Ali (Elisabeth Shue). The only problem is her ex, Johnny Lawrence (William Zabka), an arrogant karate expert who takes pleasure in bullying Daniel at every opportunity. Desperate to have the fighting skills to be able to stand up for himself, Daniel heads to the local Cobra Kai dojo, but, to his horror, he discovers it is where Johnny and his friends train. Even worse, they are taught to

Cobra Kai's John Kreese (Martin Kove) tries to face down Mr. Miyagi (Pat Mortia) in *The Karate Kid* (1984). Photo courtesy of MartinKoveOnline.com

*show no mercy to their opponents by their victory-obsessed
sensei – John Kreese (Martin Kove).*

JOHN KREESE ISN'T A VILLAIN in the traditional sense. If we were being accurate, the main villain in *The Karate Kid* is William Zabka's Johnny
Lawrence. After all, it is he and his 'toadies' that beat Daniel up and tor-
ment him at every opportunity, and whom Daniel must face in the film's
finale. However, if it wasn't for the brutal teachings of Sensei John Kreese,
Johnny might be a well-adjusted young man. Unfortunately, for all involved, Johnny and his friends have been taught, from a young age, that
pain does not exist, fear should be ignored, and defeat is unacceptable.

For most kids growing up in the eighties and nineties, *The Karate Kid*
was our *Rocky* – sure, we watched the *Rocky* films as well, but it was much
easier to relate to Daniel's bullying torments than it was Rocky's fear of
not going the distance. Martin Kove's Kreese also made a big impression.
With a massive Cobra tattoo on his bicep, his casual disrespect to Mr.
Miyagi (Pat Morita), and in encouraging his pupils to prey on the weak,
he was the quintessential boo-hiss villain.

What I always loved about the character of Kreese is the way he didn't let anything go, which inevitably led to his downfall, and that the franchise charted across three films. Due to his massive ego, Kreese would eventually lose his pupils and his dojo and come up with a ridiculous plan for revenge in *The Karate Kid Part III*. Could the man be any more petty and vindictive? Determined to find out what goes into playing such a memorable, and seemingly unredeemable character, I reached out to Martin Kove, an actor I also recalled from numerous viewings of *Rambo: First Blood Part II*, to talk about the legacy of *The Karate Kid* films, his still-strong friendship with his Cobra Kai pupils, and why mercy is for the weak!

Does a day go by when someone doesn't come up to you and quote a line from *The Karate Kid*, 'Mercy is for the weak' or 'Sweep the leg?'

[It happens] pretty much almost daily. I do autograph shows and go around the country a lot, and it was recently the film's thirtieth anniversary, and so Ralph [Macchio], Billy [Zabka], and I had to go and do different events.

The movie has always meant so much to people and I often write those lines when I sign the pictures because that's what the fans ask for! The film itself became a classic of what was in the air in 1984. People related to the fish-out-of-water story, where Daniel moves and feels quite isolated in his life, and the bullying situation. The third aspect of what has carried *The Karate Kid* for all these years is the romance, as many kids were also falling in love for the first time at that point. The bottom line is, most of the time people remember this movie because of all those factors. It was so well written.

[Director] John G. Avildsen had previously directed *Rocky* and, for many viewers, *The Karate Kid* was a 'teenage *Rocky*'. Were you surprised at the film's success when it came out? Did you think it would have the impact that it ended up having?

None of us thought that the film would be such a success. No one expected it to have the legs that it did and becoming so popular. The visionary [producer] Jerry Weintraub, who was a good friend of mine and recently passed away, had a vision and invested in the script, but no-one thought

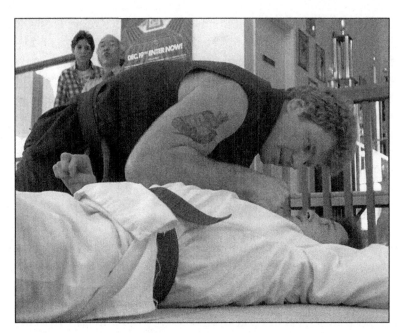

There is no place for weakness and mercy in the Cobra Kai dojo in *The Karate Kid* (1984). Photo courtesy of MartinKoveOnline.com

it would have the legs of a classic like *Casablanca* (1942) or *The Searchers* (1956).

You had been acting for a while and were known for your TV work in *Cagney and Lacey*, so how did you end up getting the role? I read that the audition process took a while and you had to turn down other roles while you were waiting.

What happened was, I got the script on a Monday and was told that the director would see me at the end of the week. I said, 'Fine,' and then the very next morning, my agent called and said they wanted to see me on set at midday. It was nine in the morning, so I was angry, as I didn't have any time to prepare. It was the 'Mercy is for the weak' scene and as I was so angry, I used that anger as an asset. I went in there and said, 'What an asshole you are John Avildsen. We wait for years to meet directors of your calibre! We fire our agents, we fire our managers, and now you don't give me any time to prepare. You are a real asshole.' I said the same thing to the casting director too!

At the height of my screaming, I went straight into the scene and they loved it. I did the same thing to Jerry Weintraub. He was late to the meeting and I berated him for being late and boom, I did the same thing again and they loved it. They said, "You've got to meet the studio head," and the rest was history! If I got it, I got it and if I didn't, I was doing *Cagney and Lacey* at the time!

The surprising thing is that, at first, the studio didn't want Pat Morita for Mr. Miyagi, but the director made a video of him and showed it to Jerry, and Jerry was completely taken by it. But at first, he didn't want anything to do with this comedian that had been on *Happy Days* (1974-1984)!

And Pat ended up getting nominated for an Oscar, so it just goes to show you never know. I read that you have black belts in Kendo and Tiger Kenpo, but was this something you developed an interest in from working on the film, or have you always practiced martial arts?

I have a foundation of karate, but [for the role] we were primarily working in Kendo. Ted Johnson, our stunt coordinator, worked with me for two to three hours a day for weeks to practice that scene where I punch in the car window. That scene was originally meant to be the climax for the first film.

When you filmed that, was that during the production for the first film or years later on the sequel?

Years later for the sequel. It was in 1986 when we finally filmed that scene as Jerry and Jon had decided to end the first movie in the tournament.

Is it true that you ill-timed one of those punches and you shattered a real window and broke your fist?

Yes. I was lunge punching and every time I hit the window it wouldn't break. I'd hit it and it was meant to break an inch before, so that when you put your hand through it, it looks like you shattered it.

[That night] was damp so when they put the gunpowder in to shatter the glass, the special effect didn't work. The gunpowder is meant to cause a ripple effect up the window, shattering the glass, but it never happened! Finally, I was told that it would work. I didn't have that much confidence, so I didn't lunge and punch, I just punched it. Sure enough, my head went right through the window glass. I pulled my hand out and I had shards of glass in my wrist. It was silly. It hurt. They patched me up, put makeup on it, and we did it again.

This time, I just stopped at the glass. I turned to John Avildsen and said, 'John, this is not the hand of The Terminator. This is not Arnold's hand. This is Marty Kove's hand.' He said, 'Okay. That's a wrap.' So, when you see the movie, the hand going through is real Marty Kove going through real glass. The shot of the hand coming out was done the next day and was fake blood.

When you first see Kreese in the Cobra Kai dojo, there's a picture of him in (I'm assuming) Vietnam. Do you think this has anything to do with his obsession with winning and showing no mercy? Did the screenwriters ever give you any insight into his background at all?

It was never written, but I created a backstory for him. In high school, college, and the army, he was never anything but a champion. He was always winning. Then he went to Vietnam, like so many of our soldiers, where he was not allowed to win. It was a political war, so when he came back he swore that he would never lose, and he decided to open more dojos. He decided that no student of his dojo would ever lose under any circumstances. That's why he was so merciless because he had to win. He was cold, cruel, and with that backstory, you could understand why he needed to be triumphant as often as possible. Also, 'sweeping the leg' is not illegal! It depends on how you use it, and what moves are involved.

What did you think of Kreese's journey throughout the three films? He tries to attack Mr. Miyagi at the beginning of *The Karate Kid Part II*, and then in *The Karate Kid Part III*, he unleashes a mission of vengeance against Daniel and Mr. Miyagi. Did you have any regrets about those films, and is there anything you would have liked to have done differently?

In *The Karate Kid Part III*, I don't think he'd changed very much during those years of life because, while he was down and out for a while, he was saved by Thomas Ian Griffith's Terry Silver, who puts him in a position where he could add more dojos. I saved his life in Vietnam, so he owes me! As Silver is very wealthy, he acts as a band-aid for Kreese, allowing him to maintain his own ego.

At the time, I was in a TV show called *Hard Time on Planet Earth* [1989], so they brought Thomas Ian Griffith to play the [main villain] and he did everything that I was supposed to do. In the film, [Kreese] was sent on vacation, so that Silver could do what he needed to do and set up a sting operation against Ralph Macchio. So, the maturation of the character didn't change very much because, once again, I come back in the same emotional condition as I was to begin with. Someone for whom winning is the most important thing. Today, I think John Kreese would be much calmer, mature, and more spiritual than he was all those years ago.

It's great to see that you're still really close with your fellow cast members and that you all go to conventions together. Has it been strange seeing these actors grow and mature from the young men they were in 1984?

I see Billy a lot and we always have a good time together, as we have the same kind of dark sense of humour. He has kids and now I have a grandchild. We're good friends.

Martin Kove and Sylvester Stallone on set of *Rambo: First Blood Part II* (1985). Photo courtesy of MartinKoveOnline.com

Ralph lives on the East Coast, but when we see him at various conventions, we always try to have dinner together. Billy and I see each other a lot more often. Ralph doesn't come out to Los Angeles unless he's working.

After *The Karate Kid*, you went straight into *Rambo: First Blood Part II*. What are your memories about making a big budget action film in Mexico with Stallone who was at the peak of his career at that point?

Sly was an old friend of mine and we had the same old clockmaker, a man called Cuno Strunholtz, who used to get us strange jobs in the early 1970s. He would get me a job as a Santa Claus in a department store, and get Sly a job as an usher in the movie theatre called The Baronet on 3rd Avenue. We were both just starting out as actors. I'd done *Death Race 2000* [1975] with Sly, so we were good friends, but then we didn't see each other for a while as I was on the TV series *Code R* (1977) and I couldn't come to the screening of *Rocky*, despite him inviting me a couple of times.

I was doing *Cagney and Lacey* and then, suddenly, I was sent this script of eighty-seven pages that was nothing but mayhem. I said, 'Okay, eighty-seven pages of action will probably make $100 million', so I signed on to do it and the rest is history.

For me, that film and *The Karate Kid* established you as one of those actors who's very good at playing villains. Throughout your career, you've played a fair number of bad guys. Is it something you enjoy or is there something about you that appeals to casting directors?

For me, the most interesting thing about playing a villain is how much they enjoy being villainous. There's a wonderful German actor named Klaus Maria Brandauer who was in one of the Bond movies [*Never Say Never Again* (1983)]. He was fantastic, and I remember seeing how much he enjoyed being evil.

Actors like Anthony Hopkins, who have that niche for villainy, must be absolutely in love with their position in life. For me, I didn't have that at the beginning of my career. I played a lot of one-dimensional bad guys, but I was physical. I had strong features in my face. I think every young actor at the beginning of their career injects a lot of anger into their roles. If you don't do it subtly, it is very easy to end up playing a lot of heavies that way. It takes someone who has a good eye to see how much more so-

As a big fan of Western, Martin has starred in his fair share. Here he
is on set with Kevin Costner in *Wyatt Earp* (1994). Photo courtesy
of MartinKoveOnline.com

phisticated and vulnerable you can be. I really don't enjoy playing a heavy
so much anymore. I like playing vulnerable characters. I cry at supermarket openings, you know what I mean?

**You've worked on eighty plus films, but there was a period during your
career in the 1980s and 1990s where you seemed to be consistently
typecast as a villain in several B-movies. At that point in your career,
were you happy to play up to that persona, or do you regret taking so
many similar roles and wished you'd played more vulnerable characters during that time?**

Yes. I have some regrets, but they are not regrets because the characters
were villains. I stopped doing small movies or independent movies, unless the role was wonderful, and I loved it as well. Right after I did *Wyatt
Earp*, I had twins and started doing movies where I was pompous enough

to say, 'Well, I can fix this role with my performance!' Many just had fair scripts, but I took on the film anyway. To be perfectly honest, if it's not on the page, it's not there. You can't enhance a movie with a performance if the script isn't very good. I did a lot of those where I kept conning myself into thinking I could make the film better.

There were roles where the characters were well-structured, but the script itself was a mess. I don't do that anymore and don't do that many heavies.

One film that I remember seeing you in and that I feel you tried to improve with your performance was *Crocodile 2: Death Swamp*.

That film was interesting because the perks were better than the movie. It was shot in India, that was doubling for Mexico. My son, who was ten-years-old at the time, came to Hyderabad, where they had a huge film studio. It was an incredible experience, but I really loved the character. I didn't have to do too much with him, so the director Gary Jones let me have the ball and run with it! It was a lot of fun because I wanted to play him as a mercenary that was there for a reason – to find a lost city of gold. They never shot a scene where, as the crocodile kills me, with my last breath I see the gold city under the surface of the water. I enjoyed the

Martin Kove with his son in India while filming *Crocodile 2: Death Swamp* (2002). Photo courtesy of MartinKoveOnline.com

movie a lot. I really did. It was a hard shoot, but I got to take my son to Kathmandu, ride on elephants, and go on safaris. It was incredible, so the perks were far superior to the quality of the movie.

I think that's the first time I've ever heard of India doubling for Mexico. As a fan of Westerns, one of the scenes I remember from *Wyatt Earp* is you getting smacked in the face by a pool ball. As someone who has played so many villains and is killed quite often on screen, do you have a favourite death scene?

[laughs] I would say oddly enough there was a movie called *Capone* (1975) directed by Steve Carver. I played a character called Pete Gusenberg, who in American Gangster history, was killed in the Saint Valentine's Day massacre back in 1929.

I remember so vividly dying in this film. It was a massacre where Capone's hitman walks into the ally and shoots us. I was part of an Irish gang, and I remember all these stunt men going down like dominoes. I get riddled with bullets and, as I'm dying, I spin and flip over the chair. It was like a *Hamlet* death! I was the only actor, everybody else was a stunt man, but I insisted on taking the hits. It was just fantastic.

Americans still have a romance with those gangster characters. There was a Roger Corman film I did called *Baby Face Nelson* (1996). I played John Dillinger and had a chase scene where I was hanging out of a car with a machine gun shooting at someone. The film *Capone* from 1974 was also a Roger Corman movie and he's famously very cheap. When I saw the movie, I realised he'd put in scenes from the 1974 film! So, there's a scene of me from 1996 chasing myself from 1974 who is shooting back at me!

Tell me you got paid twice for that?

I should've gotten paid twice, but I probably didn't.

In your opinion, what do you think makes a good villain? Do you find playing them more fun than playing a hero?

I don't know which is more fun because it all comes with the interpretation of either role. It comes down to what you do as a villain. To me, a screaming, yelling villain without charm doesn't work for me anymore. It never worked for me, but I never knew how to be vulnerable.

I once thought I was going to be Steve McQueen, but I never knew what that inner light behind the eyes was all about. I just thought you had to be cool. That inner light you really must work at, because with it you instantly have character. You also have to sit down and write out the stuff that happens between the lines that is not written on the page for you to digest. It's about what you create for yourself. A good example is, what has John Kreese done over the last thirty years? Is he the same asshole he was before? No, we've seen that. It's got to be something else.

The same thing goes for heroes. You can make those one-liners cool, but if you don't have enough charm or vulnerability, audiences are going to get tired of it. Whether you're a villain or you're a leading man, you must make sense, you must be vulnerable, you must have a certain amount of charm, and of course, the macho stuff. That goes without saying.

Superman II

"I ask you now to pronounce judgement on those accused. On this mindless aberration, whose only means of expression are wanton violence and destruction. On the woman Ursa, whose perversions and unreasoning hatred of all mankind have threatened even the children of the planet Krypton. Finally, General Zod, once trusted by this council, charged with maintaining the defense of the planet Krypton itself. Chief architect of this intended revolution, and author of this insidious plot to establish a new order amongst us - with himself as absolute ruler."

"YOU'LL BELIEVE A MAN CAN FLY" was the tagline on Richard Donner's *Superman* (1978) and, for an entire generation, we did. For millions of people around the world, Christopher Reeve became the perfect embodiment of the Man of Steel – tall, powerful yet warm-hearted, and good-humored - far from the dour portrayals that have become commonplace in most modern Superman movies.

For many, Reeve will always be the best Superman. He was a walking, talking visual effect in that he could transform himself from the hunched-over, clumsy Clark Kent to the upstanding, confident Kal-El simply by removing his glasses. It is the sort of physical acting that is taken for granted, but cannot be underestimated when dealing with a superhero hidden in plain sight. However, while every hero needs a villain, when it comes to Superman, you get three. No, we're not counting Gene Hackman's funny, but let's face it, unthreatening Lex Luthor. We're talking about General "Kneel Before" Zod, and his equally merciless companions Ursa and Non.

Non (left), Ursa (right) and General Zod (centre) arrive on Earth after escaping the Phantom Zone in *Superman II* (1978). Photo courtesy of Warner Brothers.

I must have watched *Superman* and its first sequel dozens of times growing up. I loved everything about them; John William's pitch-perfect score, the way the first movie went from a space opera to a John Ford-esque tableau, among the fields of Kansas, to the comic book adventures of Metropolis, and that fun, bordering-on-camp-but-never-not-taking-its-subject-matter-seriously tone. This is why I felt it was important to track down the actors that played the pivotal roles of Superman's adversaries in these films –Sarah Douglas (Ursa) and Jack O'Halloran (Non).

Along with Terrence Stamp as General Zod, all three actors clearly have fun with their respective roles which, while campy, are enhanced with subtle menace and a complete disregard for human life. Just watch that scene where Ursa and Non threaten to throw a bus full of innocent people to their death. They're completely unmoved by the lives they're about to end, unlike Superman, who is desperately pleading with them to stop.

Of course, the production of *Superman II* was infamously problem-atic. Richard Donner, the director of the first film, was fired mid-way through filming by father-and-son producing team Alexander and Ilya Salkind.. The first two Superman films were filmed back-to-back and

The Salkinds weren't convinced Donner would be able to deliver the final product on time, so he was fired and replaced by Richard Lester, who had previously directed *The Three Musketeers* (1973) and *The Four Musketeers: Milady's Revenge* (1974), starring Oliver Reed and Michael York.

Furious about the decision, Gene Hackman walked off the film, forcing the production to use a body double in certain scenes, which is very noticeable in the final product. Other cost saving measures were implemented, including replacing Marlon Brando with Susannah York for parts of the film shot in The Fortress of Solitude.

The result was a much more comedic sequel than Donner's first film, implementing a lot of the slapstick style comedy that Lester had used in his previous films. While *Superman II* is fun to watch, it makes you wonder what could have been and, while *Superman II: The Donner Cut* (2006), gives you a sense of where the original director would have taken the story, much of the original footage has been lost, leaving a film that feels very disjointed. As a fan, the mind boggles over what the changes must have been like for the cast, so I decided to track them down General Zod's most loyal acolytes and ask them.

Jack O'Halloran

JACK **O'H**ALLORAN WAS THE FIRST **K**RYPTONIAN I tracked down and he is as far removed from his *Superman II* character as you can imagine. Instead of a mute, Jack is a walking, talking anecdote machine. If he's not telling you about his film appearances, he's talking about his boxing career, and some of the stars he's met over the course of his fascinating life.

Jack used to party with Frank Sinatra, Dean Martin, Sammy Davis Jr. and the rest of The Rat Pack, hang out with all the A-list in Hollywood and, as the son of Albert Anastasia, the head of the Gambino crime family (one of New York's 'Five Families') has obviously seen some pretty crazy shit. Also, it's clear you don't want to cross him. If you think The Man Who Was Non might be a big pussycat, think again. It's clear from talking to Jack that he has no time for idiots and, even without his family connections, you would not want to cross him!

On paper, the character of Non doesn't seem to be a very interesting role. You're just required to stand there, look intimidating and every now and then provide a bit of comic relief. How did [director] Richard Donner describe the role to you, and what made you want to do it?

With *Superman*, Donner and I sat down and discussed the character of Non. He said, 'How do you feel about playing this guy as a mute, because he's been lobotomized? He was once this great scientist, and the elders of Krypton lobotomized him. How do you feel about this?' I said, 'I really want to do a role like that. Jackie Gleason did a picture called *Gigot* (1962) where he played a deaf, dumb mute and he won an Oscar!'

I jumped at the chance to do a role where I would just use body language and facial expression. Non was the perfect choice, because you had

Non (Jack O'Halloran) realizes he's lost his powers in *Superman II*.
Photo courtesy of Warner Brothers.

General Zod, who was this vicious commander, Ursa was a man-hater, and so there had to be somebody to relate to the kids!

How were you cast in the film? You had started off in your career as a boxer, so how did you go from that to acting?

I started my boxing career in Boston and Steve McQueen was doing a picture called *The Thomas Crown Affair* [1968]. When he was in the city, we looked after him.

As a bodyguard?

Yes. My family were Mafia guys and I was very much entrenched in that life, so we took care of him. Steve was a super kid and we became good friends. He said, 'You've got to come down on the set. I want to put you in the movie.' I said, 'I don't think so. I'm not ready for that.'

We stayed in touched and he did a picture called *The Towering Inferno* [1974] where his character's name was Chief O'Halloran. He called me on the phone and said, 'How did you like seeing your name up and lights?'

Some producers wanted me to do a picture called *The Great White Hope* [1970] with James Earl Jones, which was the biggest picture in Hollywood at the time. I'd just knocked out the number two heavyweight in the world, so I was flown out to meet the director and producer. They talked about how they would fly me out to Spain for six months, what I was going to do, and how much they were going to pay me. I said, 'I just knocked out the number two heavyweight in the world, and you want me to leave boxing and go to Spain for six months?!' They said, 'We're going to give you $1,500 a week,' which, in 1968, was a lot of money. I said, 'I give that away in tips! Listen, there's a big guy named Jim Beattie who's just retired from boxing. He lives in Minnesota. He's got six mouths to feed. I'll give you his phone number. He'll be great for the role.' So, I turned it down!

I later met James Earl Jones and he stopped me on the steps outside 20th Century Fox. He said, 'Are you Jack O'Halloran? Is it true what I just heard about you? You just told Hollywood to take the biggest movie in Hollywood and stick it? I've got to shake your hand!' and we became very good friends.

I did a lot of commercials when I was boxing, but when I started to retire, my agent called me on the phone and said they wanted me for *Farewell, My Lovely* [1975] with Robert Mitchum. I looked around at where I was and said, 'You know what? Let's do it this time.'

Mitchum was a great mentor and it was a great cast, so it was like my acting school. That's where I learned my trade. It was a villain with a lot of meat and potatoes to it. I wasn't just some lumpy guy falling down.

It takes massive balls to turn down that amount of money and tell Hollywood to shove it, but as someone who grew up in the Gambino crime family, you're obviously not easily impressed or intimidated?

My father was Albert Anastasia, the head of Gambino family, and he was probably the most feared Italian that ever came into America. He ran a little company called Murder Inc. and was, at one time in his life, the most powerful don in the country. He was partners with Charles 'Lucky' Luciano, Meyer Lansky, and Frank Costello.

It must have been fascinating growing up in that world. You must have incorporated a lot of your real-world experiences into your acting roles.

You learn the truth about life. A lot of things change in our society, and you learn both sides of the coin. In my book *Family Legacy* [2011], I write about the growth of America. It's not just about organized crime, it's about government industry, because the unions and the crime families were partners for a long time.

Publicity photo of Jack O'Halloran. Photo courtesy of Jack O'Halloran.

People don't realize that a lot of the money that these guys made, they put it back into our country. They created jobs. They had construction companies. They were the biggest shareholders in the biggest insurance companies. They funded Sears and Roebucks. They funded General Electric. They created a lot of jobs from gambling, loan sharking and extortion. You're from the UK, right?

Yes.

The UK was the same way. If you go back to the fifties, sixties and seventies, London was probably one of the safest cities in the world. A woman could walk anywhere in London night or day, except maybe Brixton, in pure safety. You could get a cab anywhere. It was an amazing place, but it was run by the street kids around London; the Krays, the Nashes, and the Richardsons. It was a safe city. You wouldn't dare commit crime and there were no guns in the streets.

Well, there aren't really guns on our streets these days.

Today, you see policemen with sub-machine guns on every corner! The city has changed drastically and America is the same way. When I was a kid, growing up, we never locked our front doors. You never had any violence or drive-by shootings, because the neighborhoods were looked after.

But doesn't that level of protection come with a certain price - namely extortion and intimidation? That's how The Krays controlled London.

I knew Ronnie and Reggie very well. Reggie was nuts. Ronnie was crazy, but they took care of their manor. In other words, East London was safe for a lot of people because of them. They were villains towards villains. They didn't kill innocent people. They didn't harm innocent people. You ever watch the way their mother ruled them? She'd grab them by the ear and walk them down the street.

You say they didn't harm innocent people, but didn't Reggie used to beat his wife Frances? I don't think it was only villains that were on the receiving end of their violence.

There's a lot of things that are taken out of context. There was also a degree of homosexuality there. He should never have been married in the first place. You know what I mean?

Not really.

He loved his wife, he really did love her. As far as beating her, I think that was taken way out of context. I think his mother would've hit him with a frying pan if he did that. I knew them better than most people did. I saw the bad and good parts of them. They were manic. Reggie went to jail after he shot a guy who called him a homosexual. [laughs]

That sounds a bit extreme.

Well, that's the way he was. He had a quick temper like that.

Are you still connected to that life these days, or is it something you've walked away from?

You never really walk away. I have a lot of respect for certain people, but I'm not in the streets running around like I did when I was younger. I still have connections, you're never going to lose that. I've had a few friends die in jail. Some have done thirty or forty years because they never opened their mouth and ratted on anybody.

It's a whole different way of life. Today, people will sell their mother out because they're scared of going to jail. They're what I call wannabees. They don't practice what they preach. The old dons used to live in their neighborhoods. They never lived in huge houses in the suburbs. They lived amongst their own and were never afraid of walking amongst their own. They were men of honor.

Do you think having those family connections ever helped or hindered your career?

After I did *Farewell, My Lovely*, I met Johnny Carson and he said, 'If you come on to my show, I'll get you nominated because I think the picture was great!' I said, 'I don't think I can do that, because you'll ask me about my father and I'll have to ask where the men's room is.' He said, 'You'd get up and leave during the show?' and I said, 'Yes, because

I don't talk about my father and I don't want other people talking about him.'

Johnny offered to change the questions and I said, 'You're the number one investigative reporter in the world and you're telling me if you have Albert Anastasia's son on your show, you're not going to ask me about him? Do I look like I fell off a turnip truck?'

Mitchum was furious! He called me the day and said, 'What's wrong with you, man! This is Hollywood! No-one cares!'

He's right. Sinatra had certain mafia connections and he won an Oscar.

Sinatra is full of shit. [laughs] The only person connected in Sinatra's family was his wife Nancy [Barbato]. She was the niece of a powerful man in Chicago, Tony Accardo. They loved Frank and the way he sang and it was my father who got him out of his big band contract. My father put a gun to the guy's head, and the guy signed the document and released him from his contract.

Like that scene Michael Corleone describes in *The Godfather*?!

My father said he was sorry that he did it, because he said Sinatra was a rat. He was right. Sinatra talked [about] him too much. He was a very talented man, but he thought that he had this power, and he didn't.

Chicago's Sam Giancana loved his voice, and he liked Frank a lot. When the role in *From Here To Eternity* [1953] came up, Frank couldn't get it because he'd romanced [studio head] Harry Cohn's old lady and he was pissed off! Frank said, 'This role is me. I can do this,' Cohn said, 'I know. You'll probably win an Oscar, but you'll never do that role as long as I own the picture.' Frank went crying to somebody because he was losing his voice at the time and was scared of losing his vocal career. You know that scene in *The Godfather* [1972] where they put the horse's head in the studio head's bed?

Of course.

Well, they didn't cut the horse's head off. They cut his balls off. Cohn had a super race horse and they gelded it. Sinatra got the picture, won an Oscar, and it launched a whole different career for him.

Non (Jack O'Halloran) and Ursa (Sarah Douglas) threaten Lois Lane (Margot
Kidder) in The Fortress of Solitude. Photo courtesy of Warner Brothers.

**Speaking of problematic studio heads and producers, the *Superman*
films are infamous for the behind-the-scenes drama that occurred during filming. The plan was to shoot *Superman* and *Superman II* back-
to-back, but then Ilya Salkind and his father Alexander, who were the
producers, fired Richard Donner halfway through, and brought in
Richard Lester to replace him, which created a lot of animosity.**

It was more than halfway through. We had shot 85% of both pictures!
We were shooting both pictures at the same time, and The Salkinds were
getting away with murder because they had everybody under contract.
People were working their ass off on two pictures, and then, suddenly,
Richard Lester appeared on set.

Why did they get rid of Donner?

Donner got carried away doing two films, and they had to deliver the first
film. The distributor, Warner Brothers, was chasing The Salkinds saying,
'We won't pick up the option for the second picture if you don't deliver the
first picture on time.'

Alexander Salkind started playing hardball, and put together a screening for distributors. He showed the fight scene of Terrence, Sarah, and myself over the city and, Warner Brothers couldn't get the rubber bands off their money fast enough!

With the Salkinds, it was all about saving money. That's why Brando was cut out of the second film and replaced with Susannah York. Who cuts Marlon Brando out of a movie?! They did it because they didn't want to pay him his percentage of the box office. He'd already been paid to do the footage for the first film, but they didn't want to pay him for the second, so they cut him out.

Let's talk about Brando. He was getting paid $3.7 million (plus a percentage of the box office) for twelve days work! While he gives a great performance as Jor-El, I've read he didn't learn his lines and had cue cards all around the set.

Brando and I became very good friends. He knew my father in New York, and I couldn't wait to meet him when he came over. I was sitting on set watching him work and he had cue cards everywhere.

A lot of people would be nervous talking to him, but I really didn't give a shit, so I went, 'What's with the cue cards? Are you that bored with the industry that you have to have cue cards?' He said, 'You've got to understand, I started this with *Mutiny on the Bounty* [1962]. I don't want the audience to think I've memorized the lines. I want to look like I'm taking them out of the air.'

He was a great actor and he could do scenes word-for-word. 'Shakespeare,' he said, 'you must know word perfect. This shit? Piece of cake!' [laughs]

But The Salkinds cut him out! They were notorious for things like that. In fact, there's now a law in the Director's Guild called The Salkind Law. You ever see their film *The Three Musketeers*?

Yes, with Oliver Reed, Richard Chamberlain and Michael York? Richard Lester also directed that for The Salkinds.

That's right, so Raquel Welch (who plays Constance in the film) wakes up one morning, and she sees an advert for a new film – *The Four Musketeers*! - she calls Oliver Reed on the phone, who's waking up from a hangover, and says, 'Ollie, did we make a movie I don't know about? They're advertising another *Musketeer* movie, with us in it, which I don't remember getting paid for?' Oliver said, 'I know I drink a lot, but I don't get that drunk!'

The Salkinds had just taken footage from the first film and made another movie! So now there's a law called The Salkind Law that stops producers from doing that. In fact, they owe us money from when *Superman II: The Donner Cut* came out, because technically it's a third movie, and we never got paid! They made a fortune off [of] us.

When Donner was fired, were you tempted to follow Gene Hackman out the door?

I almost didn't go back myself, but I ensured early in the shoot that I would get paid. We'd been working for about eight weeks, and I had four days off, so I decided to go back to America because I had written this script and I wanted to get it going. I called my accountant and said, 'I've got some things I need to do for this other picture, so how much money do I have in the bank?' She told me that she'd received a bunch of cheques that hadn't cleared.

I called Pierre Spengler, who was one of the producers on the film. I said, 'I have this ache in my back, and my doctor said that if I don't get some money in my bank account, the ache's liable not to go away for a while.' He said, 'What are you talking about? You have to be on set on Monday!' I said, 'Well, I don't have any money in my bank. I've been working all these weeks, and there's no money there. What's the deal?' Within an hour-and-a-half, there was money in my bank.

I flew back to London and went straight to Spengler's office. I reached across and pulled him across his desk. I said, 'Here's the deal. I come to work and you pay me. I have a contract that says that. Now, I don't know if you really know who I am, but maybe you should pick up the telephone and ask some people. If I have one more problem with you, I will drop you in the Hudson with a camera on your head!' I dropped him back in his chair and he said, 'Are you threatening me?' and I said, 'No, I'm making you a firm promise. I have not caused one problem on your set, so you're not going to treat me the way you treat these other people.' I never had another problem with a cheque! Pierre Spengler wrote a book about the making of *Superman* and he put that story in there!

The Salkinds never bothered me, and I didn't bother them. However, if Christopher Reeve had stood up to them and said, 'I'm not coming back unless Donner is there,' then Donner would have had to be there.

Richard Lester's scenes have a noticeable change in tone. Whereas Donner liked to adhere to the verisimilitude of the comics, Lester seemed to take a more comedic approach.

It was like night and day. Lester is not a pimple on Donner's ass. He's a television director, whereas Donner was a movie director. We were supposed to do ten pictures! When we first signed on to this thing, they were going to do ten of these things. If Donner had done five *Superman* films, the franchise would have been totally different.

Lester put too much comedy in it. He also had to put in extra scenes in order for him to have his name on the film as the director. He reshot over 50% of the picture. Donner had already shot 85% of it, so they went way back and reshot a lot of stuff. That's why Hackman never came back.

A lot of your scenes are humor-based, such as when you're trying to fry the twig, or looking at the Newton's Cradle on the president's desk. Was that Lester's influence?

That was all Donner. I did those scenes like I was a child learning how to walk. Learning how to work my eyes, and being elated when I burnt the hole in the side of the truck with the kid. I had a lot of fun with the role.

Naturally, most of your scenes are with your fellow criminal Kryptonians – Terrence Stamp and Sarah Douglas - how did the three of you get on during the shoot?

We were like family. Sarah's such a wonderful woman and Terence is a great guy. Not only is he a great actor, but he's also a really nice person. He went through a big change in his life as his brother was the manager of The Who, so he grew up around the sex, drugs and rock and roll business. He used to party for forty-eight hours, and had burnt the candle at both ends for so long it was starting to take a toll. Right before *Superman*, he went to India and cleaned up. He got very spiritual and became a completely different person.

He held out on signing his contract when it came to *Superman II*. The Salkinds were paying him a lot of money, and he kept holding out for more. The Salkinds ended up suing him stating that he put a gun to their head!

What?!

He had to pay them back! He lost the case!

That is insane. I'm surprised he didn't walk off with Hackman. I must ask you about Christopher Reeve, because the two of you apparently clashed on set.

Only once. Christopher was a very naive young kid. He came from a very wealthy family and had gone to The Juilliard School. Before *Superman*, he had never done anything. All he did was *Love of Life* [1951-1980], a television show, and he had held a spear for Katharine Hepburn in a play.

I remember when he came on the set, he was a 170 lbs., dripping wet weakling. David Prowse, the guy who played Darth Vader, oversaw his workout. Chris didn't want to wear anything underneath his costume, and wanted to have a defined body, so I said to David, 'When you're building him, just build him with definition. You don't want to bulk him up. You want to make him like Steve Reeve, the guy who was Mr. All American. Give him cuts.' So, that's what they did. He put on 20 lbs. and he looked great in the costume. There will never be another Chris Reeve. He did Superman and Clark Kent better than anyone. He [was] born for that role, but he was very immature.

In what way?

I used to take everybody from the set to this great restaurant on Beauchamp Place to eat dinner, because I knew Lorenzo, the owner, who was a dear friend of mine. It has since grown into a huge restaurant that's spreads over half of Beauchamp Place, now!

One day, Lorenzo called me on the phone, and he said, 'Jack, how well do you know this kid, Christopher Reeve?' I said, 'I don't know him well, we just work together. What's the problem?' He said, 'He's in here talking very loudly about your father and your connections in New York. I thought you should know that.'

The next day, I go to work, and when Chris came in, I said, 'Come here, we need to have a chat.' I took him into a room, just the two of us together, and I said to him, 'How well do you know me, son? What the hell gives you the right to talk about my family and talk about things you don't know anything about?' He said, 'Well, I was just telling the stories that I heard!' I said, 'Let me tell me you something: don't you ever mention my name again without saying 'Mister' first, and if I ever hear you talk about my family again, your career is over. Do you understand what I'm telling you? Now get out of my face.'

We walked out of the room and as soon as he got outside he thought he was Superman. He started screaming, 'You can't talk to me that way!' So, I pinned him against the wall and was getting ready to knock the shit out of him when Richard Donner ran up and whispered in my ear, 'Not in the face, Jack!'

I broke up laughing and I dropped him on the floor. I said, 'Boy, you just got the biggest pass in your life, kid' and walked away. That was the only altercation we ever had, and people made such a big deal out of it.

A lot of people have said that he took the role very seriously, while everyone else was having fun on set.

Marc McClure, who played Jimmy Olsen, was a super young man. He was really into music and was sitting in his dressing room when Chris walked in the room. Marc said, 'Chris, listen to this new song,' and he started strumming on his guitar. Chris looked at him and said, 'Don't talk to me unless you're talking as Jimmy Olsen!' Poor Marc! I couldn't believe he said that to him! I remember him saying, 'Wow, man, what an asshole.' It didn't endear him to people

I have to ask about the endings of the Superman films, as there is a lot of confusion, and theories about them. At the end of the first film, Superman flies around the world and turns back time and, in *Superman II: The Donner Cut*, he does the same thing again. I doubt both films were meant to end that way, so can you clarify how the films were meant to end?

In *Superman II,* after we fell into the abyss in The Fortress of Solitude, they filmed a shot of us being put into police cars and taken to jail. As we'd lost our powers, they were taking us to prison, which gave them a possible storyline of Lex Luthor manipulating Kryptonite to get our powers back and free us.

The scenes were there: we shot them, but Lester chose to end it the way he ended it. With Donner, it's sad that he didn't have the opportunity to finish that movie.

It doesn't really make sense either. In the *Lester Cut*, Superman kisses Lois and somehow wipes her memory, but in the *Donner Cut*, he travels back in time undoing all the damage that you guys did. Neither ending is satisfying, so your explanation makes a lot more sense.

We were meant to be locked up and carted off to jail. Donner just didn't have all the footage he wanted to put into the *Donner Cut*. It's a shame.

I must ask you about *Dragnet* (1987), because that is another film that I watched a huge number of times growing up, and you look like you're having a lot of fun in it as the henchman Emil Muzz.

I love *Dragnet*! *Dragnet* is one of those pictures that you can watch fifty times, and you would still miss some of the one-liners that Dan Aykroyd put out in that picture. That was also Tom Hanks' breakthrough picture, and he was great in it, and such a nice fellow. It was a very well-cast movie, and I did it because [*Superman* screenwriter Tom] Mankiewicz asked me to do it.

I said, 'Wow, man, yes. Let's have a great time, then.' And we did. We had a ball making that picture. There were a lot of great actors on that film, like Christopher Plummer.

You didn't mind being described as "big, bad and stupid-looking"?

They gave me an opportunity to add some depth to the guy, not just being a big, dumb guy. Some of the things that I did were funny, and I got away with a lot of stuff. That scene where I ran over Dan Aykroyd's toes, I got to put a load of facial expressions into it. Also, that scene in the interrogation room scene – I had a lot of fun doing that.

***Dragnet* was obviously another 'big bad henchmen' role. Do you think the *Superman* films led to you being typecast in those parts?**

I turned down about five or six films because of that. They came to me to do the James Bond movie *The Spy Who Loved Me* [1977], to play the part of Jaws. I turned it down because of typecasting, because Jaws was just this big, lump of a guy, that didn't do or say much. I turned down six pictures that made Richard Kiel's career. He did all six that I turned down!

The one picture I wished I hadn't turned down, but I was doing *King Kong* [1976] at the time, was *Silver Streak* [1976] with Richard Pryor. It was another 'big lump' part, but I liked the people involved, and it would have been fun to do it.

Do you find it amazing that a role like Non, that you played over thirty-five years ago, still resonates with so many people?

When we did the film, I knew it was going to be a great movie. No one knows how good a film is going to be, but when the chemistry of the cast and the director blends, you can feel it ,and you know that what you're doing is going to come out good. To play this big, brutish guy with a child-like manner, and learning how to walk and just use your eyes – I embraced it. I have [had] so many people come up to me and say, 'My God, you scared the hell out of me, but boy, I loved your character!'

Sarah Douglas

WHEN I MET SARAH DOUGLAS, it was at a convention where, for the first time in years, the three Kryptonian villains *from Superman II* were set to reunite! Unfortunately, Jack O'Halloran couldn't make it, but Terrence Stamp made his first convention appearance, much to the joy of fans and other celebrities like Kevin Smith who said, before realizing who it was, that it was the "best Terence Stamp cosplay I'd ever seen!"

Sarah is an old hand at conventions, often travelling the world to meet fans and sign memorabilia. While some might be content to take people's money and move fans along, Sarah takes the time to talk to all her fans and, seems genuinely interested in what everyone has to say – even this author's idea for a book!

Weeks later, we sat down for a chat and, while her character Ursa might be cold, unfeeling, and prone to throwing men through walls, Sarah couldn't have been kinder or more gracious with her time. Still, it is clear that her relationship with Ursa is a difficult one that led to hard career choices, and facing the darker side of Hollywood.

You played Ursa in the Superman films, Queen Taramis in *Conan the Destroyer* and, I read, at one point you were offered the role of Evil-Lyn in *Masters of the Universe* (1987). It seems, at one point, you were being offered every comic book villainess role under the sun.

I was never offered the role on *Masters of the Universe*, that is just one of those lovely stories on the internet. That role never came remotely near me, although I knew Dolph Lundgren terribly well. Having said that, immediately after *Superman*, in the late seventies, I made a very concerted effort not to continue playing those sorts of villain-type roles.

167

Ursa (Sarah Douglas) threatens to tear Lois Lane apart in *Superman II*.
Photo courtesy of Warner Brothers.

It was a three-year period making *Superman* and *Superman II*, so, by the time we came to be doing re-shoots for the sequel, it had been quite a long haul, so a decision was made to try and avoid being typecast in similar roles.

Back then, in the British film industry, there was the general census of opinion that one had to be very careful that you weren't pigeonholed and typecast. Just by keeping my hair long and wearing a short, cropped wig, I managed to look very different from my Ursa persona! Of course, what happened was that I was offered a lot of work in that genre. A couple of things came out of the States, which we turned down because of me not pursuing those types of villainous roles, so, consequently, I really didn't work that much.

Is that a decision you regret in hindsight?

One's got to remember that there was a great gap between when I started on *Superman* in 1977, and when the sequel came out in 1980! By the time I made the decision to go to Los Angeles, it was 1982. I had an incredible opportunity to get myself known, as I was the one that was selected to do the global publicity tour for *Superman II*. I went around the world about one and a half times to promote and sell the film, because Christopher Reeve and Margot Kidder, and most of the American cast, were furious about losing Dick Donner. They wanted to talk about it, but I was completely oblivious to it.

Did the switch of directors not affect you at all, or did you not have a close working relationship with Richard Donner?

Obviously, I realized that Donner was no longer there, but I lived in England and I didn't have the same relationship with Richard Donner that the other actors all had. They were all in each other's lives, and spent a lot of time together, but in the evening, I was going back to my little home in Shepherd's Bush.

I was thrilled that I had all this extra work, because, at the time, I thought I'd only have a few weeks shooting on the film. That was exciting enough, but it just went on and on and on. It was terrific.

So, as you didn't have the outward hostility towards Richard Lester that other cast members did, you became the perfect person to promote the film?

And I did it very successfully, and I have the letters from Warner Brothers to prove it! They were absolutely thrilled with me. There was no scandal, and there was no mention of Donner. The only problem was, that in most places, nobody knew who the hell I was!

I didn't look like my character, and so I was turning up as this little English rose and confusing everybody. It was an amazing experience, but I had to deal with problems in each country. South Africa had apartheid, and Australia was very chauvinistic, but I learned to deal with every question that could possibly be thrown at a person.

What do you remember about the reception of the film when it first opened?

Superman opened in Australia first, and then in France, as we were in Paris the night John Lennon was assassinated. It was a completely different way of releasing films. We opened in a different country every couple of weeks, which had never been done before. It didn't open in America until the following summer, so, by the time we got there, the Americans were quite pissed off. I merrily went around the world promoting it, and by the time I arrived in America, it received a lackluster reception. It wasn't the big, wonderful opening that one had anticipated.

Afterwards, I came home and didn't go back to America until 1983, when I went there for three months. By then, everyone was really interested to meet the girl who played Ursa, compared to the UK, where people weren't overly bothered! In America, they would say, 'That was a great role. What's the next great role you're going to do?'

Sarah Douglas behind the scenes on *Superman II*.
Photo courtesy of Warner Brothers.

I went out there for three months, just to feel things out and, on the day that I was flying home, I got offered the series of *Falcon Crest* [1981-1990], where they immediately put me in leather and suede, and portrayed me, as the headlines said, as a "leather-clad dominatrix"! The PR people immediately latched on to the image from *Superman* and I became the 'bad girl' literally, overnight.

After avoiding being typecast for so long in the UK, you ended up getting pigeonholed by the Americans? Typical.

They very much capitalized on that, and it was about maybe two or three months into it that I was asked to do *Conan*, and then the miniseries of *V* [The Final Battle, 1984]. Suddenly, after having had a really lean two or three years back in England, because I wasn't accepting the villainous roles, they were coming fast and furious in all sorts of different guises.

After the miniseries of *V*, there was talk of me doing the main series, but then I got a contract offer for *Falcon Crest*, so I had to make a decision. Do I appear in a night-time soap or do I do sci-fi? My agents at the time were very adamant that I shouldn't do sci-fi, because a night-time soap would get me better known. Before I knew it, I was in the press as the "super bitch", "super villain", and "evil, wicked queen". The press ran with that and I was expected to promote it and look that way. They wanted to see me looking sultry and moody, and preferably clad in leather. That was very much the Hollywood publicity machine.

It must be difficult for an actor to choose between regular work and getting typecast. Do you feel that by accepting those roles you helped or hindered your career?

I don't know. I certainly worked a great deal. Career wise, it certainly put me in one particular mold, but I'd had three years of really doing very little back in England. I suppose it was good, but I didn't really capitalize on the image. In private, I looked pretty regular, and didn't adopt that Ursa look.

I recall I was at this very famous restaurant called Le Dôme and it was after Daryl Hannah had just done *Splash* [1984]. Now, Daryl Hannah, with all due respect, is not the greatest actress or the greatest beauty, but *Splash* had made quite an impact. I remember her turning up at Le Dôme, and standing at the top of the stairs, and looking like this gorgeous mermaid. She was recreating the look, and creating an image, so people would go, 'That's the girl from *Splash*.'

The other one was Mr. T! Everywhere you went in Hollywood, there was Mr. T, with his gold chains. You probably would have recognized him anyway, but, if he was just a regular big guy walking around town, you might not be sure.

Nobody told me to go get my hair cut or to turn up anywhere looking this way or that way. That's not to say I would have turned up in black leather boots, but I certainly could have turned up and struck the pose. I could have done that very easily. I'm not saying that I ever would have done it, but I can see that's how others were really marketing themselves.

That must have been incredibly frustrating for you, wanting to be taken seriously as an actress, but having to deal with an industry that just wanted to see you as Ursa.

My early years in Hollywood I found very conflicting, because there's no question that producers and directors wanted to meet Ursa. They wanted to meet the girl from *Superman*, and I know this from many a conversation where I've been told that is who they wanted to see come through the door.

I'm close friends with Kathleen Turner, and after she did *Body Heat* [1981], she came to Hollywood and I took her out, and there was quite a flurry of press activity. Of course, she was the movie star, and she was up on a pedestal. I remember remarking to her when we got to this restaurant that all the producers and directors were coming over to talk to her, but all the busboys and parking valets knew who I was because of television!

If I had embraced my *Superman* image, I could have been more standoffish, but it's not the way I am. There was definitely this conflict during my early years in Hollywood, about who I should be in an interview: myself or this tough, mean girl. I tried it and it always felt a bit odd, because I felt like I was acting from the minute I walked through the door. If I went in as me, producers would say, 'My God, in the movies you are evil, but in real life, you're really quite funny and warm. How do you manage it?' I said, 'Well, in England, we call it acting!'

If you could do it all again, do you think you'd do it differently?

It's something that I have thought about quite often. If I was portraying Ursa right now, because of social media, billions of people would know who I was, and I wouldn't be selling myself via the press. I was very fortunate, as I did all the talk shows, but it seemed to send out a very mixed message. Having said that, I still only ever got offered villain roles. I've tried all sorts of different things, and even did a little film in Sweden, which turned out to be a student film, where I was a regular woman who was having an affair with some vicar in the 1960s. I thought, 'Oh my God. That's a real bit of acting that I can do here!'

It's very, very difficult to break the mold, especially in Hollywood. Years ago, I was at a funeral in Hollywood, and I was sat next to a director who didn't know who I was. At some point, the paparazzi started snapping pictures of me and he said, 'Why are they taking pictures of you?' Somebody else said, 'Don't you know who she is? She was in *Superman*!' This director, who had taken no notice of me up until that point, turned around and said, 'Oh my God. I wanted to fuck you when I saw you in that.'

Classy.

Yes. He was a loathsome, arrogant son of a bitch. He said, 'Whatever happened to you? You had your chance. It's so rare to have that chance where every producer or director wants to get you into bed.' Which, of course, never even bloody occurred to me! He started talking about Michelle Pfeiffer in *The Fabulous Baker Boys* [1989]. 'Look at that,' he said. 'She was just one of many actresses, but when she crawled across that piano every producer and director in town wanted to bed her.'

I was horrified, because I'd been trained at drama school and the National Youth Theatre! I was born in Stratford-upon-Avon and steeped in Shakespeare! I thought about how, after I'd done *Superman*, I was invited to meet several directors and, perhaps I was being naive, but I thought it was because they all wanted to meet me. Kathleen later said to me, 'They didn't want to meet you, they wanted to meet the sexy, leather clad dominatrix.' I think there was an opportunity, but I never would have played on my sexual prowess. I basically got to the point where I just thought, 'Well, at least I'm working.'

Do you think you were prepared for the success of the Superman films, and that they would become this global phenomenon?

Sara Douglas as Queen Taramis in *Conan The Destroyer*.
Photo courtesy of Universal Pictures.

I knew nothing about Superman and, quite honestly, back then, very few English people knew who the character was. We didn't have this love of Superman that the Americans had.

When I heard I've got the audition, I was busy working out of Pinewood on *The People That Time Forgot* [1977], which was the only film being shot in England at that time. I was full of the wonders of being twenty-seven-years-old and working non-stop. I finished working on *The People That Time Forgot* on the Wednesday, and started *Superman* on the Thursday. I just remember being overwhelmed with the idea that I was going to be working with Marlon Brando. That was gigantic. It was the first big film that I'd ever shot, and everybody was talking about it.

You've obviously never been afraid of tackling sci-fi and fantasy, with roles in films and TV shows like such *The People That Time Forgot, Superman, Conan The Destroyer, V, Beastmaster 2: Through the Portal of Time* (1991), *Puppet Master III: Toulon's Revenge* (1991) and *Space: 1999* (1975-1977).

In England, if a job comes up, you're so grateful that you do whatever it is. My very first job was *The Final Programme* [also known as: The Last Days of Man of Earth, 1973]which was a sci-fi film, but I did a lot of different little things, basically whatever came my way. I can't say that my career has gone in the way that I would have anticipated. I'm not a great sci-fi buff at all. I don't particularly enjoy science fiction, but when I get something that is in the sci-fi genre, I'm very pleasantly surprised.

In America, I know for a fact that I got the roles because I've got an English accent and I sound like I know what I'm talking about! I remember when I did *Nightfall* [1988] thinking, 'What am I doing?' as I couldn't understand the script or the story. I'd love to do something simple like an episode of *Downton Abbey* [2010-2015], rather than another sci-fi film where I'm talking about black holes! To this day, I still don't understand what a black hole is! In *Conan The Destroyer*, I had so much dialogue! I was forever having to explain The Scrolls of Skelos, or whatever the hell it was.

In *Conan The Destroyer*, you were surrounded with some of the biggest personalities, both in the physical and egotistical sense, of the eighties; Arnold Schwarzenegger, Grace Jones, and Andre the Giant. What were your experiences of working with such a unique cast?

I've only had difficulty on set one or two times, and it's because of people who are deeply unprofessional or completely up themselves. I found Schwarzenegger to be an absolute delight to work with. He was just ridiculous in his wonderful, muscular way, and he's got a fabulous sense of humor. Grace and I have remained incredibly close. We had met before and it was a match made in heaven! We still spend a lot of time together.

I was doing *Falcon Crest* while I was doing *Conan*, so I would do two or three days on *Crest* and then fly down to Mexico for *Conan*. The TV producers couldn't hold me, so they would release me to go off to do a bit of filming, then I would come back. It was fabulous working on *Conan*, because most of the crew were English, and had worked on *Superman*. We just had a blast, and I loved the outfits, and being on a horse. It was a crazy time and we made the most of it.

The *Superman* films are a major part of your career, but is it something you get tired of talking about all the time?

I get very tired of being asked what it's like to fly! I get very tired of continually people saying, 'What was Christopher Reeve really like?' I'm afraid to say I have a set answer for a couple of things that I do, but, overall, I enjoy the whole experience of going to conventions. I am a bit worried about what I may have embellished [in] some stories over the years! I know I talk about Marlon Brando sticking his lines on my forehead, but I'm not sure he did!

With those films I look at myself and think that I'm not really doing anything. There's not a lot of acting, but I must give myself credit because I am incredibly fidgety, and when I played Ursa, I was very still, so that's not bad!

But, you know what? The whole thing is bloody marvelous. The world over, wherever I go, people have seen *Superman*. In the remotest places, they've seen it. If they've not seen it on the television, they've seen it in the cinema, or they've seen it on a plane. It offered me an incredible opportunity, to travel the world, and to meet heads of states, royalty, and people in remote areas that you'd never go to, and to talk to people who actually want to meet you because they feel like they know you because of a movie they once saw as a kid. Most of the time I just feel incredibly old, but I'm very grateful, and to meet new fans forty years later is incredible.

The Terrorists of
Die Hard

"Who said we were 'terrorists'?"
> – Hans Gruber, *Die Hard* (1988).

A truck is driving through the relatively quiet streets of downtown Los Angeles. It's Christmas Eve and, while an office party is underway in Nakatomi Plaza, none of the guests nor out-of-town New York cop, John McClane, know that their night is about to change dramatically. As Michael Kamen's score begins, combining both sleigh bells and Beethoven, a truck turns into the Nakatomi Plaza underground car park, and backs up to a loading bay. The rear door flies up and out walk a group of men, each carrying machine guns, led by the stylishly dressed and noticeably unarmed Hans Gruber (Alan Rickman).

DIE HARD IS PROBABLY THE BEST action film ever made. Strong arguments can be made for the likes of *Hard Boiled* (1992), *Predator* (1987) and *Raiders of the Lost Ark* (1981), but if a bunch of scientists were to create the perfect action movie in a lab, it would probably look like *Die Hard*, and that's why the film has its own unique chapter in this book.

I can't imagine a time when I wasn't aware of this perennial Christmas classic. The film came out five years after I was born, and I probably didn't see it till I was ten-years-old (thanks Mum and Dad!) when it appeared on TV as an 'ITV Movie Premiere!', but it seems like I have always been aware of, what is widely regarded to be, "the greatest action film of all time".

Hans Gruber and his henchmen in *Die Hard* (1988).
Photo courtesy of 20th Century Fox.

Perhaps it's because I knew Alan Rickman from *Robin Hood: Prince of Thieves* (1991) and my older cousins and uncles had said, "If you like him in that, you should see him in *Die Hard*," or there had been clips of the film shown on TV, but I always knew two things about the film:

1. It was always heavily cut on TV due to the use of the word "motherfucker", and owing to the scene where a barefoot John McClane shoots a terrorist in the kneecaps while glass is being shattered all around him.
2. It was awesome.

For years, I had an edited version on VHS that I'd recorded off the TV. Instead of "Yippee-kay-yay motherfucker," Bruce Willis said, "Yippee-kay-yay kemosabe." As someone who'd seen the occasional *The Lone Ranger* (1949-1957) re-runs on Sunday morning TV, I knew that didn't sound right.

I loved everything about the film; Willis's sardonic hero, the charm and wit of Rickman's villain (who you secretly wanted to win), William Atherton's despicable reporter, Agents Johnson and Johnson (no relation), explosions, gun fights, RUN-DMC, and was that a glimpse of boobs at the Christmas party when a drunken couple are interrupted by the terrorists? Why yes it was! This film had everything!

With its reputation sealed as one of the greatest action (and Christmas) films by publications like *Empire* and *Forbes*, the film is mandatory viewing in the week leading up to Christmas Day. Sure, in our house it's primarily viewed as a Christmas movie, but for me it's the pinnacle of American action cinema.

Steven E. de Souza's script dispenses with the trope of the unstoppable, muscle-bound action hero and, instead, gave us a man who genuinely believed he might not get out of the situation alive. A man who, by

The late, great Alan Rickman as Hans Gruber. Photo courtesy of 20th Century Fox.

A publicity card of Alexander Gudunov as Karl in *Die Hard* (1988).
Photo courtesy of 20th Century Fox.

the final scene, is barely recognisable to his wife, because he's covered in so much dirt, grime, and blood – and only some of it is his.

Sure, by the third sequel Hollywood (and arguably Bruce Willis) had forgotten what had made John McClane so endearing to audiences, having him do ridiculous feats such as surfing on jet fighters, but, for many of us, the original film can't be topped, and it's just not the hero that makes it so – it's the villains.

Tragically, the actors behind the two primary antagonists, Alan Rickman and Alexander Gudunov, had passed away at the time of writing, but both left behind a body of work that showcased their incredible talent. If you only think of Gudunov as Karl, driven to revenge by the death of his brother, you should know that he was originally a Russian ballet dancer who defected to the United States at the height of the Cold War. The story was so incredible that they even made a movie about it (*Flight 222* (1986)). Not just that, but everyone who knew him said he was warm, caring, and very funny – something seen in his wonderful role in the Tom Hanks/Shelley Long comedy *The Money Pit* (1986), where he plays Long's ex-husband, Max Beissart.

As for Alan Rickman, entire books can be written about the man that was Hans Gruber (and they probably have, by now.) To many, he'll always be Severus Snape, for others, the deliciously evil Sherriff of Nottingham, but, to me, he'll also be the suave terrorist with a penchant for John Philips' suits. What of the rest of Hans Gruber's terrorists, though? What were their experiences of making the film? Did they ever recover from being shot, blown up, hurled out of windows, and knee-capped by John McClane? Writing their names on my forearm with a black marker pen, I set out to find the remaining terrorists from Die Hard: Theo, Eddie, Uli, Tony, Franco, Marco, Fritz, Heinrich, and the rest.

Andreas Wisniewski

"The fire has been called off, my friend. No one is coming to help you. You might as well come out and join the others. I promise I won't hurt you... "

— Tony, *Die Hard.*

Select Filmography

- *Gothic* (1986) – Fletcher
- *The Living Daylights* (1987) – Necros
- *Die Hard* (1988) – Tony
- *Death Machine* (1994) - Weyland
- *Mission: Impossible* (1996) – Max's Companion
- *The Scorpion King: Rise of A Warrior* (2008) - Pollux
- *Centurion* (2010) – Commander Gratus

Hans Gruber and his terrorists have seized Nakatomi Plaza on Christmas Eve, forcing New York police officer, John Mc-Clane, to flee the office Christmas party barefoot. Running upstairs, John activates the fire alarm system to alert the authorities, but the terrorists de-activate it and persuade the fire department that it's a false alarm. Tony, brother to Karl, Hans's right-hand man, goes looking for whoever set off the fire alarm system, and finds John on a floor of the building that is still under construction.

Tony (Andreas Wisniewski) comes face to face with John McClane in *Die Hard* (1988). Photo courtesy of 20th Century Fox.

THERE IS SOMETHING ABOUT PROFESSIONAL dancers and being cast in *Die Hard*. Alexander Gudunov (Karl) was a Russian ballet dancer who, while on a tour with the Bolshoi Ballet in New York City in 1979, decided to defect to the US and claim political asylum. His defection caused a major diplomatic incident between the US and USSR, and was even turned into a movie – *Flight 222* (1986).

Like his on-screen brother, Andreas Wisniewski started out as a dancer, specializing in classic dance and ballet. It was his towering height and impressive physique that first got him noticed and cast in the James Bond film *The Living Daylights*, where he terrorized Timothy Dalton's Bond as the KGB hitman, Necros. Often killing people while listening to The Pretenders' *Where Has Everybody Gone?*, Wisniewski was the latest in tall, blond, and physically imposing Bond henchmen dating back to Robert Shaw's Red Grant in *From Russia With Love* (1963).

Riding the post-Bond wave, Wisniewski was cast in *Die Hard* in the relatively small part of Tony, however, it's his character that is responsible for some of the film's most memorable scenes including; Tony being unceremoniously dumped into an elevator with, "Now I Have A Machine Gun. Ho-Ho-Ho" written on his sweater, and Bruce Willis complaining about Tony having tiny feet, "Nine million terrorists in the world and I gotta kill one with feet smaller than my sister."

It was this particular criticism that I thought would be a good starting point for my talk with Wisniewski, who was more than happy to talk about his career that has spanned everything from TV shows like *Superboy* (1988-1992) to some of the biggest action franchises of all time.

I think we should start by clearing something up. What is your actual shoe size, because *Die Hard* has, for years, been disparaging the size of your feet.

I'm a size 12.

A size 12? So, what we're saying, is that John McClane's sister must have massive feet?

[laughs] Yes.

You started off your career as a classically trained dancer, what made you decide to take up acting?

I was working at the Bavarian state opera and we had this man do a production for us, named Johan Cresnick. He is not so well-known, but he was a proponent of this method called Dodo Theatre, meaning that you use everything that's available so you can do whatever you have to do on stage.

He came from ballet himself, but he developed this style, that included acting, miming, and using whatever tools that are available. There were no restrictions. To me that was a revelation, and after that I wasn't happy going back to a stylized way of expressing myself, such as in classical ballet. I think I did another year, and then I wound it up. I couldn't face it any more.

How did you go about building up your acting experience?

I started doing local theatre, and ended up doing quite a few productions, but in the first one, I found I had no technique, so I addressed it. When I moved to London, I worked with a voice coach and discovered how to work on a text, and voice techniques, so that you can shout and not get hoarse, and so forth.

Your big break was obviously the James Bond film, *The Living Daylights*, where you starred as Necros, the imposing KGB assassin. Did

you have to repeatedly audition, or did they just see a photo of you and think that you were perfect for the role?

They saw a photo of me and that led to me being invited in. The fact was, the character description was me. I mean, it was just startling.

Big, tall, blond, and Eastern European?

I walked in there and they were like, 'Wow.' Compared to what I had to do in the States for a little television part, it was easy.

I read this book that left an impression on me, because I was getting into the psychology of it all, and reading what makes people kill. It's a book by Erick Fromm, who is most famous for *The Art of Loving* (1956), and it's all about the anatomy of human destructiveness. He analyzed what leads people to violent and destructive behavior, so that was where a lot of my information came from. It was probably overkill, but Timothy Dalton was really trying to make his mark as Bond. His take was, 'We're taking this seriously, right?' That sounded good to me, so I just jumped on the bandwagon.

In terms of what I needed to do with my body, that wasn't really that much of an issue, because, as a ballet dancer, if you do nothing else, you

Joe Don Baker, Jeroen Krabbé, and Andreas Wisniewski in *The Living Daylights* (1987). Photo courtesy of MGM.

learn how to move your body subconsciously, and that went a long way. You can use it and fake your way through a great many things. I didn't feel the need to practice being menacing or anything like that. I felt I knew how to do it, but when I look at it now, I cringe!

Are you quite a self-conscious actor? Do you not watch your own work?

I do watch it, but I cringe.

What was it like for you to be cast in a Bond film? Were you a Bond fan growing up, or was it just a job as far as you were concerned?

Not at all. I had seen them all and, basically, Bond is as old as I am! I had seen them all as the first ones came out when I was little. James Bond is huge in Germany, and always has been.

    Here was this character who just basically took what he wanted. He was a sort of reckless, misogynistic and chauvinistic character that caught people's imagination. He has a license to kill so everything he does is more or less okay. That's my theory anyway.

You were in amazing shape for the film and the filmmakers go a long way to show how much of a physical threat you are to Bond, such as with that gratuitous swimming scene. Did you have to hit the gym, or were you already in shape?

That was left over from being a dancer. I've always been very, very physically active, ever since I was a little boy. I guess they just jumped on it and thought it might work. Perhaps, if I had been less trained, maybe I wouldn't have gotten the part, who knows? I didn't find out how that swimming scene came about. I see what you mean about it being almost gratuitous, but it was in the script!

You clearly threw yourself into the action, as you have a fair number of fight scenes, including that brutal kitchen fight with the agent at the MI6 safehouse.

That was the first stunt fight I ever did. It's a minute in the film, but it took three days to film. I knocked out Bill Western, the stunt guy, at one point, and he also broke a finger! At that point, I decided that stunt work is definitely not for me! I did everything except for the parachuting stunt. I wanted to do it all as I thought it sounded exciting!

Your character, although he doesn't say much, does several accents throughout the film, including an American accent and a Cockney milk man. Was that you doing those accents, or were you dubbed over for those?

I think they dubbed a couple. Whenever I try Cockney, I'm like Dick Van Dyke! It's just not good enough.

It was your second film role (after Ken Russell's *Gothic*, 1986) and, at the time, the Bond films were these massive events. What was it like for you, at twenty-eight-years-old, to travel the world making a Bond film?

It was very exciting. I had done a couple of things with Ken Russell and I had done a student's film in Germany, so Bond was my first big role. It's just not comparable. It's like comparing a rickshaw with a Rolls-Royce! It was five-star hotels, a sit-down lunch everyday with wine, it was amazing, and I had never been treated like this. They do treat you very well.

I've heard that about the sets on Bond films, that they're like one big family, as the cast and crew have worked on so many films together.

That's totally true ,and that was amazing about the work, because there were people on set that had been working on all the Bond films, starting from *Dr. No* [1962]. Cubby's belief was, 'Why change it if it's working,' which makes a lot of sense. Everyone jelled so well. I never heard anybody shout on the Bond set, not in the three months I was on it. They all just knew each other so well and they were part of this legacy.

How about your co-stars? Were you intimidated by them at all, or were they welcoming?

Tim was great. He's a very kind man, but we weren't friends or anything. He's a very private man, and he kept his distance. The work was great, but there was nothing intimidating. It was just a blast.

I imagine your co-villains, such as Jeroen Krabbé, were good fun. The two of you look like you're having a great time driving jeeps through that final battle sequence.

In Morocco? Yes, that was fun. We were encouraged to shoot more bullets! [laughs] I couldn't really get a grasp on everything that was going on because it was such a huge scene. I just did what I was told to do. That was the only way I could deal with it! I couldn't really get my head around everything that was happening and so I almost got run over by a horse!

Really?

They said, 'Careful. There's going to be some horses galloping past you!' It came a second too late and I crossed in front of the horses! They were so close, I could have put my hand on their chests! [laughs]

When was the last time you heard that Pretenders song, *Where Has Everybody Gone*? I imagine that song must have followed you around for a while?

Yes, but it's been a while now.

Did you expect the exposure from being in a Bond film would have got you similar roles going forward, and was that something you embraced?

There was that for a bit, but it didn't last very long for a couple of reasons. After being in *The Living Daylights*, I moved to Los Angeles, but I never really capitalized on the role. I never went from one job to the next. That just never happened.

One of the advantages of being typecast, which happened in the beginning, is that you're put up for those parts, but then it just fell apart. I wasn't doing any other big movies, as those roles weren't forthcoming. I was just doing television work, appearing in little films, and doing a bit of stage work, but that didn't last. However, by way of not having a great career, I have managed to do a decent variety of things.

Why do you feel the offers dried up? Do you feel that you didn't pursue them enough?

A recent publicity photo of Andreas Wisniewski.
Photo courtesy of Kristjan Czako.

It was strange. I thought, having bagged the Bond part and, from speaking to people, I would have got lots of work playing Nazis, but I just didn't get any of it. No World War II films, no German soldier roles, nothing. It is only this year that I played my first Nazi! It's a cliché, but truthfully things just don't always go the way you expect them to go.

I assumed that you would have got the role of Tony in *Die Hard* off the back of *The Living Daylights*?

More or less. I didn't get it entirely off the back of *The Living Daylights*, but it opened the door. It's very interesting when you look back at the Bond villains. For some, it's not been a career stepping stone. There have been some Bond villains that have done well, such as Robert Shaw, but they had been established beforehand.

The same thing is true for the Bond Girls. Apart from a couple, many of the Bond girls didn't really have a career, though that has changed recently.

Actresses like Eva Green and Naomi Harris have worked hard to not be pigeon-holed by their roles.

Precisely. And Famke Janssen.

With *Die Hard*, that was such a big film, but you're in it for a relatively short amount of time. What was the shoot like for you?

I was on the film for seven weeks and on set twelve times. For five of these days I did nothing, and just played chess with Alexandra Godunov. Out of the remaining seven, I was dead for three!

You were just dumped in the lift?

Precisely [laughs]

Why did they keep calling you back? Were there reshoots or they weren't sure what they needed from you?

It was just a big movie. It takes that long, and when you have a small part, they're certainly not working around you! They work around the stars! If you happen to have a little part in a film where you show up for ten seconds in ten different locations, you can spend months on set!

Your big part in that film is fighting a barefoot Bruce Willis. It was his first major role coming off *Moonlighting* (1985). Was he nervous at all?

Putting myself in his position, I would have thought that that film was very important. I think he'd done one or two features after *Moonlighting*, but neither did very well, so there was a sense that this was extremely important for him.

We were under the impression that it was a $20 million film, which was a fairly large budget back then, but, within a couple of weeks, the executives at 20th Century Fox were so happy with it that they doubled the budget and expanded the schedule!

Compared to Necros, who is very imposing, Tony looks a little bit more on the geeky side with the big glasses. Whose idea was that look?

That was me. They were my real glasses. [laughs]

Oh, really?

Yes, I bought them and I liked them.

Was it just a way to stand out on the screen? Did you think people might mistake you and Alexandra Godunov for the same person?

I didn't concern myself with that, as we were playing brothers, and the job was to look like brothers. I don't recall thinking I had to wear something to stand out. I don't know whether that is arrogance or stupidity, but it never occurred to me!

I did have a bit of history with Alexandra Godunov, because he also was a dancer and, soon after he defected, he came to Berlin to dance with a ballet company, and I was in that company. I was only there for a year, but that's where I met him, and then it took six or seven years for us to end up playing brothers in *Die Hard*!

What was he like? I mean tragically he died far too young and, from what I've read, he was a lovely guy, and the complete opposite to Karl in *Die Hard*.

He was a really sweet man. I spent a fair bit of time with him, and we would play chess on the set when we were both not doing anything.

I have to ask about Alan Rickman. What are your memories of him?

As it happened, he and I had a friend in common. Before we started shooting, he came up to me and introduced himself. I observed him very carefully, because [he] was special, and the way he was working was unique, because he wasn't always happy with the director's wishes.

What I learned from him was that there's always a way that you can give the director what he wants without necessarily compromising what you see in the role. There's always a way to play a role so you have satisfied more than just one angle. Alan was brilliant at that. We became friends, not close friends, but we saw each other every so often.

What did he and John McTiernan disagree over?

Alan didn't like gratuitous violence, so the way he dealt with it was that he brought humor to the role, so he could take the gravity out of the violence. This was an American action movie, so there was obviously no escape from violence, and that was something that he had to deal with himself.

His decisions were for the best as he's now regarded as one of the best screen villains precisely because of the charm and humor that he exudes in the film. How did you get on with the rest of Hans's terrorists? You all seem to come from a multitude of backgrounds.

I didn't really have much to do with anyone else, except for Alan and Alexander. I didn't keep in touch with anyone except for Alan. From my experience, that's typically the way it goes. You get together, you spend long hours together every day for months on end and then you part ways. You may run into people 20 years later on another project, but that's it.

Speaking of actors that you run into years later, I wanted to ask you about your role in the *Mission: Impossible* franchise. In the first film, you starred as Vanessa Redgrave's bodyguard and then, fifteen years later, you re-appeared in *Mission: Impossible – Ghost Protocol* (2011) as, I assume, the same character. It's an obscure cameo that most people might not have picked up on, so I must ask how did that come about?

Tom Cruise had the idea that he wanted to link *Ghost Protocol* with the first film. They were trying to get Vanessa to reprieve her part too, but that didn't happen. We shot a half day and I had one scene with Tom. However, when Vanessa could make it, it didn't make sense to keep most of my role in, so they ended up keeping just three seconds of it.

It is a testimony to you that, despite them not getting Vanessa Redgrave, they decided to include you in the film. What made them decide to get you back as well as Vanessa Redgrave?

I assume because, in the first film, we were an item, so to speak. Even though I was in one tiny shot, lots of fans caught this. It linked it together with the first film and, although it was totally obscure, it did something.

What are your memories of working on the first film with Tom Cruise and Vanessa Redgrave?

The film had one of the coldest, worst shoot days of my life, and by far the hottest shoot day of all time! We were at Pinewood and it was July. It was the hottest month on record and we were filming the scene in the train. It was forty degrees Celsius outside and I can't begin to tell you what temperature it was inside, but people were dropping like flies because they had a dozen lights generating an incredible amount of heat!

They had all these air conditioners that they'd hang in the train between each take. It was extraordinary. It was so hot that from 'Roll camera' to 'Action', which is just ten seconds, I would be dripping in sweat, because I was wearing a rubber vest underneath my costume.

Why?!

It was part of the costume! It was a really neat costume, and they'd spent a lot of money to make a minor character look good, but people were fainting and that was the day I spent with Vanessa.

I imagine Vanessa was as professional as they come.

Absolutely. I had worked with her daughter Natasha on *Gothic* [1986], and I had worked with her other daughter Jolie on another film. I also knew her ex-husband Tony Richard, so I said to her, 'I need to work with you to complete the set!'

How was Tom Cruise from the first time you worked with him in 1996 to when you met again on *Ghost Protocol* in 2011? Had he changed at all?

He had changed quite drastically. He's totally professional, but on the first film, I had that bizarre experience where people would ask me what it was like to work with him and I couldn't say. It was like he had some sort of intangible quality that I couldn't grasp. Then, fifteen years later, he had changed completely. He was totally personable and very kind to me. We talked about our kids and we actually share the same birthday!

In recent years, you've moved into doing period action films like *The Scorpion King* (2002) sequel and *Centurion* (2010). Is that a genre that appeals to you?

I have never been in the position that I've been able to pick what I wanted to do. I just do what's offered me because I have to.

What do you think casting agents see in you that makes them want to cast you in those roles?

I think I've got a sort of face that lends itself to these roles, but let's face facts that most villains are cartoony, in the sense that they don't have any dimension. I'm typically in a small part, so it's very difficult to bring any dimension to it, because even if you want to take an extra breath or roll your eyes, they make you do it fast, because they need you to get off-screen so that the star can enter. That's not so fun, because it's just shallow and what's interesting is playing different and interesting characters.

When I hear about people that are in the position to be typecast, I don't know what they're complaining about! It's not something I get to complain about that because I don't get to do many roles. On smaller productions, I am sometimes lucky enough to get something with a bit of dimension. I was in the German version of *Law and Order*, and I played this man who had been poisoned with radiation. I was still alive, but I had been murdered. I'm really happy about roles like that because, in terms of acting, it's much more satisfying than playing cardboard characters.

Clarence Gilyard, Jr.

"All right, listen up guys. 'Twas the night before Christmas, and all through the house, not a creature was stirring, except... the four assholes coming in the rear in standard two-by-two cover formation."

– Theo, *Die Hard.*

Select Filmography

- *CHiPs* (1982-1983) – Officer Benjamin Webster
- *Top Gun* (1986) – Sundown
- *The Karate Kid II* (1986) – G.I. #1
- *Die Hard* (1988) – Theo
- *Matlock* (1989-1993) – Conrad McMasters
- *Walker, Texas Ranger* (1993-2001) – James Trivette

Hans Gruber and his team have Nakatomi Plaza secured, except for John McClane, who is proving to be the proverbial fly in the ointment. Eager to end the hostage situation as soon as possible, the LAPD decide to storm the building. Little do they know that their actions are being monitored by hacker and technical expert, Theo, who has taken a break from over-riding the locks on the building's vault, to report on the police's tactics as they move in.

HANS DIDN'T JUST BRING HIM ALONG for his charming personality, there's a reason why Clarence Gilyard Jr's Theo is on his team. While the

Clarence Gilyard Jr. plays Theo in *Die Hard* (1988).
Photo courtesy of 20th Century Fox.

rest of the terrorists round up hostages or hunt John McClane, Theo is breaking into the Nakatomi Cooperation's vault.

Much more laid-back than the rest of the terrorists, Theo seems an odd fit, but proves to be as callous as the rest of them when he starts betting with Karl over whether the company's CEO, Joseph Takagi, will give up the vault's codes. Despite this selfish streak, Theo is a fan favorite and also manages to survive the film when he's knocked out by limo driver, Argyle. Was it because Theo is so likeable that he got to survive while the rest of Hans's team were shot, blown up and chucked off buildings?

When I spoke to Clarence Gilyard Jr., he was enjoying an afternoon with his family, but was more than happy to discuss his time making *Die Hard,* as well as his roles in *Top Gun,* hit series *Matlock,* and *Walker, Texas Ranger.*

How did you end up cast in *Die Hard* as Theo? Did you audition for the role?

I was in-between films, because I had decided I wasn't going to do any American Television after I'd done a television series called *The Duck Factory* [1984] with Jim Carrey. After thirteen episodes, NBC didn't pick it up, and I hadn't enjoyed the daily grind of making it. It sounds disingenuous for where I was going and how I was trying to develop as an actor, but television was kind of getting under my skin, especially the pace of it. As

I was developing as an artist, the television grind was not helping, and it was a trying experience for me, so I decided that I want to take some time and study Lee Strasberg's acting method.

I went back to university, but I had just done *Top Gun*, and that film had made its way into the public consciousness. I had made my mark in Hollywood with that film, and it was iconic in a lot of ways, so director John McTiernan actually came looking for me.

You were sought out? That's impressive.

When they called, I was away! I had taken some time and gone down to Malibu Beach. When I got back to my house, there were a series of messages on my machine from my agent who was trying to find me. I'd been away for three or four days and, when I got back, I saw the light on my answering machine was flashing furiously. There were a series of frantic messages from my agent, so I called him at home and he said, 'Where the hell have you been? They've been trying to get to you! Maybe they'll still see you! Take a shower, comb your hair, get down to 20ᵗʰ Century Fox!'

Clarence Gilyard Jr. came to the attention of Hollywood's A-list after appearing as Sundown in *Top Gun* (1986). Photo courtesy of Paramount Pictures.

I arrived there at about 12:30 a.m. and Fox Plaza was still under construction, which was why we could shoot the film so cheaply. I took the elevator up and I got off on an active movie set. They had just started shooting the film. The production assistant stopped me at the door and I said, 'I've been summoned!'

I could see Bruce Willis, as they were setting up a shot against the windows overlooking Century City, and there, siting on an apple box, was the producer and the director. They came over and said, 'We're shooting this action film and we thought of you to play this terrorist. You got anything going on right now?' I said, 'No, actually, I'm free.' There was no script or anything! They just said it was a 'pretty good role'.

What was it about you that they thought would be a good fit for Theo?

John McTiernan and I talked about it because, after they made the deal with my agent, I went to my acting coach, looked at the script and decided what I wanted to do with the character. I made some notes and had a meeting with John. We talked about the lack of fear that was predicated on a heightened amount of intelligence and technology.

I gave him an outline of where I wanted the character to go, which was not necessarily scripted. He was all on board. I think he just felt that I was truthful and he liked the research that I had done.

Do you remember what the character of Theo was like in Steven E. de Souza's script? Was it a blank canvas that you could build upon, or was it very specific?

When I was assessing the screen time that the character had, and the episodic nature of the film, I noticed that when the story came back to Theo, he had to carry the energy forward rather than letting it drop. I had to build that energy as I was going through the locks [on the vault] and how I felt about it.

Also, the other personalities that I was with in the film were killers. I really felt that Theo was expendable too, unless he had something that nobody else had. The other terrorists couldn't be pedestrian with him and so I infused that into my performance, and I think it allowed that character to resonate off the screen.

Alexander Godunov and Clarence Gilyard Jr on set in *Die Hard* (1988).
Photo courtesy of 20th Century Fox.

You're right. Of all the terrorists, Theo isn't a killer, but he is callous. In that scene where Hans shoots Takagi, he is betting with Karl on whether he'll give up the password.

I think that's important, to have that diversity in your panorama of characters. You must have people that attain things in different ways, rather than having carbon copies of everyone. It's not that he couldn't kill somebody, but you just make a choice. That scene, where we're betting, and I win a dollar, that was not scripted. There was a ton of ad-libbing and a lot that was added.

Did that happen a lot throughout filming? Were you ad-libbing lines like, 'And the quarterback is toast!'?

I think that's what happens when you have a plan as an artist that you're going to use each project to grow your career. You come in with a plan, but the foundation is the script. You just imagine and create this life for your character and the production will go, 'Let's put some more cameras on him and allow him to do these things.' They'll just run the camera, and they'll decide if they want to put it in. I think that's how young actors emerge.

Most of your scenes are with Alan Rickman and Alexander Godunov. What was it like working with the two of them?

I had been on a dance scholarship when I was coming up in the business, and so to be able to play chess between shots with Alexander Godunov was crazy. The setup of shots can take up to two hours, so we would go to each other's trailers, play chess, and chat, and that was unbelievable. I didn't tell him, but I was pretty much slack jawed as we were sitting and chatting about his life and his progress in Hollywood.

Alan was interesting. The producers had seen him in *Dangerous Liaisons* (1987) on Broadway, and that's how he got the part, because of the richness of his portrayal. That blew me away, because I was really leaning towards trying to figure out how to work in the theatre even though, at that time, I was making my way in film and television. I was querying him about it, and we were talking about this and that. We would have a coffee together and, one time, I remember him getting a call from Harold Pinter [the playwright], if you can believe it.

Really?

Pinter was just emerging in my consciousness as an aesthetic and a genius. I was just blown away by that person's life and how he had progressed. The thing about Alan is that he had such a presence and such an intelligence. You should really be able to carry yourself if you're in a two-shot with somebody like that. I remember having to do scenes with him, and John McTiernan would have to intercede and go, 'Remember the status here,' because many of my lines that are on the cutting room floor were me just mouthing off at him. Whereas he would be able to say something to somebody else within the cadre of terrorists, he couldn't really say it in the same way to Theo. We had established that over the course of the shoot so that it was authentic that these two would have this kind of relaxed communication. You could tell that Theo really didn't take a back seat to him, but he did have to defer to the fact that he was the general and I was the lieutenant, as it were.

Theo is very confident in his own abilities, and knows that Hans needs him if they're going to get into the vault. I think that's why he has that more relaxed vibe with Hans than the rest of the terrorists do, because Theo knows he is indispensable.

Exactly.

As a British actor, Alan was not as familiar with guns as most American actors would be. I read he had a lot of issues when it came to firing them. Mainly, that he would constantly close his eyes, especially in the scene where he shoots Joseph Takagi.

[laughs] Yes! Yes, he did. The thing about that shot is that John McTiernan wasn't about cutting things. He was about camera movement and depth. It wasn't about him looking comfortable with the gun, but more the surprise of him pulling out the gun and just dispensing with Takagi. That shot had to be done several times, not just because of Alan, but also because of me messing up. I think we did double figures on that scene!

After that, you pretty much spend the rest of the film alone in the vault room, or watching security cameras. Was that a challenge as an actor doing those scenes by yourself?

It was a graduate course. I was the only one in the frame, but I wanted them to have to cut back to me because of the excitement of what I was doing. So, I developed it. I knew I had an internal fatigue and anxiousness going on, and so, in between shots, I would do push-ups to have a different look and convey the stress he's under, and be cinematically truthful.

It's also interesting that, by the end of the film, you are one of the few terrorists to survive. Was Theo always meant to survive, or was that decision made later because of what you brought to the role, which was a certain level of likeability?

I never really thought about it. I think there was a chance the character might have come back, but after the film I was never available. I also think it's because of his intelligence. Intelligence is more sustainable than the human body, so I think that was a factor. It's amazing that the film is over thirty years old now. Isn't that interesting? How some films just continue to have a life after they come out?

Does that surprise you? That today, it's regarded not just as an action classic, but also as a Christmas staple?

I think that of all the things that I have done, that are still out there being seen, there's; *Matlock*, that I did for four years, *Walker, Texas Ranger*, then there's *Top Gun*, and *Die Hard*. Those four alone are going to live on forever. They will be going when I will be somewhere else, God willing. Those shows, films, and characters will live on.

As artists, that's the desire to create that presence in the public consciousness. Those characters have created and are a part of me. Do you know the fighter demonstration team The Blue Angels? Have you ever heard of them?

Yes. They're the American equivalent of the Red Arrows, I believe.

They're the U.S. Navy's demonstration team. They're made up of naval and marine aviators . . . and they all know me.

Because of *Top Gun*?

Exactly. I can go to any one of those demonstrations all over the world and sit front row. Isn't that amazing? And it's all because those kids grew up watching me in *Top Gun*.

I bet you also get a lot of people coming up to you and singing *You've Lost That Lovin' Feeling*?

All the time. That's when you know you've done your job.

With your roles in *Matlock* and *Walker, Texas Ranger*, was that a conscious effort to move away from characters like Theo, that I'm sure you were offered plenty of, or just to find more regular work as an actor?

At the time, I had got married and had my first child, and as a working actor, you have a steady pay check. My agent said of *Matlock*, 'You should probably entertain this. They're really interested in you,' and so I decided to take that job. I figured that I could still do some films, but TV shows are really time consuming, when you are number two on the call sheet. I had to step back from film and once I decided to leave *Matlock* to develop a series of my own, I was approached by Chuck Norris. If he was involved, I knew there were going to be some serious pay checks!

Clarence Gilyard Jr. alongside Chuck Norris and the cast of *Walker, Texas Ranger*.
Photo courtesy of CBS.

I've interviewed a lot of people who've worked with Chuck Norris. How was your working relationship with him over that eight-year period?

I think we complimented each other, and I think that's why the show did what it did. I didn't go into it blindly, but I didn't necessarily want to stay as long as I did. I don't think I made the right decision staying with that show. You make decisions and you can't necessarily make all of them as creative decisions, but I have five kids and there was a lot going on!

These days, have you essentially stepped back from screen acting? Could we see Sundown come back as an instructor in a future *Top Gun* sequel, or is that now behind you and you're focusing on teaching?

I'm working with this theatre company, and I have a national tour of the play, *Driving Miss Daisy*. I'm thinking about how I want to go back to film, because it's time to go back. I want the next project to have an impact based upon what I've done before, that's why I am choosing when to go back. If I can just lose about 10 lbs., then I'll take the meetings that I want to take!

It's a problem we all face. That cursed 10 lbs.!

Stop eating all that junk food! But don't give up on the Guinness. Don't ever do that.

I would never give up Guinness.

There you go. That's my man.

Dennis Hayden

"Good evening officer. What can I do you for?"

– Eddie, *Die Hard.*

Select Filmography

- *Action Jackson* (1988) – Shaker
- *Die Hard* (1988) – Eddie
- *Another 48 Hrs.* (1990) – Barroom Tough
- *One Man Army* (1994) – Eddie Taylor
- *Fatal Choice* (1995) – Jim Kale
- *Sniper 2* (2002) - Klete

As Hans Gruber and his terrorists sweep through Nakatomi Plaza, Karl (Alexander Gudunov) and Theo (Clarence Gilyard Jr.) come through the front door, shooting the on-duty security guards. Taking their place is Eddie, a tall, blond American whose job is to convince any investigating police officers that everything is fine.

GRUBER'S TERRORISTS ARE A DIVERSE BUNCH. The majority are German, but you also have Chinese-American terrorist Uli (Al Leong), cocky hacker Theo (Clarence Gilyard Jr), and Eddie (Dennis Hayden), a swaggering Texan who seems to be a very odd fit with the rest of Han's "euro trash".

For years, I theorized that Eddie was German, and his thick Southern drawl was the result of watching too many American movies – he was

Eddie (Dennis Hayden) plays it cool in *Die Hard* (1988).
Photo courtesy of Dennis Hayden.

doing an over-the-top, bad John Wayne impression, which would be in line with *Die Hard*'s references to old Western films.

This was one of several questions I had for Dennis Hayden when I arranged to speak to him. Of course, not only did Dennis star in *Die Hard*, but, beforehand, he also appeared in *Action Jackson*, where director Craig R. Baxley cherry picked cast members from producer Joel Silver and director Richard Donner's assorted cinematic universe, including; Carl Weathers (*Predator*), Bill Duke (*Predator*), Sonny Landham (*Predator*), Al Leong (*Lethal Weapon*), De'Voreaux White (*Die Hard*), Robert Davi (*The Goonies*) and Mary Ellen Trainor (*Lethal Weapon*). In fact, along with Hayden, four other *Action Jackson* cast members appeared in *Die Hard*.

In the film, Hayden stars as one of The Invisible Men, a group of assassins that Craig T. Nelson's Dellaplane is using to get rid of his political rivals. He leads the group and his character, Shaker, favors a grenade launcher to dispatch his victims, meeting his demise after he attempts to barbecue Carl Weather's titular hero. His final line, 'We're going to have ourselves a little barbecue,' comes back to haunt him when Jackson disarms him, and quips, 'Barbecue, huh? How do you like your ribs?' and shoots him with his own weapon.

Dennis was wonderful to talk to, eager to discuss his most famous roles, and to regale me with anecdotes about those big budget action movies. Plus, if he's to be believed, he's got some skills when it comes to weaponry, so you don't want to mess with him.

How did you end up getting cast as Shaker in *Action Jackson*, because that is an under-rated film that I feel more people should see!

My agent called and said they wanted to see me for this film, and a limo came by and picked me up! I was introduced to Carl Weathers, the pro-

Dennis Hayden as Shaker in *Action Jackson* (1987).
Photo courtesy of Dennis Hayden.

ducer Joel Silver, and director Craig Baxley, and that afternoon they hired me! That's the way it's meant to be for an actor!

It was a great movie, man. When I first met Carl, he looked at me and went, 'Oh, so you're the bad guy, huh?' Later, when we were shooting the scene where I'm about to barbecue him, Carl was meant to kick me in the groin, and he did, accidently! The director came over and said, 'We'll have to do another one as that one didn't look real!' and I said, 'That's as real as it gets! If it was any more real, I'd be crying!'

Obviously that scene is famous for when Carl Weathers goes, 'How do you like your ribs?' and blows you away.

Yes, I get blown away by my own gun. Craig Baxley was very proud of that scene, thanks to the editing, where it goes from me getting blown up to that barbecue scene at the party, so that worked well. Going from, 'How do you like your ribs?' to me getting blown away and then cutting to a grill!

Was Carl's kiss-off line ad-libbed, or was it in the script?

It was all scripted. Carl had just played Apollo Creed, so he was already really buff from working out, so when I got there, I realized I'd really have to get in shape. He had some weights on set that were 20 lbs. a piece, so I went out and got myself a couple of 20 lb. weights, so I could also start working out! I had to compete with Apollo Creed! By the time shooting was done, I was pretty strong. Those weights felt like they didn't weigh anything!

For Carl, this film was potentially the start of a franchise. Naturally, he'd been in big films before like *Predator* and the *Rocky* movies, but was he nervous about the pressure of headlining his own film, or was this everything he'd been waiting for?

Carl was very confident. The whole script was good and the director was great. There were meant to be a whole bunch of sequels, but I believe a conflict between the writers stopped that from happening, so it never went anywhere. It's a real shame, because it's a great film. Every time it's on, I watch it and laugh my ass off. Prince's girl, Vanity, was in it and, at the time, she was pretty wild. The first day I walked into the make-up trailer, she was standing there butt naked! This was before she found religion.

Obviously, there is a lot of crossover between *Action Jackson* and *Die Hard* – Joel Silver produced both films and you and Al Leong are in both films.

I got *Die Hard* directly because I was in *Action Jackson*. Joel liked my work, and when they made the first trailer for *Action Jackson*, most of it featured me, so I naturally stood out.

I got a call to come to 20th Century Fox and go to Joel Silver's office. I drove down there and the casting director, Jackie Birch, was there. As I walked in through the door, she handed me the script and said, 'You'll be reading for the part of Eddie.'' Joel was sitting at his desk and he yelled at her and said, 'That's Dennis Hayden! He starred in *Action Jackson*! He doesn't have to read for me! I just wanted you to meet him!' He was yelling at her and I was worried, because she's the biggest casting director in town! I didn't want to get on her bad side!

Joel Silver was the biggest producer in Hollywood at that point, so it's great to have him on your side! He obviously liked you and saw something in you that made him want to put you in *Die Hard*. Do you know what that was?

I'm a great fucking actor, man! [laughs] I started out doing theatre when I first got to California, and worked for ten years before I even got into a TV show or a movie. I had my craft down.

Also, I'm a big guy, I'm six feet fucking four and I towered over Carl Weathers and all those guys. When we were shooting *Action Jackson*, Joel came up to me and said, 'Where were you when I was casting *Predator*?' I looked at him and said, 'I was in your office! I read for a part, but you gave it to the wrestler instead of the actor!'

So, you read for Blaine, played by Jesse Ventura?

Yeah! They gave it to Jesse Ventura because he was a famous wrestler. They should have given that part to me, a bad-ass actor!

Before we did *Die Hard*, they sent us to a boot camp, and the guy who ran it had trained all the top military ops people, like SEAL Team 6.

He had trained them all. We went over there for a couple of weeks and then they'd run us through these routines.

I was born and lived on a farm in Kansas, and my dad was a psychotic alcoholic that had fought in World War II. He tried to kill us every day with butcher knives, because he thought we were Germans, so we learned to hunt at an early age, because, if we didn't, we would have starved to death! Seriously, it was that bad. I've eaten possums and some [of] the nastiest shit you've ever seen just because we were hungry. Anyway, we go to this military school and we do our training, going through houses and shooting dummy pop-ups and loading our guns on the run. It was like playing 'Cowboys and Indians' like I did when I was a kid.

When we finished our time at the boot camp, everyone was saying goodbye to the trainer. I was getting my stuff to go home, he came up to me, and starts talking about all the people he had trained. He had worked with everyone on the planet who was a bad-ass, and he ended by saying, 'Of all the people I've trained, you're the best. You're the best guy I've ever trained.'

Wow.

I was thirty-five-years-old at the time, so I looked at him in shock and I said, 'Well, thanks man, you're a great trainer. You taught me well.' I started to walk off and he said, 'Seriously, if you want to do this for real, I can set you up.' I said, 'No, I'm just an actor,' but he said, 'You're that good and you did your whole training in cowboy boots!' I wear size seventeen cowboy boots, so I said, 'Well, that's my character. My character wears cowboy boots!'

What was weird was a few months later, once *Die Hard* had finished filming, I got a call from some people who wanted me to go to a third world country and take out some guy while pretending I was doing a film there. They were going to pay me huge money. It was crazy. I took a friend of mine to the meeting. They were serious about recruiting me, but I never went for it.

Hang on. Let me get this straight. Because you were an actor who was good with a gun, someone, possibly the CIA, wanted you to do an 'Argo' (2012) and, under the guise of making a film, go to a country and kill someone?!

Dennis Hayden is no stranger to weapons in *Die Hard* (1988).
Photo courtesy of Dennis Hayden.

Yes. That's exactly what they wanted.

That's incredible. You weren't tempted to say yes? Are you sure you should be telling me this?!

I'm not sure I should mention it, because it was pretty scary at the time.

That's insane. That's a movie right there, waiting to be written! I hope by you telling me that you're not going to get into trouble? Speaking of trouble, let's talk about *Die Hard*. Most of the terrorists are European apart from you and Theo, who are the only Americans. Did you ever have any backstory on why this was and how they ended up working for Hans Gruber?

No, not really. I just figured that they needed some Americans to pull this off, but there was never any backstory for the character.

For many years, I assumed that Eddie was actually German and was just doing what he thought was an American accent to fool the cops. Was that ever discussed?

No, that was never discussed, but that's a great idea!

You're also one of the last terrorists standing by the end of the film, until Bruce Willis shoots you in the head. Did they just shoot you in the head with a paint pellet?

What happened was they got a guy with a blow gun, which had wax pellets filled with fake blood, so they splattered when they hit you. Bruce was using a gun with a blank in it, so that the noise was at a quarter level of what it would normally be, so that it wouldn't deafen us. However, the guy that had the blow gun had shell shock. Every time the gun went off, he would jump.

On the DVD outtakes, I think it shows me getting shot like sixteen or seventeen times. He would jump and the pellets would hit me all over my face, and each time I would to have pick myself up off the floor, and then they would have to clean me up again. After several hours of this, Joel Silver said, 'We've got to get another guy,' so they shut the scene down and we came back two weeks later to do it. It took the new guy four or five times to get the perfect shot, but that was an ordeal to get that one shot.

It must have been a complicated shoot as it involved helicopters, SWAT teams, and explosions. Did you ever feel any pressure during the production?

At the beginning of the film, when I go to the front door and I let Reginald VelJohnson in, and I walk him back, we did that all in one take. I came back from lunch and John McTiernan was all set up, so me and Reginald did it in one take.

Afterwards, Joel Silver came on set and said, 'Are we ready to go?' and John said, 'No, we've already got it! It's perfect.' Joel looked and me and Reginald, watched it on the monitor and couldn't believe it!

When I spoke to Andreas Wisniewski (Tony), he said that despite him dying at the beginning of the film, he was on set for most of the shoot. You make it to the end of the film, so was it a lengthy process for you, too?

When I first got the script, my character died halfway through the movie, and I wasn't happy about that! I was down at the Butler Building on Santa Monica Boulevard, which had a music studio, because at the time I was involved in a lot of rock 'n' roll.

My friends were down there cutting an album and this PR lady was there. I mentioned I had been looking for someone to do some PR, and she said she had been thinking about getting into the movie business. I told her I'd been in *Murphy's Law* and *Action Jackson*, and mentioned I'd just been cast in *Die Hard,* which was about to shoot in a month. She went, 'Oh, my future brother in law is the writer of that movie!' She was marrying the brother of Steven E. de Souza (the screenwriter), so I said, 'Tell Steven to make my part so I'm the last person that Bruce shoots and I'll hire you as my manager!' A week later, she called up and says, 'I spoke to Steven and he said, that's not a problem!' So, I hired her!

How were you originally going to die?

I honestly can't remember. I'd have to pull the script out. I just remember Eddie died halfway through and they re-wrote it for me!

That's canny! That's what all good actors should do.

I've got a lot of extended parts by just walking up to the director and going, 'We could make this movie much better if we did this.'

With Walter Hill on *Another 48 Hrs*, they were casting the film and a friend of mine, Andrew Divoff, got cast in it. He told me they were casting on the Paramount lot, so I went down there. This was all pre-9/11 when you could just walk around on the lot, so I drove through the front gate, looked around, found Walter Hill's office, walked through the door and found him at his desk.

I had met him once before, with Nick Nolte many years before, and so he knew who I was. I said, 'Hey man, I heard you were casting a movie and I'd love to be in it.' He said, 'I'm sorry, it's already been cast. Maybe the next one?' A week later he called and said, 'I've just written you a part!' He knew

Dennis Hayden on set of *Die Hard* (1987). Photo courtesy of Dennis Hayden.

Nick and I were friends but didn't tell him, so when I showed up to work, Nolte had no idea! It was the same with *Wild Bill* [1995]. I called up about a role and they wrote one for me! If they like you, they'll write you parts.

I have to ask you about Alan Rickman and Alex Gudunov. What are your memories of working with them?

Alan wasn't nervous one bit. He was a trained theatrical actor and had been on the stage his whole life. It's hard to intimidate someone who has done theatre for most of their life, because you work in front of a crowd every night, so you don't worry about a camera. Alan was an all-round great guy. He read the script for Joel Silver's *Road House* [1989]and came up to me and said, You'd be perfect for this film.' He told Joel that I was meant to be in the film, but I was so much bigger than Patrick Swayze, they didn't think it would work!

Gudunov was great. He was cool, but he'd get lost. We'd have to go find him as he drank quite a bit, but we hung out every day on set. We all got on great together.

There have been many comments about how much you resemble Huey Lewis in *Die Hard*. In fact, I believe you played him in *The Cleveland Show*'s parody episode, "Die Semi-Hard". Did this happen a lot in your career that you were mistaken for each other?

Not now! Back then I was, but, as we've both gotten older, we look very different. In that parody for *The Cleveland Show*, they got Huey Lewis to do the voice over for that. I never got paid for that! I never got a dime! They gave it to Huey, which was bullshit. Every Christmas, when they play the hell out of it, I get calls, but I never got paid for it.

When *Die Hard* came out, one of the major newspapers said, 'Huey Lewis was great in *Die Hard*,' so all the Hollywood people thought that it was him! I swear to God! I went to a couple of agencies, and this was before the IMDb when you can prove you were in a film, and when I told them I was in *Die Hard* they said, 'That wasn't you! That was Huey Lewis!' They were so rude about it, so I left! However, now, the older I get ,though, the more I look like Tommy Lee Jones!

You've been a steady working actor over the past few decades, do you think being cast in such a well-known film like *Die Hard* stereotyped you at all, or was it a stepping stone to a wider range of roles?

I can work a lot more if I want to, but now I just work if people call up and ask me. I've done fifty or so national commercials, but it's no fun to audition, so if someone wants me, they'll call me. I'm not going to play that game. I'm too old for that crap.

You've been cast as a lot of villains over the years, such as in *Sniper 2*. Do you think it's more fun to play bad guys?

It makes no difference to me, I play both: good and bad. I just dig into what the author wants. That's the whole thing behind acting. Make the writer happy and everything falls in place. If I read something I like and I want to do, I'll throw 100% of myself into it at all times. In *Sniper 2*, they flew me to Hungary, and that was Craig Baxley again! He said he needed me for this scene and I got the call!

That's great that directors remember actors for roles they did years ago and hire them for roles they'd be perfect for.

Yeah, if an actor never works with the same director again, it's probably because the director doesn't want them. I can't say enough good things about Craig Baxley.

Al Leong

"Endo, meet Mr. Martin Riggs. Endo here has forgotten more about dispensing pain than you and I will ever know."
— Mr. Joshua, *Lethal Weapon* (1987).

Select Filmography

- *Big Trouble in Little China* (1986) – Wing Kong Hatchet Man
- *Lethal Weapon* (1987) – Endo
- *Die Hard* (1988) – Uli
- *Bill and Ted's Excellent Adventure* (1989) – Genghis Khan
- *Black Rain* (1989) – Yakuza Assassin
- *Showdown in Little Tokyo* (1991) – Yoshida's Man
- *Rapid Fire* (1992) – Minh
- *Last Action Hero* (1993) – Vivaldi Gunmen
- *Beverly Hills Cop III* (1994) – Car Mechanic
- *The Shadow* (1994) – Tibetan Driver
- *Double Dragon* (1994) – Lewis
- *Deadly Target* (1994) – Guard
- *The Replacement* Killers (1998) – Terence Wei Gunman
- *Lethal Weapon 4* (1998) – Wah Sing Ku Triad Member

Riggs and Murtaugh have been captured by Shadow Company, a heroin-smuggling operation run by General Peter McAllister and his chief enforcer, Mr. Joshua (Gary Busey). Eager to find out how much they know about their plans, Mr. Joshua brings in Endo (Al Leong) to torture Riggs for information.

Mr. Joshua (Gary Busey) introduces Endo (Al Leong) in *Lethal Weapon* (1987).
Photo courtesy of Warner Brothers.

WHETHER YOU'VE SEEN HIM fighting Jean-Claude Van Damme in *Death Warrant*, taking over Nakatomi Plaza in *Die Hard* or torturing Martin Riggs in *Lethal Weapon*, it's fair to say that Al Leong is the most recognizable gun for hire in action cinema. Yes, I know I've put Al Leong in the *Die Hard* section of the book, but let's face it, that's probably the film he's best known for even if he says nothing in that film. Actually, he says nothing in *Lethal Weapon* either.

For decades, Al Leong has been a constant presence in action movies, often portraying henchmen of few words, but of furious fists. Al's distinctive long hair and Fu Manchu moustache has seen him appear in over sixty-five TV shows and movies as a fight choreographer, stuntman, and actor. In fact, Al's filmography reads like a list of the best eighties action films ever made.

Tragically, Al was diagnosed with brain cancer in the late 1990s and, despite fully recovering at the time, he has since had two strokes that have left him paralyzed down one side of his body and caused some memory problems. However, when we spoke, he was full of stories and listening to him was an inspiration. He stands as living proof that, no matter what obstacles, physical or otherwise, you can always overcome them.

Al has even written a book, *The Eight Lives of Al 'Ka-Bong' Leong* (2011), detailing his early life and his time in the movies. If you enjoy this interview, it is worth tracking it down. Incredibly, for a man who is best known for his martial arts prowess and fighting ability, Al never wanted a life of action and, as we spoke, he revealed another passion close to his heart…

Despite your action-packed career, is it true that, growing up in St. Louis, you were more into mechanics and music than martial arts?

Al Leong is skilled in Sil Lum Kuen (Northern Shaolin kung fu).
Photo courtesy of Al Leong.

My whole life came together during high school. Mr. Harwell, a P.E. teacher, once screened a 16mm film about him and two friends riding Bultaco dirt bikes in the Mojave desert. It's what motivated me to later buy my own dirt bike, a Yamaha 125!

I also took shop classes that are unheard of today in schools – print shop, electric shop, wood shop and metal shop. For some reason, I really got into metal shop. At the end of the year, awards were given out for outstanding students. It was determined by points, so these two guys decided to combine their projects together so they would win. By doing this they overshot me in points, so, to beat them, I built my projects from scratch instead of using existing designs. It was then I realized there that was nothing I couldn't do.

I also loved rock 'n' roll. There was only one band at school, so I used to sit in during their practice sessions.

If your passion was always for the music, how did you end up becoming such a proficient martial artist?

My dad took me to New York and then I started training out of the On Leong Tong, which is the Chinese Association of my family. My teacher always said, 'You are good enough to be your own person so don't be afraid to do your own thing.'

As the years went by I did just that, and there has been no stopping me. Later, my family moved out to Los Angeles, and I started training here in Chinatown. Originally, I didn't want to do martial arts, because there's no money to be made except in the movie business.

Also, if you're Asian, it's another thing you must deal with. I wanted to be a Motocross racer because Asians never did that, but I could take down anyone, and that was a fact. I'm not afraid of anything or anybody and I wanted to do something away from martial arts because that was all Asians were known for. I wanted to do motocross and race because there was money in that. However, Douglas Wong asked me to join his martial arts team on the professional circuit and, as I knew he was good, I agreed.

What about your second passion, music?

That's another thing Asians don't do. Asians are known for martial arts and that's it. I wanted to be in a rock band. I played guitar, but I wasn't great, as my brother taught me, but I had spent a long of time training as a martial artist which helped me in whatever else I wanted to do.

It's ironic that you didn't want to do martial arts because you thought that, as an Asian man, it would be too cliched and, yet, it's what you ended up becoming famous for.

In the States, there are no Asians that are known for racing motorcycles, or being in rock bands. I wanted things that were far away from the traditional Asian look and thinking. For a while, I ended up painting cars. My car got hit badly and, when I took it to the body shop to get it fixed, the painter came up to me asked if I could paint designs on cars, so that's how I got into that business. We were working seven days a week, working fourteen-hour days, however long it took to get things done. We blew the doors off every other company on Van Nuys Boulevard.

How did you go from that to appearing in TV shows like *The A-Team* (1984-1986), *Airwolf* (1985) and *Knightrider* (1984)?

I first got into the business as a grip behind the camera. A friend of mine was doing it and he suggested I put in an application at Warner Brothers, and they just happened to be hiring. I got a call a few weeks later and worked on TV shows for the next three years. I got to see how hard all the people work behind the camera.

On one show, the director asked me if I knew any martial arts, and when I said yes, he asked me to train these four girls for a fight scene. Once they were ready, the director asked me to get in front of the camera with them, and a week later I was in the Screen Actors Guild!

The industry then got super busy, so I was working quite a bit. Whatever I was asked to do, I did it! I worked with a great group of stunt guys that are still working today on the *Fast and Furious* films and Jerry Bruckheimer's action features. They included Henry Kingie, Cory Eubanks, Craig R. Baxley, and a ton of great stunt guys.

Craig R. Baxley was the stunt coordinator on *The A-Team* and *The Warriors*, and he invited me to work on many TV episodes. He directed Joel Silver's *Action Jackson* and I got a role in that too!

So how did you go from choreographing fights and doing stunt work to becoming an actor?

I'm a stunt guy, I'm not an actor. I'm not an actor at all. I always tell people that. I'm not a trained actor. When it comes to jobs, I pick and choose what I want to do. If I work now, I may not work for another year. Plus being Asian is even tougher, because studios are more selective about what they choose you for, because the fact is, if the story doesn't deal with Asians, they don't want to see you.

A lot of times, if you're Asian and you're asked to do a show, you're going to do it no matter what. When I started reading the scripts I asked if I could make changes. If the movie sounds like junk, and there's a lot of junk out there even though it costs millions of dollars, I would say, 'No thanks'. No other actor would ever do that! They know that once you lose a job, you might not get another one for a long time, but I didn't care! That's how I ended up doing a lot of big movies.

Your big break was John Carpenter's *Big Trouble In Little China* as one of the Wing Kong Hatchet Men. How did you end up in that film?

Every Asian in Hollywood was hired for that film except for me. John Carpenter came up to me and asked if I was working on it. When I said 'No,' he said, 'Do you want to?' He was the one that put me in it, but that was after everyone was already hired! I was walking through the set with him and he said, 'What would you like to do?', and we talked about crashing James Lew through the window and doing the fight on that street set. John is fantastic, he's an incredible guy.

I worked with him again on *They Live* [1988] and on a couple of other films. Jeff Imada became his stunt coordinator and he bought me in on those other films.

The role that you're probably most famous for is Endo in *Lethal Weapon*. Did you end up in that film because producer Joel Silver knew you from his previous project, *Action Jackson*?

The first thing I worked on with Joel Silver was *Action Jackson*. Craig R. Baxley, who was the stunt coordinator on *The A-Team*, directed that, and that's when Joel Silver saw me. Joel is the type of guy who's on the set every single day and he oversees everything!

I got in *Lethal Weapon* because the stunt coordinator, Bobby Bass, needed someone to take out Mel Gibson! After that, Joel took me straight on to *Die Hard*!

John Carpenter and Al Leong on set. Photo courtesy of Al Leong.

In *Lethal Weapon*, you torture Mel Gibson's Martin Riggs, and work closely with Gary Busey who played Mr. Joshua. What was it like working with the two of them? Gary has always had a reputation as being a bit crazy.

Gary wasn't too crazy then! He did a great job and, at the time, everyone was fine. I've heard all this stuff about Gary Busey, but both he and Mel were great.

The two of them have this big fight scene at the end, which is one of the first instances where Hollywood used mixed martial arts. Did you have anything to do with that?

I had nothing to do with that, and I'll tell you the truth, I didn't like it! I just didn't think the fight at the end looked very good at all. Everyone has their own choice, and everyone has their own thing, but I didn't really care for it. I thought it was a big waste of time!

It's interesting to note that, despite Endo being killed in *Lethal Weapon*, you show up again in *Lethal Weapon 4* as another henchman. How did that happen?

I was meant to have a big fight scene with Danny Glover. We spent a whole week doing this fight, but I don't think they wanted to take anything away from Jet Li, because he was one of the main draws, so they cut a lot of my scenes out of the film.

You then went to *Die Hard*, where you played the infamous candy-stealing henchman, Uli. Was that scene ad-libbed by you, or was it always planned?

It was not planned. I asked the director, John McTiernan, if I could do [it] and he said, 'Yeah!'

Were you actually hungry?

No, I wasn't hungry! Joel Silver called me directly to come work on the film. I worked for twelve weeks and got paid a lot of good money, but then I got a call asking me to go to England to fight Stallone for the opening fight scene in *Rambo III*. Unfortunately, the *Die Hard* producers didn't know when they might need me, so I couldn't go!

What memories do you have of the late Alan Rickman and Alexander Gudunov, who played Hans Gruber and Karl?

Alan was great, but here's the thing, when he was doing his dialogue, I thought he was talking way too slow! I'm not an actor, and I'd never seen anyone do dialogue the way he did it. I wondered how he could say his lines so slowly, but he did an incredible job. It was unreal when I saw it on the screen.

Why do you think you kept getting cast as a henchman in all these films, what do you think made you so appealing to casting agents?

Most of the time I didn't come through casting directors. I would get a role because someone already knew me, like the stunt coordinator, and they would call me.

Some directors override everything and don't have a clue what they're talking about. They'll over-rule stunt coordinators who know what they're talking about, and that's what I don't like. I was working on a series up in Canada for two years, and some of the directors that came on the show were clueless. There were three or four directors that were great, like John Cassar, who went on to do *24* as an executive producer. I was really happy with his work and that's how I ended up in *24* for a bit.

You've taken a lot of flak from the Asian community about being typecast in certain roles. Do you know what their issue with your roles has been?

I was supposed to work on *Cobra* [1986] with Sylvester Stallone, and some Asian groups complained to the studio about having an Asian bad guy, so they cut me out. They cast me, gave me the part and then I was told the part was cut because the Asian community didn't want a negative image of an Asian person, so I was cut.

Were you looking forward to the role?

I definitely was! I've never gotten the chance to work with Stallone, which I would have loved!

Do you feel there are lots of challenges in Hollywood for Asian actors? Chow Yun-Fat and Jet Li had limited successes, Donnie Yen and Jackie Chan built upon their pre-existing fanbases, but there's a new generation of actors like Daniel Wu that have done well in recent years.

Many successful Asian actors come from China, so that's a whole different situation. A lot more Asians are working now, especially in the last five years. I've seen a lot more on TV shows, but I think we're still getting cast in roles that American audiences are used to seeing us in. However, everyone is desperate for work, so many people just take these roles because they need a job.

Chow Yun-Fat was a great guy to work with. When filming *The Replacement Killers*, we were in downtown Los Angeles, and there were big rats all over the place. We were doing a scene in the alley and I was standing up against the wall and saw this rat coming towards me! The rat decides to walk across my foot, and so I kicked this rat up and it hit the stunt coordinator in the chest! He had no idea and he freaked out!

You're Chinese-American, but you're often cast, in films like *Black Rain* and *Godzilla*, as a Japanese person. Does that sort of lazy casting by Hollywood ever bother you?

It doesn't bother me.

Saying that, one of my favorite roles of yours is in *Bill and Ted's Excellent Adventure*, where you play Genghis Khan. You look like you're having a lot of fun in that role.

Everybody on that film was great fun. Stephen Herek, the director, was fantastic, and so were the crew. It was great fun.

That scene in the mall where you're wearing the sports equipment, chasing people and biting the baseball bats to test their strength, was that all you doing your own stunts?

Not all of it was done by me, but most of it was.

When you were working with Keanu Reeves at the time, did you have any idea he'd go on to be such a big action star?

I thought Alex Winter would be the big star! I thought he'd be really big, but I had no idea that Keanu Reeves would go on to do what he's done. He's doing an incredible job.

Al, I would like to ask you about when you were diagnosed with brain cancer. As someone who leads such an actively lifestyle, what went through your mind when you were told?

It was in 1990, and I walked outside to my car, and I started coughing really bad. I had no idea what it was. I thought it was mosquito spray that they'd just sprayed the whole of Los Angeles with. I thought it was in my lungs and that was what was bothering me. I went to a friend's and he took me to the hospital and, once I was there, they told me I was in the final stages of brain cancer. For over a year I was in and out of hospital with the cancer but once I came out, I fought Brandon Lee in *Rapid Fire*!

The strokes have been worse because I can't work anymore. If I go down, I can't get back up, so that's when I stopped working, and that's what bothered me the most. The strokes were the ones that crippled me and took me out of the business. I cannot do anything anymore and it does really bother me.

Have you made peace with that at all or is it a daily source of frustration?

I don't know if I've made peace with it, but life is great, and I just try to keep moving on. I don't know if there's an explanation, I'm not a religious person at all so you've just got to do what you got to do.

Why did you go straight back to work once the cancer had cleared up? Did you not want to take a break?

During the cancer treatment, I hadn't worked for about a year and a half, so I wanted to do something! I was tired of sitting down and doing nothing.

Of all the henchmen you've played, do you have a particular favorite?

I was happy with *Rapid Fire* and all of John Carpenter's films that I worked on. I like those two the most because, when you go on set, it's often not a choice on what you get to do.

In *Rapid Fire,* you have that final fight with Brandon Lee. What is it like working with him, as he obviously left us far too soon.

Brandon was great. He was incredible. It's so tragic he died so young. Life is so strange. You really don't know what's going to happen.

I was brought onto that film by Jeff Imada. I read for Tzi Ma's role, but they gave me all this dialogue and I couldn't do it! So, they called me back again, and they gave me more dialogue and again I blew it! Then, three weeks later, they call me in again to read even more dialogue, and I couldn't do it! No one told me it was so much dialogue!

I think mine and Tzi Ma's character was originally one character, but once I blew all the dialogue, Tzi Ma came in to do it and then they added my character so I could do the fight work.

You then did *Death Warrant* where you fight Jean-Claude Van Damme in the laundry room. What are your memories of working with him?

Al Leong fights Brandon Lee in *Rapid Fire* (1992). Photo courtesy of Al Leong.

He likes to triple-cut his kicks, which I hate. I don't think he did that with me, but he throws a kick and then they reshow that cut several more times. He's done that in several of his films, where he'll do a jump spin and, in the film, they'll show it three times in a row! I think it's a waste of time and it looks fake.

Originally, Jean-Claude didn't want to fight me. He went, 'I've got this guy in Santa Barbara that I'll fight,' so I went 'Fine.' I'm just a stunt guy, so I didn't care, but Jean-Claude later decided to fight me instead, and the fight was good.

That's weird. Why didn't he want to fight you?

No idea. I'm just a stunt guy. I say just yes or no. I came in, did the fight, and it was fine.

I've heard stories about Van Damme where, sometimes, he doesn't pull his punches with stuntmen. Did you have any problems with that?

I had no problems with him at all. I'll tell you who I've heard stories about and that's Steve Seagal. Over the years, I'd been offered to work on a couple of films with him and I've turned them down. I'd heard from other stunt people that he was difficult.

You worked with pretty much every major action star including Schwarzenegger, Willis, Lundgren, Gibson and The Rock. In your eyes who was the most professional, proficient, and fun to work with?

Brandon Lee was great, but if I'd had problems with anyone, I'd have gone! If things don't work out with the people I work with, I leave, so I always try and get a script so I can see the story. Actors do this. Look at Bruce Willis. A lot of his stories make sense because he knows what's he looking for, but a lot of actors choose money over good stories.

As one of cinema's most infamous henchmen, you've obviously died a lot of times on screen. Do any stand out?

Yeah, yeah, I die all the time! I can't remember one off the top of my head.

For me, it's *Last Action Hero* where you're killed by an ice cream cone.

That was a fun film to work on, but probably not my favorite death scene!

How about getting squibbed? Obviously, you've been shot numerous times in movies, and I've often been curious about what it feels like!

You know, it's not too bad, they pad you up so much it doesn't hurt too much, but I've never had anything that was too painful!

Do you think playing bad guys is more fun?

Nice guys finish last!

Hans Buringer and the Rest

WHILE ANDREAS WISNIEWSKI, Dennis Hayden, Clarence Gilyard Jr., and Al Leong were all actors and veterans of the film industry, many of the young men that made up the rest of Han's team weren't. They were bit-part players, boxers, footballers, and even nutritional experts. Many aren't working in Hollywood today, so it was hard to track them down, but I tried!

Heinrich (played by Gary Roberts): a.k.a the blond, curly-haired terrorist who is carrying the detonators, before McClane shoots him. Despite his all-American name, Gary Roberts is a German actor who hasn't appeared in a film since 1998. Interesting fact, he plays an Australian cop at the end of *Point Break* (1991).

All attempts to track down Gary failed.

Marco (played by Lorenzo Caccialanza): a.k.a the terrorist who McClane shoots through the table (after shooting Heinrich) and chucks out the window to get the attention of Sgt. Al Powell! Caccialanza was formerly a professional Italian football player before he traded sports for acting and moved to the States. There are rumors he dated Jane Fonda in the eighties and still appears in the occasional film.

Unfortunately, I was unable to track Lorenzo down for this book.

Franco (played by Bruno Doyon): a.k.a the terrorist that McClane shoots in the kneecaps before he falls headfirst through a glass window! With only four acting credits to his name, *Die Hard* was Doyon's last on-screen appearance before he disappeared from the silver screen.

I tried to find him. I failed.

Alexander (played by Joey Plewa): a.k.a the terrorist who fires the missile at the LAPD armored vehicle, before McClane drops C4 down the lift shaft, killing him. Plewa followed up *Die Hard* with a role in *Road House* as 'Bandstand Tough Guy' before becoming a music video producer.

I couldn't track him down for a chat.

James (played by Wilhelm von Homburg): a.k.a the terrorist who interrupts the couple who are having sex on the desk, and is later killed by McClane throwing C4 down the lift shaft. Formerly a German boxer and wrestler, Hornburg later turned his hand to acting, and not only appeared in *Die Hard*, but also in *Ghostbusters II* as Vigo the Carpathian!

Unfortunately, I was unable to get an interview with the man who was the scourge of Carpathia and the sorrow of Moldovia, as he died in 2004.

Kristoff (played by Gerald Bonn): a.k.a the terrorist who, other than Theo, was the only terrorist to survive the film, as he was knocked out by McClane while running from the vault with an armful of negotiable bearer bonds.

The French (I'm assuming!) actor hasn't worked since 1993 and couldn't be tracked down.

Fritz (played by Hans Buhringer) With his gorgeous long flowing hair, Fritz stands out amongst Hans' terrorists, and is often seen protecting his boss from any possible threats. Unfortunately, he's killed when Hans' plan to ambush John fails, and Fritz is shot as soon as he steps off the elevator.

Fritz stands out in the film as he discovers Tony's body in the lift and, aside from Karl, appears to be the terrorist who is most trusted by Hans Gruber, until his eventual demise.

Unfortunately, Buhringer was never a professional actor, he was a nutritionist at the time, which immediately led to me wanting to know more. Thanks to social media, I eventually tracked Hans down and asked how he went from practicing nutritional medicine to storming Nakatomi Plaza.

So how does a non-actor, such as yourself, get cast in a 20ᵗʰ Century Fox blockbuster?

Because of my nutritional counselling in Los Angeles, and my celebrity girlfriend at the time (who shall remain nameless), I met Hollywood's most influential figures either privately or through my work. I knew and was friends with producers Larry Gordon and Joel Silver and, during the call-back auditions, I read for the part as one of the bad guys, and I was hired on the spot as Fritz.

Did you have any previous acting experience at all?

Years before I arrived in LA, I pursued a dream I had as a singer and song-writer. In the seventies, I was signed to the United Artists label in Germany, and published two singles. When I arrived in Hollywood, I took acting classes, and some stage training to prepare me, but after a year of no success in the business, I pursued my second passion, which was nutritional science.

I still think I got the part, not just because I knew the producers and spoke German, but also because I gave a good reading in front of the casting director. She was the one that recommended me for a call back audition. Throughout the shoot though, Alan Rickman helped me with some scenes, and was very open to assisting all of us when we asked.

How did John McTiernan feel about his producers putting you in to his film?

John was a technical director, and so he expected the cast to rehearse on their own, and show up on set well prepared. He never really guided the actors, only the scenes.

I assume you also had to go through weapons training along with everyone else? How was that?

The weapons training was cool but intense, partly because, a month earlier, Jon-Erik Hexum accidentally shot himself on the set of *Cover Up* (1984-1985). What a shock. He was a real nice guy, and we knew each other from celebrity tennis tournaments.

As Fritz, you share most of your scenes with Alan Rickman and Alexander Gudonov. What are your memories of working with the two of them?

I already knew Alexander quite well, before we got on the set, because his girlfriend, Jacqueline Bisset, was a good friend of my girlfriend, and we enjoyed many parties and dinners together. We would play chess in between scenes, and he was a formidable player.

You are not the first person to tell me that!

By the time principle photography was over, our scores were equal, but we never played again. Soon after, I met my first wife, got married, and moved to my ranch in Santa Barbara, and we had a daughter. When I heard of his passing I was very saddened and surprised.

Alan and I met several times after we wrapped in LA, London, and Cannes during the film festivals. He was a very nice and conscious man with sincere and deep values that are generally not seen in Hollywood, or among film stars. When he passed, I mourned his loss. I didn't know he was battling for his health, because I had lost contact with him, like many of the others, save Dennis Hayden.

What made you and Dennis bond on set?

Dennis and I both had our children at the same time. He visited me on the ranch, and whenever I came to Los Angeles, we'd see each other. He has been a very good friend for all those years. Andreas Wisniewski and I met in London once, and drank single malt scotches while reminiscing over the past. We kept in contact for some time after.

There is a story that you didn't shoot your own death scene and, as such, you never died on screen. How did that happen?

It was very late that night, and we were already on triple time according to the Screen Actors Guild's rules, so they decided to use an experienced stuntman for my death scene.

After the success of *Die Hard*, were you tempted to pursue a career in acting?

I had many readings, some for good or leading roles, but I didn't get them, or the project was shelved. The ones I was offered, I did not see a future in, and turned them down.

Later I wrote a screenplay that got good feedback, but I could not procure financing, especially with me in the starring role, so I simply let it go! I was fortunate that I was financially independent, and I realized early enough that the U.S. was no country for old men, especially in Hollywood. Most of the cast got a good start from *Die Hard*, they worked hard to get where they are now, but some got lost in Hollywood, like so many souls before them.

When was the last time you saw *Die Hard*? Are you surprised at how the film has endured over the years?

The one and only time I saw the film was the studio premier at the AMC theatres on Wilshire Blvd. I was initially surprised it was so successful, but very pleased as it pays out so much in royalties, year after year!

And now you're an artisan baker?

From the start, I missed good European breads in California. When my Austrian friend, Wolfgang Puck of Spargo, brought in a pastry chef, to teach his chefs artisan baking, I learned the basics and, once I moved back to Austria, I refined the craft by using 100% whole grain flower and homemade sourdough. Now I'm remarried to a wonderful woman, and we've just had a son. I still research longevity medicine and nutrition, as well as practicing spiritual awakening, baking bread, and enjoying the present moment.

The Outsiders

WHILE MOST VILLAINS have a team, there are others that prefer to work alone; the psychopaths, the serial killers, the bounty hunters, and, in some cases, the bureaucrats.

While Hollywood was looking at body builders and martial arts experts to physically intimidate their heroes, there was plenty of work for established stage and character actors to be a more intellectual obstacle.

Whatever they lacked in size, these characters often more than made up for in unpredictability, and a certain level of perversity. After all, why punch the hero when you can terrify them, stalk their family, or threaten to close down their whole operation?

Never knowing what these characters would do next made these actors so fascinating to watch. More often than not, their years of theatre experience gave them a whole arsenal of skill sets to unleash on the audience, whether it was a simple nod, or casual sneer.

Today, many are still working in the theatre, on screen or, in some cases, teaching, so it was wonderful to speak to all of them about the roles that transformed their career for the better, and, in some cases, for the worse.

David Patrick Kelly

"WARRIORS! Come out to plaaaaaaay!"
– Luther, The Warriors (1979).

David Patrick Kelly – Select Filmography

- *The Warriors* (1979) – Luther
- *48 Hrs.* (1982) – Luther
- *Dreamscape* (1984) – Tommy Ray Glatman
- *Commando* (1985) – Sully
- *Twin Peaks* (1990-1991) – Jerry Horne
- *Malcolm X* (1992) – Mr. Ostrowski
- *The Crow* (1994) – T-Bird
- *Last Man Standing* (1996) – Doyle
- *John Wick* (2014) - Charlie

> *The Warriors have spent the night evading rival gangs after being framed for the murder of Cyrus, the leader of the Gramercy Riffs. Waiting for them on their home turf of Coney Island are The Rogues, led by the psychotic Luther, who was the one that actually killed Cyrus, because he 'likes doing things like that.'*

DAVID PATRICK KELLY IS ONE OF THOSE ACTORS that disappears into his roles. For years, I knew him primarily as Sully from *Commando*, and Luther in *The Warriors*, but it was only relatively recently that it clicked that he was also T-Bird in *The Crow*.

David Patrick Kelly plays the evil Luther in *The Warriors* (1979).
Photo courtesy of Paramount Pictures.

A chameleonic actor, David is perhaps best known for playing the murderous Luther in Walter Hill's *The Warriors*, where his gang, The Rogues, frame their rivals for murder, and pursue them across New York City. Famously, he improvised his sadistic, taunting cry that many remember from the end of the film but, it has always seemed to me, that he never quite escaped the shadow of that first iconic role.

In person, David is unbelievably warm, charming and well-read, seemingly an expert on everything from psychology to art, he is best known for playing sadistic and evil men, and it was this very typecasting that I was eager to talk to him about – as well as what it's like to be dangled upside down by Arnold Schwarzenegger. I spoke to David for over two hours, discussing everything and anything. He's a wonderful man to talk to, plus he pronounced my name correctly, straight off the bat. Knowing he was a fan of Shakespeare's *Timon of Athens*, I expected nothing less.

Speaking via Skype, he was immediately struck by a map hanging in my office. Glimpsing it from behind my head, he asked what is was....

It's a map of Middle Earth. My wife is a big *Lord of the Rings* fan.

I've only read *The Hobbit* [1937], though I should say, I only stopped at the first of the movies. I'm not a big sequel fellow. *The Hobbit* was very informative back in the sixties, when I was in high school. I was in-charge of our – in high school, our dance, and we called our junior high school dance, Eventide at Mirkwood!

I notice, these days, you seem to be more into your music than acting. Was music something that you were always into, or was it an equal love between the two?

It's always been parallel. My mother gave me a mandolin on St. Patrick's Day in 1964, my name day, and so music has always been a part of my life. It's such a blessing for me, because I wanted to go to Juilliard in Yale. I ended up not going there when I finished my undergraduate college at the University of Detroit. I came here to New York and I couldn't go to those schools, but CBGB (a New York music club) was happening right then, in the seventies, and I played and played and played.

Magically, my graduate school was a club called Max's Kansas City. This was an amazing club and was the major showcase for anybody with a single or a record, so I saw an incredible and unbelievable list of musicians. It was just the best graduate school ever. I saw Bruce Springsteen, who, at that time, had one record out, and opening for him was a little band from Jamaica called The Wailers.

As in Bob Marley and The Wailers?

Yes, Bob Marley and the original line-up. Nobody had heard of them in the early seventies. Then there was the Charles Mingus Quartet, Billy Joel – but it was also the beginnings of the punk movement. It was 1974 and Patti Smith, The New York Dolls, and The Ramones were playing there. Downstairs was a restaurant where all the artists, like Andy Warhol, and all the movie stars would go. Anybody uncool was not allowed in there. Debbie Harry worked as a waitress down there!

If you were so into music, how did you get into acting?

I came up in the late sixties, being inspired by Peter Brook, and being inspired by Grotowski's physical theatre and circus techniques. Everybody in my generation wanted to go to circus school. Musical theatre was happening, but I am not a musical guy, I'm a physical theatre guy.

When I got to college, the experimental film scene just exploded. I got into all the experimentalists like Jordan Belson and Kenneth Anger. I was constantly investigating film and got into the classics like Kurosawa and Bergman. I then got deep into Chaplin and the silent comics. I was fascinated with what could be communicated with no words at all, and how the idea of the gesture was so important. So, my passion for film, music, literature, and theatre always ran parallel.

With all those influences, what did you aim to bring to the character of Luther in *The Warriors*? Did Walter Hill give you any guidance on that? As it was your first role I can only imagine that the whole experience was quite intimidating?

I'd made little movies in high school, so I was familiar with some of the language, but it's quite a different thing when they've got all the big toys! However, none of us were paid very much, and we all dressed in one tiny trailer, and then we were on our feet for twelve hours. We were really out there.

Walter had come to see me in this play on Broadway with Joel Silver and Lawrence Gordon. He saw me play guitar and sing James Taylor songs. Then he saw me do this incredible monolog from Studs Terkel's book *Working* [1974]. On the surface, he is a sweet, hippie, copy boy who works at a newspaper, but he is, in fact, seething with rage, at all his employers, his own frustrations, and his own inability to get anywhere in his life. It was really funny and great material, and that's what he saw. When I went to the meeting for *The Warriors*, I think that they were originally thinking of me for one of the Warriors, but I'd grown my hair quite long which, in 1977, was not cool. 1977 was punk! It was chopped hair or John Travolta disco hair. I looked so different, and something in this monologue said to them that I was in the spirit of the movie, and they cast me as Luther, which was a great blessing.

How did you prepare for the film before shooting started?

Walter mentioned *Richard III* as an inspiration. He was like a football coach in many ways. He loves football, and he said we had to have stamina because it was going to be a long shoot. It turned out to be much longer than they planned, because they lost some footage, and it was a difficult shoot in many ways. Walter told me how to pace and take care of myself, because I had only a few scenes, but they really meant something. Everything that was in the script that they'd written was there,

Luther (David Patrick Kelly) leads rival gang The Rogues in *The Warriors* (1979). Photo courtesy of Paramount Pictures.

except for the additional 'Come out to play' scene, which we just added on the day.

Walter was very clear about what he needed. He was quite choreographed, which I was used to from Avant-garde theatre. You bring your own self to it from the inside out when you're constructing the character.

The Warriors is a pretty extreme film, from the concept to the violence to the outfits. Even our heroes aren't the nicest of characters. With Luther, did you feel you could take the character right to the edge in terms of what might be acceptable, or did Walter have to rein you in? Or did he encourage you to push it even further?

I think it was both, but he was really hands off. There were a couple [of] directions where he told me to do less, but I don't recall him ever saying to do more, because we just went for it.

It was really important to me to find my own voice, to find something unique, because that was a big part of actor work then – to stay within yourself. When we did the 'Come out to play' scene, the sound of it was a combination of so many different things. There was nothing in the script, Walter just said, 'I need you to make something up. We want to make more of a moment of it.' I said, 'What am I supposed to say?' He said, 'Would you sing him something?'

I thought it's not going to be a lyrical thing, so it's got to be something different. At the time, I had a neighbor who lived next to me, he was an unusual guy, and I would say to him, 'Hello, Rich, how's everything?' And he would say, 'Dave . . . Daaaave . . . DAAAAAAAAVE,' and that's it.

Well, that's creepy.

Yes. It was one of the creepiest things I'd heard, so I just added that in, but put a lot more behind it.

Obviously, fans of *The Warriors* know that you ad-libbed that chant, but I read an interview with Walter where he said the first option you came to him with involved two dead pigeons.

That's true. He wanted me to make something up, so I searched around for something to make a gesture that silent comedians would make. At the time, I saw these dead pigeons and I said, 'Well, that's sort of symbolic.'

The pigeons in Coney Island were poisoned as they were seen as a nuisance. I thought that could be something, but Walter didn't like it. Then I came up with these tiny beer bottles that they used to make. We found three of them and we just did it. I think it works because it rattles the palette of the movie. It was beautifully orchestrated by Walter, but I was surprised that they kept it in to be honest! We filmed the scene twice, and that was it.

People have asked me many times over the years to do it again for various things and I never have because you want to keep the performance in context. When *The Warriors* first came out and it was number one, having that energy come back at me was quite scary. I'd go into bars and people would want to fight me because it tweaked them. I never wanted to have a catchphrase, but I'm very grateful that people remember it. It's always been a blessing and, over the years, it's become an amusing thing for people to do. I really appreciate people remembering it.

Where you surprised at both the positive and the negative reaction to *The Warriors*, as the violence drew a lot of criticism?

In the seventies, there were Roger Corman movies where you'd see Bruce Dern as a Hell's Angel, or actors like Jack Nicholson in small parts, but they were 'Grindhouse movies', as Quentin Tarantino would call them.

That's what I thought *The Warriors* was, and I was happy about that as I love those movies. But then it debuted at number one.

The cult around the film began that first week, as did the controversy about the violence, and I was very sad about that. However, Pauline Kael, one of my favorite critics, wrote an amazing review of the film, and it meant so much to me. I'd read her books, *Bang Bang Kiss Kiss* [sic, *Kiss Kiss Bang Bang*, 1968] and *I Lost It at The Movies* [1965], in high school, and when I saw her review in *The New Yorker*, it was just thrilling. I actually didn't see *The Warriors* for years.

Really?!

I saw the rough cut. They asked us all to come and see that, but I did not go to see it for many, many years. Finally, when I saw how Walter Hill directed it, and how it was orchestrated, and everything came together, it was thrilling. I saw what Pauline Kael was talking about it, when she compared it to *Rock Around the Clock* [1956] and those kind of teen movies.

Are you surprised that the film still has a massive cult following? The film has a devoted army of fans and, in 2017, there was a big conclave in Birmingham (UK) featuring a cast reunion, which you opted not to attend. Do you ever go to any of these types of conventions?

David Patrick Kelly doesn't pull any punches in his first film role in *The Warriors* (1979). Photo courtesy of Paramount Pictures.

No, I never have. Like Eli Wallach, I'm of the generation where you do your work and that's enough. Many of my friends do it, and they make good cash, but it's a lot of work to stand there and say the same thing over and over. It kind of diminishes it in a way, for me. I like to leave it with the work and not try to change it into anything else. I'm happy when people show up at other things I do, but some people come with suitcases full of stuff and say, 'Can you sign this?' I simply say, 'I'm sorry, I don't want to do that, but I'll give you one. That's it.'

I think that's fair enough! You've had several other collaborations with Walter Hill, such as playing Doyle in *Last Man Standing*, and another character called Luther in *48 Hrs.*, which I'm going to assume is a coincidence, unless that was like an in-joke between you and Walter?

I never thought of it as the same character. It was quite a different situation. I think it was just a nice thing Walter did as a kind of tip of the hat, because [of] the reaction of our first film.

It was wonderful to come to San Francisco again, with Walter and James Remar. There was a great jazz saxophonist named Art Pepper, who had a rough and tumble autobiography called *The Straight Life* [1979]. Remar shared that with me and I shared Malcolm Braly's prison novels with him. We're living there at the Chateau Marmont during the making of *48 Hrs*. It was quite a thrill.

When I last re-watched the film, I was surprised at how brutal Nick Nolte appears to be with you in your scenes together. He appears to be really going for it when he's slamming you against the car. What was it like filming that scene, as I hear Nick Nolte really gets into his roles?

[laughs] I think Walter assumed I could take it because I pushed my dear friend Joel Weiss around quite a bit in *The Warriors*. He said, 'Okay, your turn!'

Nolte is a big guy who played football, but I could take it. I have to confess, I did not fly over the car. That was a wonderful stuntman whose name I can't recall. I did land there and, as Nolte was wearing cowboy boots, I had an imprint of a cowboy boot on my chest for about a week and a half! He was punching me around – I think a little blood came out of my nose at one point.

I think it really motivated my lines for that scene, as we were improvising a lot. It was Eddie Murphy's first movie and, when he saw the fighting going on, he said, 'Oh my God. This is how you guys do this stuff?' And I said, 'Yes, that's how we do it!'

The stunts in *The Warriors* were stylized but, in *48 Hrs.*, we were keeping it as real as possible. I had a great time in that, and I was really touched when people would come up to me and say, 'We were so moved by the relationship between you and Rosalie.'

You never actually find out what happens to Rosalie in the film. I think her fate is left unclear, but it's assumed that Ganz (Remar) kills her?

Yes, I think so. Or she was left to run away. Somebody noted that the cool part of *48 Hrs.* is the contentiousness of the men and the women in it. You see that in Nolte's relationship, with Jonathan Banks complaining about his wife, the horrible relationship Remar has with the poor girls, and then you see Rosalie and I arguing about buying furniture before she's kidnapped. Maybe it's an idea for a sequel? I don't know, I'm not a big sequel guy as I said.

Well, you didn't crop up in *Another 48 Hours* so I'm going to assume Walter considered your character dead! With the success of *The Warriors*, and as it was your first big role, did you find producers thought of you as being perfect for creepy villain-type roles, like Tommy Glatman in *Dreamscape*? Was it something you embraced, or actively resisted?

I came up in musicals and things like that, so I had never done violent, scary characters before. You never think about your character being good or bad. You think about the story as a total.

I was in the midst of critiquing the dominance of method acting in the seventies, and this gave me an opportunity that I never really expected. I was rebelling against it, because I thought it subverted the story to the personality and the psychology of particular actors. This is real 'Actor Studio' stuff, but I think at its worst, it can affect the larger story and the poetics. I was rebelling against that, and they say you should never judge your character, but I judged Luther. Walter had mentioned *Richard III*, so I made him evil, and chose the things that were creepy and evil to me.

I've never felt typecast and, over these years, I've played in so many different genres. I've done war movies, I've played Harry Truman in *Flags of our Fathers* [2006] and done films like *K-Pax* [2001]. I never really worried about typecasting. I still don't to this day. I've had a really blessed career on the stage where I played some amazing things. Speaking of villains, it was only seven or eight years ago where I finally got to play Iago [in *Othello*].

You said you judged Luther, but characters like him and T-Bird are out-and-out evil. How about more morally ambiguous characters? Do you ever try and relate to them at all?

I'm a nice Catholic boy from Detroit, Michigan, so I think people were shocked when I started doing these kinds of parts. I think I was well-prepared for trying to look at evil and what it means in the world.

You try to do good acting no matter what kind of style you do, and so you must bring your own emotions to it, and your own expressiveness to it. I was trying to do a particular style with Luther. A more theatrical kind of style. When playing T-Bird, the style was quite external. You always have to find the parts that you identify with, but a good part will open up an avenue of research for you.

With Luther, I read so many different things. I'd read Hubert Selby's *Last Exit to Brooklyn*. Being from Detroit, I had to research New York. Part of my research was of a wonderful French photographer who came in the sixties to New York, named Martine Barrett. She lived in Harlem for years, and she's photographed boxers and gangs like The Latin Kings and The Roman Kings, so that was a big influence.

The world that I lived in, down lower in Manhattan, was rife with gangs. Luther's a combination of some of the kind of gangster people that were involved in the rock and roll business that I was meeting. There was a band called the New York Dolls, and their guitar player was a guy named Johnny Thunders. The way he talked and the way he moved was a big influence on Luther as well. These are the observational things that, as an actor, you can combine and change when you do your homework.

Obviously, you worked with Joel Silver on *The Warriors*. Was he the reason you got cast in *Commando*, or did you audition for that?

No, I never had to audition again after *The Warriors*. I had to go two or three times for *The Warriors* I think, until they decided to make me Luther. After that, *48 Hrs.* and *Commando* were all just offers. The producers, Lawrence Gordon and Joel Silver, offered the role of Sully to me and it was great. Really fun. Arnold is a very nice, humble guy, believe it or not. We had a wonderful time working on that film. Rae Dawn Chong was so beautiful, and charming. I didn't meet Alyssa Milano really, but Charles Smith, who played Enriquez, my buddy at the airport, he was an actual Vietnam veteran.

The day we were at LAX putting Arnold on the plane, they finally had a parade for the Vietnam veterans. This was 1984, and it had taken them that long to finally have a parade to welcome home the veterans of that war. Charles was really moved by that, so I always remember that from making that movie. Other things too, like when Arnold helped me over the cliff at the Griffith Observatory!

Is he actually holding you then? I'm mean, he's a big guy, so was he picking you up and dangling you by your leg?

I'm sorry to spoil this for you Timon, but no he wasn't! It was a cable that went up my leg. I had a lot of blood vessels going crazy in my head, because we were up there for a while. It was fascinating because we filmed it at the Griffith Observatory, which was the iconic place where James Dean had the fight in *Rebel Without a Cause* [1955]. I was also working with one of the late, great stunt guys, Bennie Dobbins. He had a leather tool belt, that had his name on it, and it went under my trousers, and was attached to the cable.

David Patrick Kelly as the slimy Sully in *Commando* (1985).
Photo courtesy of 20th Century Fox.

Bennie told me the stories about when he was playing Native Americans in fifties Westerns. They did this technique where they'd shoot you, and you would have to fall off the horse, but they wanted to make it look real, so they did this method called 'the one-legged jerk off'. They would pull him, and he'd fly off. I was honored to wear his belt. But, *Commando* was memorable for that, and even though I'm only in it for a little while.

Everyone remembers Sully, not just because of Arnie's final line to you, but because the character really stands out, for many reasons. One of them is that he's incredibly sexually aggressive to Rae Dawn Chong. As soon as she spurns Sully's advances, he takes it very personally.

Yes. I'm not quite sure where that came from. I just thought it would be another thing to add so that people want to see him gone. In terms of stuff that was in the news at that time, when Sully is in the restaurant, he's buying doctored passports. It really gives you the creeps about what's possible. In fact, Steven E. de Souza, who wrote that movie, was called into a commission to give possible scenarios for what could possibly happen in the future, after 9/11.

When I was playing Sully, it was a fascinating peak into the mercenaries of the world, which is a big story. The big book I read when researching Sully was by Christopher Dickey. His father, James Dickey, wrote *Deliverance* [1970] and was poet-laureate of the United States under President Carter. Christopher Dickey, his son, became an investigative journalist and, during the eighties, he lived with the Contras for a long time in Nicaragua. His book, *With the Contras* [1985], is all about CIA involvement in counter-revolutionary activities. With the Freedom of Information Act, I got a book about the CIA's manual of counter-revolutionary activity in Central and South America, and I gave that to Joel Silver. It's all about how to neutralize leaders within revolutions. Sully was part of that international mercenary army, that you now have with (private security contractors) Blackwater. I have two or three books on my shelves about these private armies where former military personnel go out and create policy for whoever pays their bills.

Is that what attracts you to roles - the level of research that you're able to do, or is there something else that gets you excited about a project?

I'd always loved directors like [Martin] Scorsese, who really bring a sense of their own home to their films. One of the reasons I did *The Crow*, even though it was a fantasy, was it was set in Detroit, which is my hometown. Many of the elements I was totally familiar with, such as Devil's Night. You know what Devil's Night is?

I know what it is because of *The Crow*, but it's not really something that happens here in the UK, so my entire knowledge of it is *Crow*-based.

[laughs] Devil's Night is a real thing and it still goes on. It's the night before Halloween, when you go out and you play tricks. You can put toilet paper around people's trees, throw eggs at houses, things like that. In Detroit, it took a particularly over-the-top turn as people would set whole neighborhoods on fire. We go every year.

You must be greeted like a local celebrity because of the film?

People treat me very well there, but I don't go specifically for Devil's Night. We go to visit family and hang out. My wife said that Detroit is a lot like Berlin now. It's become a big art and high-tech community, and the music of course is still rolling there. It's a great place.

***The Crow* is a film that Hollywood is constantly trying to reboot, but because of its troubled production, and the shadow that looms over it from Brandon Lee's death, it's one of those films that should probably be left alone. What are your thoughts about it these days?**

It was a tragedy. Really shocking, and it ruined some people's lives, but we decided to finish it for Brandon's sake. In fact, Chad Stahelski, who later directed me in *John Wick*, was the double for Brandon. In the few moments that we had to film when Brandon wasn't there, that's Chad Stahelski standing in.

They had a couple of close-ups of Brandon that they used and then they just used Chad in the shadows. Brandon was just a wonderful guy, he was really gifted, and so generous, and I'll never forget all those days, coming up to him the first time and saying, 'Your father was a big influence on me,' and he said, 'Me too!' I was going for my first black belt, as I started karate at an advanced stage, but Brandon would always offer to train with me.

It was all so heartbreaking. We, and Eliza, his fiancé, wanted to finish the film for him. Everybody was so devastated by it. I have to say that my faith really helped me, and helped me to reach out to people who were suffering. The day that Brandon passed, we stayed up all night at the hospital with him, and nobody knew what would happen. I went to a church at 6:00 a.m., which had always been locked before, but that time it was open. I went in and there was this beautiful light coming in through the glass, and there was this amazing paradox of the inconsolable, and the consolation of God, and that carried me through that horrible tragedy.

What made you accept the role of T-Bird in the film in the first place, because he is not a pleasant character?

James O'Barr's script was the reason I wanted to do it in the beginning. To be frank, I wasn't a graphic novel fan, but there was so much emotion in the original book. When I read it, and found out that it was based on his tragic loss of his girlfriend I said, 'There's something here and I'd like to be involved.'

It was such a bizarre and unusual story. Despite the rather low budget, it was one of those films which saw people come together at a certain point in their careers. Graeme Revell did this amazing score, Dariusz Wolski was a great cinematographer, and my crew included the late great Michael Massee (Funboy), who recently passed away.

It was really a rewarding experience, being able to give a little bit of advice to [director] Alex Proyas about Detroit. For example, there's a moment where T-Bird comes in and talks about Lake Huron being set on fire. I brought that line in because I'd read about how it was so polluted at one point, that it actually caught on fire. I hope I don't sound too immodest about the film, but it became for that generation a kind of *Rebel Without A Cause*. I'm very proud of it, and would prefer that Brandon was here, but we finished it for him.

It's a film that I adore and, despite watching it from the age of fifteen, it was only a few years ago that I realized it was you playing T-Bird. I knew you primarily from *The Warriors* and *Commando*, and I think it was the scene where you were stubbing the cigar out on your tongue when it finally clicked. I'm going to assume that cigar was fake?

It was real, but we put it out before I did it, just faked it.

I have to ask about *Dreamscape*, which we mentioned earlier, because, as concepts go, that one is pretty out there – you play a man who is trying to kill the President within his dreams.

I love *Dreamscape*. I grew up as a huge fan of Ray Harryhausen, and when I saw *The 7th Voyage of Sinbad* [1958], and the skeleton fight in *Jason and the Argonauts* [1963], I coined a phrase called 'cinemetampsychosis'. It's that feeling you get, or you used to get, where you're in a movie theatre, and suddenly it's like the character comes over you. Ray Harryhausen's effects did that to me!

We had this wonderful process where my character [Tommy Glatman] becomes a Snakeman, so they put me in a body cast, and then they sculpted the transformation of Tommy. This was another role where I got to be theatrical. I love the scene where Eddie Albert's president sees me as I'm halfway into becoming the Snakeman, and you can still see my face. It's kind of like Kabuki acting, in a way. It's wonderful what I was allowed to do, and it was another genre for me. For the film, I went to Princeton to a psychic research facility and they gave this personality test to see if I could potentially move things with my mind.

Could you?

They wouldn't reveal their findings to me.

David Patrick Kelly as Tommy Glatman, the dream assassin in *Dreamscape* (1984).
Photo courtesy of 20th Century Fox.

That seems very one sided.

[laughs] I know, but I liked doing the test. It must've been before *Ghostbusters*, because Dan Ackroyd had joined The American Society for Psychic Research. It was a wonderful library just across Central Park, and I joined that as well. They had a lot of wonderful material over there to look through. I also went to Bellevue Hospital and hung out in the prison ward. Do you know what Bellevue is?

Again, the American pop culture influence means that I vaguely know what Bellevue is. It's essentially a prison for the criminally insane, isn't it?

Well, if they think you're nuts they say, 'Send them to Bellevue'.

***Dreamscape* is one of those rare films where you're front and center as the main protagonist, but I'm guessing it's not the role you're best known for? Would I be right in thinking it's between Luther or *Twin Peaks*'s Jerry Horne?**

It's still Luther. That role has got me so much, but T-Bird is also a big one for people too. A few years [ago], I was at this vegan restaurant in Harvard, and there was this giant tattooed kid in the kitchen. He came out and said, 'You were in my favorite film.' I said, 'Oh, what was that?' He said, '*The Adventures of Ford Fairlane*' [1990]. I said, 'Wow, that's a first!' But that film actually got me into *Twin Peaks*.

I played a character called Sam the Sleazebag. Dice Clay was, of course, Ford Fairlane, the rock 'n' roll detective. While researching that, I hung out with the autograph hounds at NBC and met an artiste from Athens, Georgia named Joni Mabe. Joni is a wonderful painter, and did a show where she made suitcase shrines to all the Country-Western stars. They'd open up and there would be all this paraphernalia from the different stars. I thought Sam the Sleazebag should have a suitcase shrine to the girls that he's stalking, so I called up Joni, commissioned her, and she made me this bizarre suitcase. It was a blue and pink suitcase and, when you opened it up, there were all these twinkling lights and paraphernalia of women in there. It was so bizarre. When I got a meeting to go to meet David Lynch, I took the suitcase and showed him. After that, he wrote me into *Wild at Heart* [1990], and then later into *Twin Peaks*.

In regard to Jerry Horne in *Twin Peaks*, what is a smoked cheese pig?

[chuckles] There used to be a wonderful gourmet market down in the village called Balducci's. They had so many different items. One of them was an Italian smoked pig. I said, 'I'm going to take this,' and it survived the flight to Los Angeles, and we used it in the scene.

Were you excited to come back for the revival?

Yes, and it was really a blast. It was really something. It's sort of the fulfillment of Jerry's vector in life. Jerry Horne was inspired, in my mind, by The Kennedys. I'm a Kennedy Democrat, and my father took my brother and I to see Bobby Kennedy speak when he was running for President in downtown Detroit.

It was amazing, but Jerry Horne was based on everything bad you've ever read about the Kennedy brothers. All the rumors and conspiracy theories – that's what I put into Jerry Horne and Ben Horne.

Do you feel characters like that are more fun to play than clean cut heroes?

I've played good guys on stage, and had some great parts in relatively few films. I see people with 150 films and, for a few of my films to be remembered, appreciated, and respected, is a wonderful feeling. It just is about the poetics.

I've always been a fan of one shot wonders, the great character actors who bring that one scene and make it pop, and make the whole thing have importance and balance, like Eli Wallach and Peter Lorre. It's just wonderful that you can contribute something that means so much to folks in the larger context of this story. The great thing about villains is they make you ask what would you do to defeat them, and they implicate you in their passion. They make you think about 'There but for the grace of God go I', and that's what usual about them.

Andrew Robinson

"Don't pass out on me yet, you dirty, rotten oinker! Do we understand each other? If you want to know where the girl is. Okay? Now listen... I've changed my mind. I'm going to let her die! I just wanted you to know that. You hear me? I just wanted you to know that before I killed you!"

– Scorpio, *Dirty Harry* (1971).

Andrew Robinson – Select Filmography

- *Dirty Harry* (1971) – The (Scorpio) Killer
- *Cobra* (1986) – Detective Monte
- *Hellraiser* (1987) – Larry
- *Shoot to Kill* (1988) – Harvey
- *Trancers III* (1992) – Col. Daddy Muthuh
- *Star Trek: Deep Space Nine* (1993-1999) – Elim Garak

A killer is on the loose in San Francisco. Calling himself Scorpio, the killer has been shooting people using a sniper rifle, but has moved onto kidnapping. With a teenage girl missing, rogue cop Harry Callahan (Clint Eastwood) is determined to do everything he can to find her and bring the killer to justice.

FOR YEARS, I ONLY KNEW Andrew Robinson as Garak *in Star Trek: Deep Space Nine*. As an avid *Star Trek* fan, his portrayal of the morally-ambiguous and mysterious Cardassian spy-turned-tailor was one of the

Andrew Robinson as the killer Scorpio in *Dirty Harry* (1971).
Photo courtesy of Warner Brothers.

best things in the show, equally at home trading witty barbs with the righteous Starfleet crew members, or killing Romulan ambassadors in the name of the greater good.

It was astonishing to me, when I first saw *Dirty Harry*, that the vile killer Scorpio was played by the same actor. Sure, Garak was a killer, but he was a delightful one! Scorpio was pure malice and evil, someone you were happy to see Harry Callahan blow away with his trademark .44 Magnum by the end of the film.

Of course, playing such an unlikeable character inevitably influenced Andrew's career. For years, Andrew received death threats from weirdos unable to separate movies from reality, and was typecast by the industry as psychopaths. In fact, in the Sidney Poitier thriller *Shoot to Kill*, he was cast alongside other notable 'bad guy' actors (Clancy Brown (*Highlander*, 1986), Frederick Coffin (*Mother's Day*, 1980) and Richard Masur (*Who'll Stop the Rain*, 1978), so the audience wouldn't know who the real killer was.

Today, Andrew is a Professor of Theatre Practice in Acting at the University of Southern California's School of Dramatic Arts. When we met, he was in London for the Film and TV Comic Con, where thousands of fans were eager to meet the actor they know from *Star Trek: Deep Space Nine*, *Hellraiser*, and so many other classic genre movies.

You're about to be besieged by hundreds of adoring fans that know you from a multitude of projects that you've done. What's the character that most fans associate you with?

It would be Garak, but then, in England, *Dirty Harry* was enormously successful. I should also say *Hellraiser* because, over the years, different generations have come through and discovered that film. So, it's a tie between those three!

At the time you made *Dirty Harry*, the Zodiac killings [upon which the film was based] were still very prominent in San Francisco, and no-one knew who was behind them. How did you go about portraying a killer that was based on someone real, yet who was still at large and that no-one knew anything about?

I always try to come up with some backstory for my characters, and for the Scorpio Killer I got it from the costume that they gave me. They gave me a belt with a peace sign buckle and paratrooper boots. They were the same kind of boots that my father wore in World War II when he was a paratrooper, and so I basically came up with the backstory that he had been in Vietnam and the war had driven him crazy, and he had come back this deranged person.

For someone so evil, you obviously had fun with the role. You ad-lib a lot of lines, such as when you take out his gun and go 'That's a big one', or when you go, 'Hubba Hubba' . . . .

'. . . Fascist Pig!' [laughs]

Exactly! Was Clint ok with your ad-libbing, as he's known as being very methodical as a director and does very few takes? Was there a clash of styles at all?

No, not at all. I hate doing a lot of takes too, and being from the theatre, I don't need a lot of them. Once I know what I'm doing, I love just doing it. As I say, 'Hitting it and quitting it!'

I think the great contrasts between Clint and myself were the temperaments, and who we are as people. He really is a very contained man: very professional, and doesn't have a lot to say, unless you're a good-looking woman, and I wasn't! It's also the way that the characters were written. Don

Siegel [director of *Dirty Harry*] let me develop the character, because I would come up with ideas or bits of action, and he just went with it. When he found out that one of my theatrical backgrounds was physical theatre, he would set up shots where I would be on the move, such as sliding down a banister.

You go all out with Scorpio and play him as being completely unhinged, like when he's yelling, and slapping the children on the bus. When you're playing a character like that, do you think it's scarier when they're more of a loose cannon, or when that menace is bubbling just under the surface?

Honestly, that performance surprises me, because it had every pitfall that you can imagine. It would have been so easy, especially in those moments you've mentioned, when he's going off the deep end, for it to become operatic and over the top, but it didn't, and I'm eternally grateful for that.

I think it's because I did plug into something, into my own rage, and stayed true to that, so that it never became theatrical. If you take a character like Garak, I tried to stay true to what the core was. Garak, unlike Scorpio, was all about the internal, working from a subtext, and keeping that containment of the character within.

Harry Callahan (Clint Eastwood) comes face to face with Andrew Robinson's Scorpio killer in *Dirty Harry* (1971). Photo courtesy of Warner Brothers.

The thing that makes Scorpio terrifying is that, because he's so angry and full of rage, you never know what he's going to do next. It clearly hit a nerve with audience members as, when the film came out, it was a big hit, but you personally received death threats. What was their major grievance with you, and how did you feel about it?

They were just insane people and, for whatever reason, I became a source of their rage. It freaked me out so much. I had to have my telephone number unlisted.

It's a bizarre testament to you, obviously doing a great job of portraying a psychopath! After the film, did you feel that the film's success was a boost to your acting career, or got you pigeonholed into those more sinister roles such as in *Child's Play 3* (1991)?

Well, it gave me a film career, but it took it away at the same time. A woman, who was the Head of Casting at Warner Brothers, admitted to me years later that I had an appointment to meet with her shortly after *Dirty Harry* came out. She was looking out her window, and she saw me coming down the path to her office, and she said to her assistant, 'Who's that?' She said, 'That's Andy Robinson, that's your next appointment,' and she said, 'Cancel it, I can't meet with him.'

Because you terrified her?

Exactly, and I guess she thought, 'What the hell is this guy like, that played that character?'

Your portrayal of Scorpio was so disturbing that people wouldn't want to cast you because you disturbed them too much? I would have thought you'd be getting roles for precisely that reason.

I think it was both.

You did too good of a job!

[laughs] The thing about playing someone who's insane, is that you have to go to that place. Sometimes the people who are sitting in the theatre, whether it's a film or a live production, know the difference. Even if they

are untutored, if they have not been educated in terms of what acting is about and so forth, people should be able to tell the difference.

Is it fair to say that, for many studios, you were an actor that was only good for playing villains? For example, in *Shoot to Kill* (or *Deadly Pursuit*, as it's called in the UK), you were cast alongside several actors who were also known for playing bad guys, so the audience wouldn't be sure who the real killer was. Was that frustrating for you, or had you accepted the route your career was going down at that point?

I did get really upset about how I was received and perceived, because I was a trained actor. I went to drama school, and I worked on stage for several years before I did *Dirty Harry*, and so to be perceived like that was very confusing to me, and was very upsetting.

By the time I did *Shoot to Kill* I was fine with it. I got to the Canadian Rockies, it was several weeks of being in a beautiful place, they paid me well, I got to meet Sidney Poitier, so fuck it! That's how I felt at that time.

Andrew Robinson in a publicity photo for *Shoot to Kill* (1988) with a cast of known villain actors including Clancy Brown, Richard Masur and Frederick Coffin. Photo courtesy of Warner Brothers.

Typecasting and studio perception might have handicapped your career, but do you enjoy playing villains?

Oh, I love playing villains. It's just that *Dirty Harry* put me in a box for a while, because that was more than just your customary villain. It was a first of its kind – that kind of psychotic raging murderer.

When you were offered the role of Garak in 1991, how did you feel about science fiction at that point? For some actors it's a genre that is often sneered at.

I knew nothing about *Star Trek*. I think I saw maybe an episode or two of the original series, and I thought it was really cheesy. Originally, I went up for Odo [played by René Auberjonois] because it was a regular role. They called me back three times and it was going great, and then René got it. He was the right person, but when they called me up about Garak, I didn't want to go in. My wife said, 'Don't be an idiot, we still have bills to pay!' Thank God she did! She's done that to me many times in my life.

At what point did you know they were going to bring Garak back as a recurring character?

It wasn't until the second year and, even then, they were being very coy about it. They said, 'Well, we have interest in you for some upcoming episodes,' and I said, 'Fine, but I'm not going to wait for you to call.' And I didn't. Sometimes they would call and I would be off someplace else!

The character of Garak is probably one of the most layered in, not just *Deep Space Nine*, but all of *Star Trek*. What's it like to play a character who, like the audience, you discovered more about as the series progressed?

It's wonderful to play that part because it's all about subtext. It's where I learned how to work with an active subtext. It's the first time on film where I had a character that I could pull that off [with]. With film, you have such power if you have a strong subtext, so you can play internal actions.

Thanks to services like Netflix, the show is seen by whole new generations, and it's why I'm here at events like this. Next year will be the twenty-fifth anniversary and it's going to be wonderful!

Andrew Robinson as Cardassian spy/tailor Garak in *Star Trek: Deep Space Nine*.
Photo courtesy of Paramount Pictures.

Finally, I must ask you about your appearance in *Cobra* with Sylvester Stallone?

Oh, Sylvester. He changed the ending of the entire film, because he had killed so many people during that film. I was supposed to have my shirt ripped off to reveal a big satanic tattoo, and then get killed, but [Stallone] said that was boring. So, I said, 'How do you want to end this?' and he said, 'Well, why don't I just punch you?' I just said, 'Ok!'

It's not my least favorite film, but another one that was weird was *Child's Play 3*, where I got my throat slit by a puppet. That was pretty weird.

It's a very memorable way to go!

Yes, it is!

Jeremy Bulloch

"What if he doesn't survive? He's worth a lot to me."
— Boba Fett, *The Empire Strikes Back* (1980).

Select Filmography

- *The Spy Who Loved Me* (1977) – HMS Ranger Crewman
- *Star Wars: Episode V – The Empire Strikes Back* (1980) – Boba Fett/Lt. Sheckil
- *For Your Eyes Only* (1981) – Smithers
- *Star Wars: Episode VI – Return of the Jedi* (1983) – Boba Fett
- *Octopussy* (1983) – Smithers
- *Robin of Sherwood* (1984-1986) – Edward of Wickham
- *Star Wars: Episode III – Revenge of the Sith* (2005) – Captain Colton

Han Solo should have paid Jabba the Hutt back when he had the chance. For the past few years, he's been helping the Rebel Alliance and ignoring his financial obligations to the galaxy's most notorious criminal overlord. Now, it's come back to haunt him. Eager to capture Luke Skywalker, Darth Vader has recruited the best bounty hunters in the Outer Rim Territories, including the mysterious Boba Fett. Tracking Han and the rest of the rebels to Cloud City, Fett is eager to take Solo back to Jabba the Hutt, but Vader wants to freeze Han in carbonite to see if it'll work on Skywalker, his true prize.

267

Boba Fett (Jeremy Bulloch) gets concerned about whether he'll be able to collect
the bounty on Han Solo's head in The Empire Strikes Back (1980).
Photo courtesy of LucasFilm.

LIKE MANY OF YOU READING THIS BOOK, *Star Wars* was a massive
part of my childhood. My parents had recorded it on TV at some point
in the early eighties, and the VHS included *The Wizard of Oz* (1939) and
The Valley of Gwangi (1969). This meant it was probably one of the most
watched tapes in our house.

I could wax lyrical all day about how the worlds that George Lucas
created have inspired generations of writers, filmmakers, and people all
around the world, and how we were all equally disappointed when he sul-
lied his own franchise with the prequels. Especially when it came to Boba
Fett – the most fearsome bounty hunter in the galaxy.

When I first saw *The Empire Strikes Back*, I thought Boba Fett was
like The Invisible Man. I thought he wore all-over body armor because
he was invisible and that was the only way people could see him. Later, I
realized that being invisible would probably be the greatest attribute for a
bounty hunter, so it made no sense for him to wear armor when he could
just walk up behind his unsuspecting target and smack them over the
head with a stick.

Still, that left the question of who, or what, was under that helmet?
Was he human? Was he disfigured? Was he even a he!?! Boba Fett could
be a woman, forced to wear armor so she doesn't have to deal with any

of the galaxy's assorted gender politics! Leia does it in *Return of the Jedi* (1983) when she goes undercover in Jabba's Palace after all.

But no, George Lucas had other plans. Turns out Boba Fett is the blueprint for Imperial Stormtroopers and, when audiences first meet him in *Star Wars: Episode II - Attack of the Clones* (2002), he is a small, petulant boy. What a letdown. If I felt that all this unnecessary backstory was debilitating to a previously awesome character, how did the man who played Boba Fett in the original films feel about it?

Jeremy Bulloch has been a staple on the convention circuit for years, and has appeared in countless documentaries talking about his experiences as the famous bounty hunter. In fact, I was wary about approaching him as, even though his character is only on screen for a probable total of ten minutes across two films, he's surely been asked every question under the sun ad nauseum. That was the case when I met him at the London Film and TV Comic Con. Hosting a panel with other Boba Fetts (the stand-in for *Star Wars: Special Edition*, a stunt Boba Fett, and someone else), he was asked all the questions I predicted he would be asked: 'What's Harrison Ford like?', 'How heavy was the armor?', 'Are you surprised that the character is so popular after so long?', 'Are you upset you were killed by a blind man?'

Jeremy must have heard all these questions at least a thousand times, yet he answered them with good humor and enthusiasm, and trotted out the anecdotes he must have told at every Star Wars convention around the world.

I'm sure he did the same with me, but I'm going to kid myself in pretending I asked him questions he had clearly never been asked in the decades since he first donned that iconic Mandalorian armor.

Boba Fett is a man of action and few words, and that's what I love about the character, and you underplay him spectacularly. So much seems to go into something simple like a nod. Did you actively try to articulate the character through movement, or am I just reading far too much into it?

Well, they didn't give me many lines! I do remember in the scene in Jabba's palace [in *Return of the Jedi*], walking up to Jabba and just very slowly clasping my own hand and just giving a slight nod to Carrie Fisher - just a slow turn and a look as if I'm saying, 'I know you' – or something silly like that!

It was great because there were no lines in that scene, I just had to give Carrie something to feed off. It was fun, but it wasn't like I was thinking, 'This is what Boba Fett would do.' It was just a case of quietly giving a nod, standing still, and acting strong.

Less is more.

Yes, you've hit it. I've said that so many times about Boba Fett. We don't know what he is; whether he is stronger than anybody, or how he does what he does, but he's definitely among the top ranked.

I thought the best thing to do was just to stand there and hold the gun in a certain way. I can't remember why I was doing it. I just held the gun and stared at people. But that's the strength he has; he doesn't need to go any further than that. I got the stare from my time at drama school. There were some young teddy boys who would look at you and try to pick a fight. I would do the stare and say, 'Are you talking to me? Well, don't!' I'd love to say I was too young at the time, but honestly, I was too old! Luckily, it never went much further than that!

You go to conventions several times a year and, when it comes to fans, few are as passionate as those who love *Star Wars*. Is it ever overwhelming, the amount of attention that you get?

People make such an effort! They travel a long way just to be there and say, 'Is it all right if I shake your hand?' It's terrible when I hear that some people say, 'No, you can't!'

Once they get over the fact I was Boba Fett, I just give them a couple of nods and say, Maybe one day you can be Boba Fett,' and they say, 'Oh, thank you Mr. Bulloch!'

Also, there are many people that go to a tattoo parlor after I've signed their leg or knee! They always ask, 'Can I get this done?' and I say, 'What do you mean, 'done'?' And they said, 'To have it as a tattoo!' I just back off slightly and talk about the weather! I once had forty people come down from London specifically to get Boba Fett tattoos done! I said, 'You're all mad!' and they all said, 'Well, we thought that's what Boba Fett would do!' I said, 'He would be a bit cooler than that, I think.' One man started going, 'Why didn't you tell me!?' [laughs]

The *Star Wars* films were primarily shot in the UK, and you were act-

ing on the stage at the time, so how did you end up in the sequel to the biggest film of all time?

It's a wonderful thing that happens perhaps once in your life. I was working in the theatre at the time, and I remember getting a call from my half-brother, who was an associate producer on *Star Wars*. He said, 'We're filming today and there's this role available. It's not a big role, in fact, it's very small, but just to let you know, you might get a call. I can't say any more!' I told him that I was in the middle of a good theatre play and wasn't interested if it was just one line.

Did you not know it was a *Star Wars* sequel at that point?

No! I asked the director of the stage play if I could go to the studio and he said, 'That's fine, but you must be back here by 6:00 p.m. at the latest because curtain goes up at 7:45 p.m.!' At first, I thought, 'This is terrific: two jobs at once!' But then I thought, 'No, that's going to be quite tough to do, both filming and theatre,' but it worked out, thanks to my half-brother!

I went to the studios and they were right at the beginning of the filming. My half-brother came up to me and said, 'Jeremy, we're going to meet George Lucas,' and suddenly my heart was pumping! I was very excited and said, 'I can't stop my heart from beating!' George came up to us and said, 'Good morning Jeremy, it's not a big role, but I think you'll have some fun!'

I went up to another actor on set and asked him what the film was, and he said, 'It's the second *Star Wars* film!' I asked what it was called and he said, '*The Empire Strikes Back!*' I said, 'That sounds like a good one!', and that was it! We started filming, and I had to make sure I left on time at 6:00 p.m. to get back to the theatre. It was great to be able to do both. I gave them - everyone - a bottle of wine as thanks, if I remember correctly.

How aware were you of the *Star Wars* phenomenon at the time? Did you have any children that were fans of the first film?

I had a very young son and my wife was pregnant with a second one at the time. It was a very exciting time, and I was grafting, as you always do, in the theatre. My son had seen *Star Wars*, but he was still very young. I took him to set and said, 'I'm going to take you to see some props. Whatever you do, don't drop it, and then give it back quickly!' [laughs] He had a great time!

You must have been the coolest dad in school. You were in *Star Wars* with Harrison Ford and Mark Hamill! I bet your kids were overjoyed.

They absolutely loved it. It was a dream come true, really, and now, it's the same for my grandsons!

When you first arrived on set, did George Lucas and Irvin Kershner give you any backstory about your character?

If I remember, there was no backstory. George was always on set, though, if I had any questions. When I first started, I felt nervous for about half an hour, and then I thought, 'Right, you roughly know what you're doing, so do it!' I always talk to myself before a scene's about to start!

Did you know when you got the role that, not only would you not have many lines, but you'd also be wearing a helmet that covered your entire face?

No, I never knew that! I thought I may have to pull down the visor occasionally to be quite moody. I remember the helmet cutting my face and being too heavy, but I was wearing a lot of interesting gear that I never

Jeremy Bulloch (right) also appeared as Imperial Officer Lt. Sheckil in *The Empire Strikes Back* (1981). Photo courtesy of LucasFilm.

got to use, such as the gun on the belt and the jetpack. At first, I thought I would hardly be able to lift the costume up. The jetpack wasn't heavy, but the gun was, so I just dropped it on my arm and just gently held and played with it.

I've always thought of Boba Fett as a science fiction version of Clint Eastwood's character in the Spaghetti Westerns, The Man with No Name. No one knows anything about him, he works for money, and he's a bit of a bad-ass.

You hit on that very well, because I remember seeing A *Fistful of Dollars* (1964) and it's why Boba Fett has his cloak draped over his shoulder. That's the typical Clint Eastwood look!

Did you have any thoughts of what Boba Fett might look like under the helmet? For years, I believed he was either horrifically disfigured or was like The Invisible Man, and wore a complete suit of armor so people could see him – which is pretty stupid in hindsight. Did you ever have any thoughts about what might be under the helmet?

I thought he would be some deformed creature, because why else would they cover his face? He could have been severely disfigured, you never know! At the time, I thought he could be either an alien or human, and I know it was something that people were waiting for. Whatever was under the helmet, I hoped they would go, 'Oh no, he isn't as handsome as Mr. Bulloch!'

It reminds me of years ago, at the cinema at Saturday morning pictures, when you'd see your film and you didn't know what it was going to be. Often, it wouldn't be what you thought. It's the same with Boba Fett, but whoever plays him in the future, I'm looking forward to seeing it.

How did you feel when the prequels revealed his backstory, the fact that he was the template for the Imperial Stormtroopers and that he'd end up looking like Temuera Morrison? Were you surprised?

The role just moves on, and Temuera is terrific. He is a smashing guy, and if he continues to play Boba Fett, I'd be thrilled to bits, because he's a cracking guy. You never know what might happen, but I'm the kind of person who sits down to watch a film and goes, 'Right: entertain me!'

Did the two of you talk about the role at all?

I think I said he'd be very quick and sharp, but we talked about a lot of things, mainly family. I haven't seen him for a while, but it's great to see him when [I] do. It's all moved on now; there's Boba Fett, there's Jango Fett, it's getting complicated, but that's what I like!

It must have been frustrating for you when Lucas replaced your voice in the re-release of the original films with Temuera's? It's almost like he was erasing your performance.

People have asked me that, but it doesn't worry me at all. If someone wanted to change my face, then I'd say, 'It's fine, you can do that. It's part of the film!'

I think it's because I have quite a soft voice, so that's fair enough! I'm quite a straightforward person, so I never complained that they did it. It's just what happens in filmmaking. I'm also always looking forward to the next film or the next role. If it makes the film better, that's fine, if it's bad, you can say it's a bit disappointing, but I never think it will be.

In *The Empire Strikes Back*, you also have another role as Lt. Sheck-il, the Imperial Officer that drags Leia away during the shoot out on Cloud City. How did you end up getting that role, too?

It was a case of 'Quick, quick! We need someone!' The assistant director came up to me and said, 'Jeremy, we need you to go into wardrobe and dress as an Imperial Officer.' I said, 'But I think I'm already in this scene as Boba Fett!' They just said, 'Do you want to do it?', and I said 'Yes', so I appeared as Lt. Sheckil, too!

At that point, the character didn't have a name, but was given one in a *Star Wars* card game years later. So, overall, in *Star Wars*, I've had three parts: Boba Fett, Lt. Sheckil and Captain Colton in *Episode III*. In that film, I was flying a spaceship, and it was difficult to remember what I was meant to be doing and what I was meant to be saying! Lots of people have said they've seen me in *Rogue One*, but I wasn't [in it]. I did enjoy *The Force Awakens*, but I couldn't take my youngest granddaughter. It was just quite violent at times!

I'm sure she'll love it when she's a bit older.

Yes, she will absolutely love it.

People have said that George Lucas is a not an actor's director, but that wasn't the case with [*Empire Strikes Back* director] Irvin Kershner. How did you find working with him?

Irvin has passed away now, but he was a good director, no question about that. We'd have a chat at lunchtime and I'd ask how the filming was going. He'd say, 'So far, very good, but it can always change!'

There was some controversy about how Boba Fett dies (or possibly doesn't die) in *Return of the Jedi,* where he's hit by Han Solo, who's blind at the time, and falls into the Sarlacc pit. Were you disappointed with the way Boba Fett dies, or do you even think he's dead?

First, I was like, 'God, I think he's gone. He's dead!' But I was waiting for him to return, like a Clint Eastwood character!

People are always asking, 'Are you going to be in the new film? Is Boba Fett going to be in the new film?' I always say, 'I hope so!' If it happens, it happens. If it doesn't, it doesn't. It doesn't worry me, because I've played so many parts on film and stage. It doesn't worry me at all.

There have been lots of rumors over the years that they want to make a standalone Boba Fett film at some point. What do you think that film should be, if it's ever made?

I'd like to see whether they can do something where we see his family and children. It would be nice to do that.

Boba Fett: The Next Generation?

Yes, Boba Fett's son! Whoever plays it, they will have a ball. I'd like to see them do the occasional nod of the head, but it's got to be exciting, like the Saturday morning pictures I used to watch. However, what I'd really like to see is him taking off the helmet, looking around and it's just an hour and half of Jeremy Bulloch! [laughs]

As an actor who has been in everything from *Doctor Who* (1965-1974) to *Agony* (1979-1981), are you happy that, for millions, you'll always

Jeremy Bulloch appears as a submarine crewman in *The Spy Who Loves Me* (1977)
before appearing in two later films as Q's assistant Smithers.
Photo courtesy of MGM.

**be Boba Fett? Or would you rather be an actor that's remembered for
all of his many different roles?**

I think, at my age now, and I'm getting on a bit, I'm happy with just being Boba Fett. I've been treated so well by people, and fans all around the
world. Russians, Germans, Americans, the English, all of them love the
character. I recently wore the outfit to raise money for Great Ormond
Street Hospital, so that was wonderful.

**As a fan of the James Bond films, I must ask you about your involve-
ment in them. You've been in several, as a sailor at the beginning of
the *Spy Who Loved Me* and in a couple more as Q's assistant, Smithers.
How did you end up in those films?**

Even then, all those years ago, you still had to go for an interview. I went
and asked what the role was, and they said it wasn't a huge part, but I
was told it was fun, and I'd help Bond on his cases! I did three films and I

loved every second of it. Desmond Llewelyn was hysterical, and Sir Roger Moore, who has sadly passed away now, was too. Desmond would be telling Roger off, and telling him to behave, and complaining about his difficult lines. Roger would tease him all the time.

I heard that Desmond used to write his lines down on cue cards, and Roger would hide them.

I used to giggle at the two of them misbehaving! Roger was fantastic, and so funny. He was an absolute delight. I remember saying to him, 'This film *Octopussy* is filming in India. I've never been there!', and he said, 'Well, you won't be going on this one!', I said, 'Fair enough! It was worth a try!' That was the sort of banter that happened on set. He made the studio floor fun. If you're working with someone who gees up the studio and gets everyone going, then it's lots of laughs.

I've had so many roles and have gone from one to another and worked with so many good people. If you're right for a part, then you'll be picked. If you're wrong, and it's not quite working, you shouldn't have been interviewed in the first place. I think I've been terribly lucky and I'm still going!

William Atherton

"Frankly, I've heard a lot of wild stories in the media and we want to assess any possibility of dangerous and possibly hazardous waste chemicals in your basement."

– Walter Peck, *Ghostbusters* (1984).

Select Filmography

- *The Sugarland Express* (1974) – Clovis
- *Ghostbusters* (1984) – Walter Peck
- *Real Genius* (1985) – Prof. Jerry Hathaway
- *Die Hard* (1988) – Richard Thornburg
- *Die Hard 2* (1990) – Richard Thornburg
- *The Pelican Brief* (1993) – Bob Gminski
- *The Crow: Salvation* (2000) – Nathan Randall
- *The Last Samurai* (2003) – Winchester Rep

The Ghostbusters are cementing a reputation for themselves as the first choice for New York City's supernatural elimination needs, but some people aren't happy – specifically Walter Peck of the EPA. Concerned that the Ghostbusters are a bunch of charlatans, Peck visits their headquarters to investigate whether they are really the con artists he thinks they are. Of course, he isn't expecting the sarcastic and flippant attitude of Dr. Peter Venkman (Bill Murray).

The Environmental Protection Agency's Walter Peck (William Atherton) tries to wrap Dr. Peter Venkman (Bill Murray) in red tape in *Ghostbusters* (1984). Photo courtesy of Columbia Pictures.

NOT ALL VILLAINS CARRY GUNS or are trying to take over the world. In a bizarre testament to what was regarded as a nuisance in the 1980s, one of the main antagonists in *Ghostbusters* (1984) is just a stuck-up bureaucrat that wants to make sure the Ghostbusters aren't polluting the environment – a justifiable reason, I think you'll agree! The only problem is that the EPA investigator is Walter Peck, played with a sense of sneering superiority by the wonderful William Atherton.

Already curt, rude, and patronizing, Peck becomes even more of a problem for our heroes when he is faced with Peter Venkman who, let's face it, is equally curt, rude, and patronizing. If only Venkman had taken the time to show the Ghostbusters facility to the uppity pencil pusher, then maybe they could have avoided unleashing a Sumerian God on the Big Apple!

It really is Venkman's fault, but the fact that Atherton plays Peck as such an unlikeable prick makes us immediately take the Ghostbusters' side. It is that ability to convey such unlikability that also got him cast as the greasy news anchor Richard Thornburg in *Die Hard* – a man willing to do anything to get the story, even if it means putting McClane's children in danger.

There have been rumors for years that Atherton's role in *Ghostbusters* led to people picking fights with him in bars, and children calling him 'Dickless' for decades. It apparently got so bad that he had to shave off his trademark beard so that people wouldn't recognize him. Of course, many of these stories are probably nonsense, so I decided to track down Atherton to find out.

I imagine it doesn't happen so much these days (or maybe it does), but when *Ghostbusters* came out, was there a day that didn't go by when someone would yell, 'Dickless!' at you on the street?

The first time it happened, I remember I was performing on Broadway. I had left the Minskoff Theatre's rehearsal studio and, across the street, I saw that *Ghostbusters* had just been released. I was walking down the street and there were all these school buses parked up. In New York in the summer time, you have the Fresh Air Fund, where kids go to camp outside the city to get fresh air and enjoy activities, but on this day, they were bringing them into the city to go to the movies.

I was walking under the theatre's marquee and suddenly, about 8,000 children go, 'Hey! Dickless!' That was the first time I had ever heard that, and it upset [me] at the time, but after about two hours I said, 'Well, this movie is making money!'

I'd done a lot of movies that had received good critical reviews, like *Sugarland Express* and *[The] Day of the Locust* [1975], but they hadn't made nearly as much money, or made that much of a splash. That's why it's a double-edged sword.

That's a hell of a way to find out that the film is a hit – with 8,000 children calling you 'Dickless!'

It is, but you as they say, 'All recognition is better than none.'

For years, Ivan Reitman has said that, after the film came out, you called him to complain that people were picking physical fights with you because they hated the character so much, is that true?

No, but I told him the story that I just told you. I was a little upset at the time but I related the story as more of an ironic concept than a complaint. I think that he took it as a complaint, which I didn't mean because I like Ivan a lot. Irony doesn't go very far in Los Angeles. You're either one thing or another.

Before we get into the character of Walter Peck, how did you end up getting cast in the film, as before *Ghostbusters*, you had appeared in several dramas and were an established stage actor – how do you go from that to appearing with the cream of *Saturday Night Live* [1979-]?

It's a complicated picture. I began as a leading man in the seventies. Then, by accident, I became the 'funny bad guy' in *Ghostbusters*. I'd known all those guys in New York, as I knew Gilda Radner, and because of *Saturday Night Live*, she, Bill Murray, and Dan Aykroyd were iconic. They were signature comic people, and culturally important at that time, because nobody had ever seen that kind of satire.

I knew them and they asked me to play this part. It sounded fun, because it was mostly in New York, and they had a lot of other very cool local actors in it, and then it just became this monster!

It changed the business's perception of me. What happened after that was I did a movie with Val Kilmer called *Real Genius*, which became a sleeper hit. Then there were the *Die Hard* films, up until the early nineties, and then there was *Bio-Dome* [1996], *The Last Samurai*, and things like that.

With *Ghostbusters*, the leads were signature comic actors. So, what am I going to do? Try and compete with them? It's absurd! I decided that the best move for me was to be like what Groucho Marx used to talk about with Margaret Dumont, in that she didn't know why it was funny. She didn't understand the comedy of it at all. That's why she was so great as a straight woman. I thought about that, and I felt I would have to be a male Margaret Dumont. So, that's what I decided to do.

William Atherton plays the straight man to Bill Murray in *Ghostbusters* (1984). Photo courtesy of Columbia Pictures.

You simply reacted to them?

Yes. Any time anybody thought they were funny, or awry, or trying to get away with something, I just didn't find it funny. I found it reprehensible, confusing, or stupid.

You do it very well, but how hard is that to do with the likes of Dan Aykroyd and Bill Murray, who are obviously very funny guys?

Not at all.

Not at all?!

No, because I just played the straight man to them. The more I played the straight man, the more dimension my character took on, and they could riff on me. 'Dickless' is a line that was made up. Not everything was scripted, a lot of it was improvised. The scene in the Mayor's office was filmed while we were on a roll!

Then, when Bill Murray goes, 'Yes, it's true. This man has no dick,' and you lunge at him, that was all completely ad-libbed?

Yes, that was all improvised.

[laughs] I'm surprised you say that because it's almost out of character that you'd want to punch Venkman in the presence of the mayor, but I guess it's entirely reasonable that you'd want to.

I was taking this as a drama, as a melodrama. I felt that you couldn't get cute with it. You just had to go with it.

In today's political environment, the EPA is vilified by certain right-leaning politicians. Do you ever think you might be responsible for slandering the good name of the agency? Perhaps Trump's opinion of the EPA was formed in 1984 when he first saw _Ghostbusters_?

I don't think, intellectually, Trump has that much resonance. [laughs] I just don't think there's any dimension where we would have registered with him at all! It would be helpful if he got anything intellectual at all from *Ghostbusters*, but I don't think that's the case.

Walter Peck is last seen being coated with melted marshmallow as the Stay Puff Marshmallow Man explodes above him. What were they dumping on you for that scene?

Shaving cream. It's interesting because they had this massive bag of shaving cream, and I asked what is was. The crew said, 'It's shaving cream, but it's *only* shaving cream.' I said, 'Well, I remember in science, from when I was twelve, that 100 lbs. of feathers weights as much as a 100 lbs. of lead!' The crew thought I was just a pussy actor, so they said, 'Ok, we'll test it with a stuntman,' and it knocked him flat! [laughter] So, they gave me half as much, so that I could do it!

Were there ever any plans for you to return to the sequel, because there's a similar character in there played by Kurt Fuller, and I was wondering if it was originally written for you, and you simply opted not to return?

No, I don't think so. By then I'd gone on to *Real Genius*, and then, later, the *Die Hard*s.

Let's talk about *Die Hard*. When you were cast in the film as Richard Thornburg, the character was, again, a professional dick. Did you have any reservations about taking on the role? Or did you think you were pretty good at playing the level of arrogance that Thornburg embodies?

I was more arrogant in the second film (*Die Hard 2: Die Harder* [1990]). In the first film, Thornburg is just this guy trying to get a story, and doing everything he can to do that. There was a Columbia School of Broadcasting, and there was this guy there who helped me out a lot. I would start reading things off the old AP [Associated Press] wires, and would just practice doing that, so I would get the American wannabe local newscaster cadence.

The first *Die Hard* was a great movie. It's just structured wonderfully; there are two different stories going on at the same time. There's no other movie really like it. The sequel was more centered on Bruce's character. People always ask what was it like to work with him, and I say, 'I don't know! I didn't work with him.'

Thornburg (William Atherton) will do anything for a story in *Die Hard* (1988).
Photo courtesy of 20th Century Fox.

You barely share a scene together.

Because we were in two different movies. In the first one, it was just that last shot at the end. At the time, a lot of news people were commenting about my character, as there was this foreign newscaster for CBS, called Fred Francis. He had this column in the *Los Angeles Times*, and he really went after my character, saying that no newscaster would ever put anybody's life in danger – which we all felt was such a crock of shit! The *Los Angeles Times* called me and they said, 'Would you want to do a rebuttal?', and I said, 'No, I'm not going to write it, but my wife will!'

My wife, Bobbi, is a copy writer, and has worked for all the big ad agencies in New York. She worked for the studio and would do the trailers, one sheets, and all of that. In her article, she essentially wrote, 'Get a grip here! It's a comedy, and it's all about somebody who wants to be ambitious. Obviously, you don't get to Mr. Francis's position without a little ambition, do you?', and that was kind of that!

There are stories that, due to the film's non-stop shooting, they had to give Bruce Willis some time off, so expanded the roles of a lot of the supporting characters. Was the role of Thornburg expanded at all during production?

I don't remember [if] there was any difference from the original script, but things are rewritten all the time. It was technically a very difficult shoot. The whole structure of shooting a movie is so much different now than it was then. Now, the movies aren't made by movie people. They're made by accountants, lawyers, and executives. The sad thing is, they think, 'If we can shoot *Downton Abbey* [2010-2015] in ten days, why can't we do *Ben-Hur* [1959] in ten days?'

As someone who's played several villains over the years, is there a secret to playing them well? Do you just make them relatable or do you feel that going 'full evil' is the best way to be?

I think about what I would do in the same position. Every part is different, but you have to ask yourself, 'What is it about you that is the same as this character?' We all have dislikes, resentments, bad days, bad moods, and grievances. My feeling is, nobody is immune from that. I'm certainly not, so why not use it?

Do you find it's more fun to play those characters than the standard 'good guy' roles?

The true mark of a villain – putting your career before a family's safety!
Photo courtesy of 20th Century Fox.

Yes, I always did. The straight-arrow [sic] good guy role never really appealed to me. Ever. I don't think they really appeal to most actors who play those roles. It's not just black and white, the way it used to be. All the younger guys, like Ben Affleck and Matt Damon, they have characters with shades in them all the time. If the arc of the story depends upon your character, then that makes you the lead – at least in my opinion. For example, in *Dracula* , he's the main drive of the story.

If I do play a villain, I have to be very sure that I'm not repeating myself, because you don't want to pollute and become a parody of yourself.

With the success of *Die Hard* and *Ghostbusters*, did you find that you were offered similar roles afterwards, and that appearing in those films colored how audiences, and studios, saw you?

At the time, I thought it was a little annoying because, when you're young, you want to be Gary Cooper. But it was very fortunate, because it gave me an entire other life, and a very myriad one. I was in New York for twenty years and it turned out to be a boon for me. I didn't expect it to be, but it was. It can be a lot of fun playing those guys, because you're not spending the whole time staring off into the sunset looking sensitive. It was something you can have some fun and play around with. I was really lucky because I was given the movies that came in order.

When we were doing *Die Hard*, we all knew it was going to be a big movie, but we didn't know it was going to be another signature event. I was never the bad guy with a gun. Well, I was bad, and carried a gun in a lot of nineties indie movies, but I was never putting bamboo shoots under the heroine's fingernails or anything like that. I was lucky that way, too. Particularly with the *Die Hard*s, because they were fun. I took them as comedies because, essentially, that's what they are. If you want to look at it in strictly classical sense, *Die Hard* is a comedy.

Billy Drago

"Your friend died screaming like a stuck Irish pig. Now you think about that when I beat the rap."
        – Frank Nitti, *The Untouchables* (1987)

Selected Filmography

- *Pale Rider* (1985) – Deputy Mather
- *Invasion U.S.A.* (1985) – Mickey
- *The Untouchables* (1987) – Frank Nitti
- *Delta Force 2: The Colombian Connection* (1990) – Ramon Cota
- *Diplomatic Immunity* (1991) – Cowboy
- *Guncrazy* (1992) – Hank Fulton
- *Tremors 4: The Legend Begins* (2004) – Black Hand Kelly
- *The Hills Have Eyes* (2006) – Papa Jupiter

As the enforcer for Al Capone, Frank Nitti (Billy Drago) is responsible for killing people that don't pay on time, power rivals and police officers trying to take the crime lord down. Unfortunately for him, one of the police officers he has killed is Jim Malone (Sean Connery), one of the founders of The Untouchables, and his partner Eliot Ness isn't happy about it...

WHEN IT COMES TO ACTORS who have cornered the market in playing sinister villains, Billy Drago is at the top of the list. With a smile that sends shivers down your spine, Billy Drago has faced off against the likes

Frank Nitti (Billy Drago) mocks Eliot Ness during the finale of *The Untouchables* (1987). Photo courtesy of Paramount Pictures.

of Clint Eastwood, Kevin Costner and Chuck Norris in action movies. Sure, he always loses, but with that playful grin, you get the impression that was always his plan all along.

Originally a stuntman, Drago got his start in relatively low budget movies and villain roles in TV series, before being cast as one the evil deputies in Clint Eastwood's *Pale Rider* (1985). After that, parts in films like *Vamp* (1986), *Hunter's Blood* (1986), Freeway (1988) and True Blood (1989) solidified his reputation as a perfect foil for heroes. Chuck Norris clearly thought so and cast him in three of his films (*Invasion U.S.A.*(1985), *Hero and the Terror* (1988) and *Delta Force 2: The Colombian Connection* (1990)) as well as a guest role in *Walker, Texas Ranger* (1993). For many readers though, Drago will be most familiar as Capone's enforcer Frank Nitti in The Untouchables who is unceremoniously hurled off the room of the courthouse by Eliot Ness.

I was eager to talk to Drago about these roles and being typecast as a villain, but at the time of writing this book, he was unavailable. However, film writer Owen Williams interviewed him a few years ago about his career and has kindly let me use their interview for this book.

Where do you most enjoy working?

Acting is like running away to join the carnival. Wherever they set the tent up you do the show and try and make a couple of bucks from the rubes and then make your escape! I've shot a lot of pictures in Asia: for whatever reason they like me there a lot! But I only finally got to shoot in Japan relatively recently, with Takashi Miike for the Masters of Horror series. It never played in the States. It was going to, but whoever figures these things out looked at it and said, 'We love it, it's fantastic, but it's just too unsettling!' Why hire Takashi Miike to direct your picture if you don't want it to be unsettling? It only came out in the States on DVD, but it was a great experience. Takashi doesn't really speak English and I don't speak Japanese, but we spoke Film, in a sense; we understood what we were going to do. And we got to shoot kind of off the beaten track. When you think Japan you basically think Tokyo, and you don't think about the mountains and the rural areas. There are so many islands and each one's a little different, so we saw swamps and mountains. That was a great experience.

What got you started in movies?

I was a disc jockey for a number of years and I eventually ended up with a syndicated radio show that played 300 radio stations around the country, playing late night blues and jazz. Every now and again I'd go around to some radio station and make nice with the sponsors, and one of them in Kansas was a big theatre company. I'd always wanted to be an actor, but I come from such a little town that I didn't have any idea how you would go about doing it, so just for the hell of it I asked if I could stand on the stage and audition for a part, just so I could say in my head one time I had a real try-out for a professional acting gig. And I did it and went back to the radio station. And the next day they called up and said if I really wanted it, the job was mine, and they were leaving for Denver on Monday, to tour Canada for six months!

It was like the gods of fate saying there's your opportunity, take it or leave it! I called my attorney and told him to sell the house, sell the show, sell everything, because on Monday I'm going to go be an actor! I'm outta here! And when the tour was finished I got a train ticket to New York, which was a two-week trip, and gradually got plays at Lincoln Centre and bits and pieces. And after a while I took the bus from New York to LA, and that's how I ended up in movies!

Pale Rider **was one of your first movies…**

It was. I had long hair at the time, because I'd just finished my first movie, *Windwalker,* with Trevor Howard, which was set in the 1600s. I'd gotten a job on *MASH*, and the *Pale Rider* people were deciding whether they wanted me to have long hair, and the *MASH* people were telling me to cut it, since I was supposed to be in the army. I said, 'I can't!' It didn't matter, because it became this classic *MASH* episode called "POV", where you never see my character; it's shot entirely from my point of view. So, I kept my long hair, and I got to do *Pale Rider*! You can't get much better than being killed by Clint Eastwood in a Western. I've killed great people and been killed by great people!

Is it really Eastwood that shoots you though? It's just a hand coming out of a horse trough: is it not just a stunt-hand?

No, it really is Eastwood! It's not a stunt hand! He's right there, hiding in the trough. I almost got blown up because of that shot. They glued a dime to my neck and then put the plastic explosive on the dime, and then they wired it and made it up so you couldn't see it. And the wires went down my pants leg all the way over to the FX guy.

So, they set all that up and then we broke for lunch, and in the meantime, out there in the desert which was so hot, the plastic explosive started to melt and a little bit slipped off the dime onto my neck without me realizing. So, I'm there and this gun comes up and BOOM, all of a sudden I realize that's not stage blood! That's really me!

Billy Drago (second from the right) as one of Marshal Stockburn's (John Russell) deputies in *Pale Rider* (1985). Photo courtesy of Warner Brothers.

Eastwood is like two different people. There's this kind of middle-aged director in a stalking hat and a big coat, behind the camera, and then he would step away from the camera, and he'd take off the big coat and his costume would be underneath, and he'd put on the hat, and after about ninety seconds, there would be Clint Eastwood! He's a wonderful jazz musician too. We were up in the mountains staying at this ski lodge, and I went into the bar and someone was playing the piano really beautifully. And I sat down to listen, and looked over, and it was Clint, just casually playing the piano in the hotel bar.

I have really fond memories of that film. John Russell who played the lead bad guy came up to me the first day of shooting and put his arm around me and said 'Son, this movie's gonna pay off for you like a slot machine!' And he was right. The residuals from late night TV and DVD or whenever there's an Eastwood boxset or a Western box set it's in there. Those residuals are still very nice.

And from *Pale Rider* you went straight to *The Untouchables*…

That was one of those films where even the things that went wrong went right. It was a difficult shoot in that it was period and we were actually shooting in the city so you have to periodise all those blocks. It was huge. And the studio didn't know it was going to be a hit, and they actually called De Palma and shut it down. They said, 'Okay we've seen the footage, you've got enough, we don't want to spend any more money, that's it, after the weekend you're home', and there were a whole load more scenes we were supposed to shoot.

That's when they went and shot the Odessa Steps sequence in the train station, with a load of raw film stock that De Palma had stored up. That wasn't even in the script. We were supposed to shoot at the race track and a lot of other stuff, and he said, 'We can't shoot any of that stuff, so everybody pack up, but in the meantime I'm going to shoot my version of the *Battleship Potemkin* scene with all this film I've stolen!'

The first scene we shot was where the little kid gets blown up. So, I'm outside waiting on the street where they're lighting, and some older woman comes up with a little boy and asks for a picture, so I put my arm around the little boy and all that. And the next day in the newspaper I found that the picture was there! And the little boy was Nitti's great great grandson!

The guy who was my stand-in was the great grandson of a guy who'd had a Nitti contract out on him! And his grandfather had hidden out in the middle of Illinois until Nitti had died, and survived the hit. But even after that, he got ill and he was in the hospital, and the nurses complained about him because he was sleeping with a pistol under his pillow, because he was convinced he was still gonna get whacked!

I got to know the Nitti family. They still live in the Chicago area and they have grocery stores and businesses: regular businesses; they're not mob connected anymore! They called the hotel where I was staying, which was the actual hotel that had been owned by Capone and Nitti during that period (in fact the very phone booth where Machine Gun Jack McGill was killed was right outside my door). I was down in the lobby and the concierge came over to say that the Nitti family would be by to pick me up at 8 o'clock. Nobody asked if I actually wanted to go! It was an offer I couldn't refuse! But it would have been too interesting an adventure to turn down anyway. So, at eight o'clock I'm down in the lobby and a limousine pulls up and a guy gets out and introduces himself as someone who works for the Nitti family, and we drove around every Blues club in Chicago, and at every one it was like royalty had arrived. 'The Nitti family is here!' It was great fun, but they were making me a little nervous because they gradually started treating me like I really was Frank Nitti. They made sure my back was to the wall so I could see everybody, and all the young Italian Turks would come by to pay their respects, and they'd all say 'Sooooo, playin' Uncle Frank huh? Lookin' good, lookin' good!' It gave me a bit of an insight into what it would have been like and what had gone on.

The family didn't mind how Nitti was portrayed in the film?

They didn't mind Frank being portrayed as such a villain; the legend is so big. They had to move Nitti's grave several times because people kept digging it up to make sure he really was dead; they were so scared of him. Only the family knew where his grave was for a while. I wore a white suit in the movie because we thought of him as the angel of death. I talked to a very elderly gentleman once who'd been a policeman undercover, and he said that Nitti had found him out, and tied him up in a basement and put a gun in his mouth and waited to see if he would sweat. Nitti had a very famous saying: 'I never killed a man who wasn't afraid to die.' So, if he'd sweated he would've been killed, but he didn't so Nitti said 'Ok, he's not afraid' so he let him go. My mother never quite forgave me for killing Sean Connery. Mom, I had to! They paid me!

You've made more horror movies than any other genre. Do you have a particular love of horror, or do those roles just find you?

I like horror. I like to be scared. I grew up in a rural area with a very limited number of movie theatres, so my parents would drive 20 or 30 miles occasionally to the bigger neighbouring town, and drop me off at the movies while they went about their business. It was a movie theatre that had really gone to seed. The city had declared the building dangerous and they were getting ready to close it down, but they were still showing every one of the old classics, so I got to see Phantom of the Opera and Dracula and Frankenstein and the Mummy. I became a big fan of Vincent Price because they showed all his old films. And it was great to see William Castle come on the screen and say, 'Take your insurance so you won't die from fear!' They weren't reruns from my point of view: it was the first time, in this scary old theatre.

But I didn't think of it as horror so much. Just movies. So that's stayed with me. I tend not to think 'Oh, this is another scary movie.' I just look for interesting roles. The only real exception to that was *The Hills Have Eyes*. I'd seen and loved the original when it came out, and I actually called them up for that one and asked if they could find something for me to do! I didn't care what the part was. I just wanted to be in it, to complete that circle of being there at the beginning then being in the new version.

The design sketches for *The Hills Have Eyes* show your character, Papa Jupe, with a Siamese twin. We don't see that in the film. Did it go any further than the drawings?

I don't appear to have a mutation in it, but that's really because it didn't end up on screen. A lot of the scenes that we shot were about Papa Jupe's family, and the executives were getting a little worried and they were saying 'Y'know, they seem too sympathetic, they seem like a real family!' So, we had to edit it so they didn't seem so family-like. So some of those scenes got cut out.

It was a great cast though, and we got to go to Morocco to shoot. Of course, I couldn't go to Morocco and not go to Marrakech, but I got stranded. Somebody asked me if I wanted to go, and we hopped in the car and drove there, but he lost all his money in the casino, and the next thing I knew I was in Marrakech for three days with no money and no passport! And I didn't have the phone number of the hotel because I hadn't thought to take it. Finally, at about 6am on the last morning I walked past some nightclub and the musicians had finished their gig and were coming out, and they happened to know me from the movies, and they asked what I was doing and I said I was stuck there! So, they told me not to worry and they took me to a hotel lobby and sat me down and talked to the hotel people and fed me; I hadn't eaten for three days! And the hotel people found some little eleven-year-old boy who had relatives in the town we were filming, which was hours and hours away through the mountains, and they gave him a car and the keys, and said 'He'll drive you home!' We got in the car and he drove through the mountains. And we were filming during what they call the wedding season, so there were all these wedding celebrations happening in all these Moroccan mountain villages, incredible parties all night long, and he knew all of them. So, on the way back we'd drive through the mountains and stop in some little village and there'd be musicians and we'd party there for an hour or two, and then we'd get back in the car and drive to another little village and finally we made it back. It was completely insane, but most movies are, in that sense.

Speaking of insane, what about *Vamp*, with Grace Jones?

Vamp was a really interesting picture. For me it's always interesting who's involved in the project. Grace Jones is such a legend, so to not only get to hang out with her but work with her… We'd shoot from sundown to sun up, and then she'd always invite everyone over to some place she'd rented for a party, and the crew and everybody would be over there and there'd be champagne in the bathtub. And then she'd just disappear, like she really was a vampire and couldn't be out in the light. Everyone would keep on partying at her place until they got tired and fell asleep, and then they'd wake up and go and shoot again. If I wasn't going to her place I'd have to drive back to my house from downtown LA. It'd be really early in the morning and I'd just rush out from the studio without taking off the albino make-up so I didn't get stuck in the rush hour traffic. And I'd be wanting a cup of coffee so I'd stop at a little Chinese supermarket and forget that they'd bleached my hair and my eyebrows and my eyelashes. I got some really alarmed looks!

There's a film on your CV that we couldn't get hold of, called Re-vamped. Is that connected to *Vamp*?

It isn't. I wanted to make sure they weren't somehow ripping that film off, so I made sure to get a good look at the script before I said yes. But the title is just coincidence. That was one of a big batch immediately after *The Hills Have Eyes*. It just happened that a lot of my friends had projects going suddenly at the same time and they were saying 'Billy! Come and do this!' That was my chance to do my version of Dracula. The cast was all American character actors that have been working for thirty years, and so it was a great chance for all of us to get together, because we'd all worked with one another at one time or another, but we'd never worked all together! The director just called every character actor he could think of to make this kind of scary-with-a-sense-of-humour film. My favorite line was 'Just because I'm immortal doesn't mean I have all the time in the world!' I made that up and they let me keep it in.

Getting to play classic monsters is great. I've done my Dracula, and I got to play the classic mad scientist in a movie called Zombie Hunter that Peter Maris directed. He'd been up into northern California near the Cicoya national forest and bought an abandoned winery – this big spooky abandoned old building – that he'd turned into a studio and wanted to use to get some projects going. I said okay, just so I could play the mad scientist!

Billy Drago in *Angel of Fury* (1992), one of several films he appeared in with Cynthia Rothrock. Photo courtesy of Rapi Pictures.

Do you have a favourite role, of the more-than-a-hundred you've played?

I like the weird ones. I made a film called *Moving McAllister* where I played a gangster called The Lady, and nobody ever mentions why he's dressed like he is. He runs a gambling place where they have people fighting almost to the death in a ring, and he plays the piano, but I'm in a very beautiful sort of purple outfit, and we never go into why this deadly gangster is like this! He was a real interesting character.

I also did this picture based on a Spanish comic book called *El Muerto*, The Dead One. And in that one I play an eighty-year-old woman! Like, I'm not playing a guy in drag, I'm actually playing an eighty-year-old woman. There's a lot of physical activity because it turns out this old woman is this bad demon spirit character. I have fight scenes, and the director looked at a lot of eighty-year-old actresses, but none of them could have done it, and it wouldn't have looked right to have them fighting with a 22-year-old. So he said 'I know! I'll get Billy!' It's based on the Spanish celebration of the Day of the Dead. I did that and then went right into playing The Lady. I was like, 'Hmmm, maybe it's a new career path.' My career path is to always say yes!

The Final Boss

IN MANY WAYS, AMERICA has never gotten over the American Revolution (or the War of Independence, depending what side of the Atlantic Ocean you're on). How else can you explain Hollywood's constant casting of British actors as villains?

Whether it's Alan Rickman, Joss Ackland, David Warner, or Steven Berkoff, British actors have long dominated the villain scene in American action films. In many cases, Hollywood utilize these skilled actors' penchant for accents by casting them as Russian, French, German, and, in some cases, American. Either way, if there is a role for a greedy CEO, a rogue colonel, or an evil mastermind, odds are they'll be played by a British actor. Sure, you can say it's down to the world-class training many of them have gone through at Royal Academy of Dramatic Arts (RADA), or the Old Vic, and because they're often cheaper to hire than their American counterparts, but, deep down, we all know it's because there is an inherent mistrust of British accents!

Jokes aside, tracking down actors at the top of the villainy food chain was a delight. From the list I complied for this section, I managed to secure several. From talking to actors sunning themselves in their Venice beach-homes to interrupting a Shakespearean acting class, each of these actors was a delight to talk to about why they are so appealing to casting agents as The Final Boss!

David Warner

"I'm bored with corporations. With the information I can access, I can run things 900 to 1200 times better than any human!"

— Sark, *TRON* (1982).

David Warner – Select Filmography

- *The Omen* (1976) – Jennings
- *Cross of Iron* (1977) – Hauptmann Kiesel
- *The Thirty-Nine Steps* (1978) – Appleton
- *Time After Time* (1979) – Stevenson
- *Time Bandits* (1981) – Evil
- *TRON* (1982) – Ed Dillinger / Sark / Master Control Program
- *The Man with Two Brains* (1983) – Dr. Alfred Necessiter
- *Star Trek V: The Final Frontier* (1989) – St. John Talbot
- *Teenage Mutant Ninja Turtles II: The Secret of the Ooze* (1991) – Professor Jordon Perry
- *Star Trek VI: The Undiscovered Country* (1991) – Chancellor Gorkon
- *In the Mouth of Madness* (1994) – Dr. Wrenn
- *Titanic* (1997) – Spicer Lovejoy

Kevin Flynn (Jeff Bridges) has been trying to hack the mainframe of his former employer ENCOM, ever since Ed Dillinger (David Warner) stole several of his video game ideas for himself, leading him to be promoted to Senior Executive VP. With Dillinger's Master Control Program (also

David Warner as Sark, right-hand man of The Master Control Program (also David Warner) in *TRON* (1982). Photo courtesy of Buena Vista Distribution.

David Warner) illegally acquiring government and corporate secrets, Flynn and his friends Lora and Alan digitize and download themselves into ENCOM's mainframe. There, they face the MCP and a host of hostile programs led by the MCP's chief enforcer Sark (again played by David Warner).

WITH OVER 220 FILM AND TV CREDITS to his name, it's fair to say that David Warner has done everything – period drama, horror, sci-fi, animation – if you can think of it, he's probably done it. However, with so many roles to his name, it's those where he played the villain that have stuck in my mind.

Sure, he was trying to expose Damian in *The Omen* (and lost his head as a result), but there's something about David's voice and cold stare that just exudes menace. Terry Gilliam picked him to play the personification of Evil in *Time Bandits*, for God's sake!

It was that role, and his multiple roles in *TRON*, that cemented David Warner's reputation as a terrifying actor in my young brain. Was it because he always seemed to be so calm, collected, and in complete control? Was it his soothing, hypnotic voice? Or was it the crazy costumes (especially in *Time Bandits*)?

I was determined to find out, so I tracked David down, and enjoyed a wide-ranging conversation with him, from appearing in one of the biggest films of all time (*Titanic*) to doing voice work for DC Comic's animated shows.

David was quick to point out that he hasn't just played villains, and that it was a bit odd that I primarily thought of him as such. He's right. With so many acting credits, he is the very definition of a working actor. I blame his performances in the bigger-budget movies for having him typecast in my mind.

Of course, with so many roles on his resume, we couldn't touch upon them all, but, it was wonderful to speak to a British legend who, at the time of writing, had just finished filming on *Mary Poppins Returns* (2018).

You started your career at the Royal Shakespeare Company, which must have given you many opportunities to play literature's greatest heroes and villains.

I didn't play any villains. I played Hamlet and Henry VI, and some other roles, but none of them were villains. I haven't done Richard III, I haven't done Iago, I haven't done any of those guys. I've always played more of the more sympathetic Shakespeare parts.

Really? That surprises me.

It's interesting that you're surprised that I didn't play any villains, because, of all the movies that I've done, villains are really in the minority.

Yet it's those roles that stick in my mind. Mostly likely because I saw them when I was younger and more impressionable. I assumed that, as you started as a stage actor, you'd have done the classic villain roles and taken that persona to the silver screen.

That doesn't happen in the theatre so much. It happens on film and [in] television. There was a film that Judi Dench did, where she played the villain, and everybody was so surprised because she wasn't known for that. The point I'm making is, that's what we do. We play different parts! I hope I'm not being patronizing.

Not at all. I think it was growing up and seeing you in all these films as the villain that meant I just assumed that was how you were generally cast throughout your career.

For every villain I played, I like to put in something not so villainous to play in-between. For example, in George C. Scott's *A Christmas Carol* [1984], I played Bob Cratchit. But then, I was in a huge miniseries years ago called *The Holocaust* [1978], where I played a real-life Nazi.

Reinhard Heydrich.

Correct, but then before I did *The Holocaust*, I played William Wordsworth the poet. You'd go mad if you only played villains!

There goes my question about whether you ever felt you were typecast in such roles!

I think a lot of people think that I was pigeonholed, but if those are the main films you've seen me in, it is quite natural you'd think that that's what I do. Tell me the films that come to mind when you think of me?

Time After Time, Time Bandits, TRON, **obviously,** *Titanic . . . .*

You know who Warner Brothers wanted to play Jack the Ripper in *Time After Time*, and the director, Nick Meyer had to talk them out of it?

No.

They wanted Mick Jagger for that part! Then it was going to be Jonathan Pryce, but he wasn't available, so I stepped in. It was also an opportunity to work with my old friend Malcolm McDowell, who was at Stratford at the beginning his career the same time I was. To suddenly find ourselves in Hollywood was quite a strange moment.

The concept of *Time After Time* is pretty out there – H.G. Wells travels to the future to stop Jack the Ripper. I can't imagine it was like anything you'd done before. Was that what attracted you to the role?

Well, actors love to work and, I've got to be honest, it's not as if I had a hundred scripts piled up on my desk. When someone said, 'Would you like to work with Malcolm McDowell? Would you like to work with Nicholas Meyer? It's a wonderful script,' I said, 'Okay, I'll do it!'

I've always loved how you bring a lot of nuance to your roles, especially Jack the Ripper. You don't play him as an out-and-out psychopath. You play him as someone who feels he is, literally in this case, not in the world he's meant to be in. As he says, 'Eighty years ago I was a freak, today I am an amateur!'

That's right. That famous line as he's clicking the old remote control. That was a wonderful thing to do. You must weigh up the discomfort. Some people love playing villains. Christopher Lee, although he played many other roles, would always say, 'By the way, I have done other things!'

Vincent Price or Boris Karloff would play with the personalities of their villains, making them quite gentle creatures. However, being cast as villains started with *Time After Time*. After that, I was cast as Heydrich, and you really can't enjoy playing a character like that.

You can't get more evil than playing Evil in *Time Bandits* (1981).
Photo courtesy of Avco Embassy Pictures.

You played him twice, didn't you?

Yes. First in *The Holocaust* TV series and then in *Hitler's SS: Portrait in Evil* [1985]. That second time, I really had to pay the mortgage!

I didn't want to do it when I was asked to play Heydrich, because he was a real person, responsible for awful things and it really pained [me] doing it. I didn't want to play it, then I realized that if I didn't play it somebody else would, and whatever discomfort I might feel playing him is nothing [compared] to the discomfort in history for all [of] his victims.

It was after *Time After Time* that some typecasting began. I was asked to do a film called *Masada* [1981], where I was the villain. I tried to give it a bit of color, but I thought that this was what my career was going to be. When you don't have a hundred scripts on your desk, and you have a family, you just have to go with it sometimes.

Then came *Time Bandits*, which, despite you literally playing Evil personified, must have been a fun experience?

The opportunity of working with Terry Gilliam and the Monty Python team was why I did *Time Bandits*. There was quite a lot of comedy in *Time Bandits*, even though, as a kid, you feared my character, if you look at it now, he's a bit of a fun. He's a fun villain.

I think what stuck with me was the dark ending where Kevin's parents touch a piece of you and they blow up! It's such a unique film, how did Terry Gilliam pitch the role to you?

Oh, he didn't have to! My agent said, 'Would you like to work with Terry Gilliam in *Time Bandits*?' and I said, 'Yes!' It wasn't a question of having to be persuaded. Of course, it was a very uncomfortable costume, but, for Terry Gilliam, you did it! You couldn't sit down and the costume was heavy and the long fingernails were uncomfortable, so they constructed what they called a leaning board. In between takes, I'd just lie back on this wooden plank that they constructed for me. Plus, with the long nails, going to the bathroom was quite difficult!

Do you find that many casting agents or directors make the mistake that I do, that they primarily see you as someone who's played villains, and that's the main image that they have of you in their mind?

Well, don't forget, now I am seventy-five-years-old, so I'm not exactly running around looking for work! I think, in England, they appreciate that you can do different things, but I have heard from casting directors and producers that many uncreative executives on a project will say, 'You can't have that actor in this film because he plays villains, and the public won't accept it!' Of course, that's an insult to everybody, but I've never felt that casting directors or producers see me only as being suitable for villains. After all, I was cast in a Steve Martin comedy!

Sure, *The Man with Two Brains*. That's a great movie.

That's correct. So, I don't feel totally typecast. Of course, villain roles come in my direction, and I've turned down a lot. I don't really want to play child molesters and slashers. At one point, all the scripts I received were for those types of roles.

I read that you were almost Freddy Krueger in *A Nightmare on Elm Street* (1984)?

That is not true. Many people ask me that because there's a photograph on the internet of me supposedly in the makeup of Freddy Krueger, but that's not me. It's one of those things that gets out there on the Internet, but it never happened – unless I had a blackout for six months or something, and they put the makeup on me and I wasn't aware of it!

What I've loved about your career is that you've never been afraid to take on genres like science fiction and fantasy that some actors might think are beneath them. Is there something that particularly attracts you to genre or do you just take the roles you're offered?

I'm just a working actor. Some of the science fiction I've done, I haven't understood a word that I say. Like in *TRON* – I didn't understand a word!

What was it like working on a film like *TRON*, where they were doing things that no one had done before? Was it hard to put your faith into such an experimental production, or were you fascinated by the entire process?

I must be honest and say I didn't understand what I was talking about or what was going on, not only because of the CGI or the visual effects, but, also, I knew nothing about computers even though, at the time, it was at the birth of the computer.

For me, it was really a question of being guided. As Robert Mitchum used to say, 'Just put me in the suit and point me in the right direction and I'll just do the very best I can!' [laughs]

I suppose I was a little bit curious to see how it would turn out, but, with every job you do, you think about that. I'm not the kind of person that rushes to see myself on the screen. With *TRON*, people had faith in it, and it [was] obviously something that was going to be interesting, but, as with *Time Bandits,* you have no idea who's going to turn out to see it! People come up to me and ask about *TRON*, but I haven't looked at the film for a long time, so I wonder what they see in it.

From an acting point of view, you're playing three roles – Ed Dillinger, Sark, and the Master Control Program, who are all essentially different sides to the same coin. Did you shade your various performances for those roles at all?

Well, it's always good to play multiple parts in a movie, but I never really thought of it in those terms because, and I'm not denigrating the film or anything, but it wasn't really an actor's film. We're hired hands and, if you accept the part, you accept the part. It was simply all part of the brief!

I'm just a jobbing actor, and *TRON* was another job and another genre that I'd done. I'd done horror, comedy, war movies, so, with *TRON*, I was saying, 'Oh, I've done science-fiction – this is fantastic!'

You said you didn't understand what was going on in *TRON* and, at the time, it didn't do well at the box office, but it's one of those films where it's developed a cult following over the decades. Is it the film that people most want to talk to you about, and does that surprise you?

When I go to conventions and meet the fans, *TRON* is very popular. I always say what I'm saying to you, 'I didn't understand what was going on!' [laughs]

Were you invited to come back for the sequel that they made a few years ago?

No, not to my knowledge.

David Warner appears as the Federation ambassador (far right) in *Star Trek V: The Final Frontier* (1989) in one of his many appearances in the sci-fi franchise. Photo courtesy of Paramount Pictures.

In terms of the science-fiction genre, you've also appeared in *Star Trek* several times. Once as the Federation Ambassador in *Star Trek V: The Final Frontier* (1989), and then as the Klingon Chancellor in *Star Trek VI: The Undiscovered Country*, where you played the Klingon version of Gorbachev.

Gorbachev and Abraham Lincoln! That's where the beard came from!

Of course! However, both of those characters are eclipsed by your performance in the *Star Trek: The Next Generation* episode 'Chain of Command', where you play a Cardassian interrogator who tortures Patrick Stewart's Jean-Luc Picard. That episode received a lot of acclaim for your portrayal, and for the show's chilling use of torture. What's even more incredible is that you were apparently cast at the last moment?

You know all [about] how that episode was put together?

I've heard cue cards might have been involved?

Yes, absolutely. I have no secret there. There was no way I could learn all that stuff in three days. People were holding cue cards all over the place for me. It was a wonderful experience to see a whole crew, including Patrick, holding cue cards for me. It wasn't like I turned up unprepared, but I had to tell them, 'Look, I can't learn these lines in so short a time.'

It's chilling how you play the character – someone who is so detached from torturing people that he even brings his daughter to work so she can see what he does.

I suppose the nearest you could compare it to, without going too deep and heavy about it, is Reinhard Heydrich. He was a monster, but he loved classical music, he loved literature, he had a family, he wrote love letters to his wife, and yet, he was one of the most evil men in history. How do you account for that?

That evil never looks how you'd expect it to.

Absolutely. These people can love, have families, love their children, and play classical music. I can't explain it. It's something I don't like to think about too much. I didn't heavily think about that during working with Patrick. However, when it came out, it was one of those extraordinary things that worked.

It says something that Patrick Stewart was willing to strip completely naked for that scene, because he trusted you as an actor and the relationship that you two had previously from your stage work.

I met Patrick at the beginning of his career at Stratford. At the time, I was playing *Hamlet* and Patrick was not. [laughs] He had just joined the company and we got on well, so years later, when he was the mega star, I was the replacement that stepped in with three days' notice!

Were you cast because you had a relationship with the producers of *Star Trek* after your previous appearances in the films?

I don't know about that. I'm one of those actors who does the job and then retreats, but to have the opportunity of working with Patrick was influential in me taking the part.

You're obviously not afraid to don heavy make-up and prosthetics considering you've played a Klingon, a Cardassian, and even an ape in Tim Burton's remake of *Planet of the Apes*. I'm guessing they never make a performance easier.

It's a four-hour make-up session from 5:00 a.m. in the morning. They've managed to get more sophisticated with it over the years, but they're not comfortable!

It takes three to four hours to put on, and one hour to take off. They can't just rip it off as it's stuck to your face, so they have to brush it gently with spirits to take it off. After a long exhausting day's work, you have to sit there and still have another hour to go before you can get out of the studio, but that's part of the game.

You've worked on low budget films like *Beastmaster III* or *Wing Commander*, but how does the experience change when you go to work on, what was at the time, the most expensive film of all time – *Titanic* – where you played Spicer Lovejoy, Billy Zane's butler-slash-bodyguard?

David Warner appears in one of the biggest box office hits of all time, *Titanic* (1997). Photo courtesy of 20th Century Fox.

At the time, *The Hollywood Report* or *Variety* had a daily budget report on *Titanic*! The film was constantly going over budget, but when it was released, it made more money at that time than any other movie.

Hollywood tends to do that a lot with James Cameron. Before each of his films are released, there are always articles claiming that this will be the film that will flop and end his career, and each time he ends up making billions.

They wanted him to fail and he didn't, but that was never in my thoughts. I think you may have read things about how the atmosphere was for certain people.

James Cameron allegedly has an infamous temper, should you get on the wrong side of him.

Absolutely. For some reason, I never got on the wrong side of him, but I saw it, and I had to hold my peace. It's not like I was playing the lead, but even so, it wasn't all that pleasant because we were working at night for six months.

One of my great friends at the time was an English stunt man, and he'd been out there for four months in Mexico, rehearsing certain set pieces. I didn't do many of my stunts. I was just waiting around in water. In fact, many of my scenes were cut out. There was a scene where I had a fight with Leonardo DiCaprio in the water. The ship's going down and Cameron said, 'I think we have to cut this out because it's just illogical.' With all those things going on, to have a fight while the boat's sinking, just didn't work.

That's a shame, because that would have been great to see – you beating up Leonardo DiCaprio while the set is sinking.

It was great! I was fighting the great Leonardo DiCaprio! He's a great actor and was a lovely bloke. We got on so well, he was so funny, we couldn't stop laughing. That's one of the great bonuses of being in *Titanic*. You got to meet a couple of smashing people, like Leonardo and Victor Garber. Lovely actors, lovely people. That's what I like to come away with.

With *The Omen*, I was travelling a lot on location with Gregory Peck. Those are the things I remember. Bearing in mind that I was at an age

David Warner is still acting and has appeared in over 220 productions.
Photo courtesy of Lisa Bowerman.

where I used to go to the cinema and see Gregory Peck! Who would've thought that I would be travelling first class to Israel and sharing a hotel suite with Gregory Peck?! Those are the things that I love in this business, the good things. There are bad things and difficult people, but not in those instances.

I bet he had some wonderful stories?

Yes, which I can't go into! But he was a wonderful man.

With *Titanic*, were you surprised at the global reaction to the film, or was it not something you really focused on or concerned yourself with?

I didn't really focus on it. I did go to the premiere, which is something I don't do anymore. Nobody was interested in interviewing me because the publicist said, 'This is David Warner, he's playing the butler.' Now who's going to want to speak to the butler in a film that no-one has yet seen!

One question someone asked was, 'Was it worth all the money?' But, at that point, I hadn't seen the film yet! I said, 'Well, it's a business. I can't tell you if it's worth the money, but at least it didn't go to financing a war somewhere in Asia. It's just a film!'

Over the years, you've also done a lot of voice work for villains, such as doing Ra's Al Ghul in DC's *Batman* animated films. When it comes to doing voice work for such infamous villains, do you have a method to playing them?

No, it's just my voice! They say, 'Go!', and I do it! There's no big method going on there! [laughs]

I really don't want to play villains anymore. Now, I really do turn them down, because they did get a bit heavy for me. I think people have the respect to know that I can do other things. Friends in America would often say, 'Are you ever going to play the good guy?', so when my agent came to me with a role in *Teenage Mutant Ninja Turtles II: The Secret of the Ooze*, I jumped at it! I was a friend of the heroes! Luckily for me, I think for every villain I played, I managed to play somebody who wasn't.

Paul Freeman

"You and I are very much alike. Archeology is our religion, yet we have both fallen from the pure faith. Our methods have not differed as much as you pretend. I am but a shadowy reflection of you. It would take only a nudge to make you like me. To push you out of the light."
— Belloq, *Raiders of the Lost Ark* (1981).

Select Filmography

- *The Long Good Friday* (1980) - Colin
- *Raiders of the Lost Ark* (1981) – Dr. Rene Belloq
- *Falcon Crest* (1984-1985) – Gustav Riebman
- *Twist of Fate* (*Pursuit*, 1989) – SS-Oberfuhrer Mittendorf
- *Aces: Iron Eagle III* (1992) – Kleiss
- *Mighty Morphin Power Rangers: The Movie* (1995) – Ivan Ooze
- *Double Team* (1997) - Goldsmythe
- *Hot Fuzz* (2007) – Rev. Philip Shooter
- *Centurion* (2010) – Governor Julius Agricola

It seems, no matter what he does, Indiana Jones always ends up losing out to his professional rival Dr. Rene Belloq (Paul Freeman). After failing to secure the golden Fertility Idol at the start of the film (if only he spoke Hovitos!), Indy is not surprised to learn that Belloq is also helping the Nazis in their search for the mythical Ark of the Covenant. After believing Marion (Karen Allen) has been killed, Indy is drinking alone in a Cairo bar when Belloq finds him and

Belloq (Paul Freeman) taunts his professional rival Indiana Jones (Harrison Ford)
as they both search for the Ark of the Covenant in *Raiders of the Lost Ark* (1981).
Photo courtesy of Lucasfilm.

reminds him why they are both archaeologists, and why
they are more similar than either of them would like to ad-
mit.

RAIDERS OF THE LOST ARK is probably my favorite film of all time.
Sure, the top position is occasionally held by *Jaws* (1975), *Die Hard* or
Lawrence of Arabia (1962), but 97% of the time, gun to my head, I'll pick
Raiders of the Lost Ark.

Indiana Jones (and by the same token, Lawrence Kasdan, Steven
Spielberg, and George Lucas) have a lot to answer for – my love of history
(which I studied at university), my interest in the paranormal (not that
I believe any of it) and my belief that if you can speak more than three
languages, you are quite simply a walking God (I'm awful at learning new
languages).

One-part James Bond, one-part Flash Gordon, and one-part Allan
Quartermain, Indiana Jones is what every young boy wants to be: travelling the world, saving the girl, and defeating Nazis, all with that wry-Har-

rison-Ford grin on your face, and the knowledge that you're just making it up as you go along. That said, Indiana Jones is completely ineffectual in his own film.

If he had never had rocked up, the Nazis would still have found the Ark of the Covenant, and their faces would have melted off. As it stands, he just upsets their schedule by going straight to Marion's to recover the Eye of Ra. In fact, he hastens everything. Good job, Indy.

The redundancy of the hero aside, my parents had a copy of the film recorded on VHS, and I can't even guess how many times I watched it. It was inevitable, then, that in planning this book, I wanted to track down the villain of the piece – Paul Freeman, a.k.a Rene Belloq.

Now, you can argue that Belloq is just like Indy – he just wants to find the Ark, seize the professional glory, and make history, but, he sides with the Nazis, so that makes him a bad guy in my book! Of course, unlike Indy, Belloq is far more refined, smoother around the edges, and even has his own wine label. Most importantly, he also speaks Hovitos.

Having starred in so many films throughout his career, including more Nazis than he'd care to remember, Paul Freeman was full of great stories and was a delight to speak to. When we talked, he was enjoying the sun from his home in France, but was more than willing to answer all my Indiana Jones fanboy questions and talk about appearing in the likes of *Iron Eagle III*, *Hot Fuzz*, and working with Jean-Claude Van Damme in *Double Team*!

Hollywood is an industry that loves casting British actors as bad guys, and you've played several such roles throughout your career. What has made studios think of you as such a popular choice for villains throughout the years? Some say it's your talent for accents.

Well, there was a time when I played a considerable number of Germans, but I've also played other accents too, so yes, that is a part of it, but there is something else. Steven Spielberg once said to me that the English are not trusted by the Americans. That's why they think we make good villains.

They just can't get over that whole American Revolution, can they? I read that when you were auditioning for the part of Belloq, you completely winged your French accent, and you weren't completely confident in it? Is that true? How dodgy was it?

I'd already been offered the part, but then Spielberg asked to see me at the last minute, so I went down to the studio in Elstree, because he was already in England at that point, ready to start shooting.

He just said to me, 'I forgot to ask you if you could do a French accent.' I just went [puts on mock French accent], 'Oh well, yes, sure. I could do something like this . . .' He said, 'Fine,' and that was it, end of meeting!

How was the film pitched to you at the time? Obviously, it was a throwback to the pulp adventures of the 1930s, and you were playing the anti-Indiana Jones, an archaeologist who is charming but very self-motivated. Was it something that appealed to you as they were no longer making those types of films in Hollywood?

It was the script that appealed to me, and that was all. I had a meeting in Los Angeles with George and Steven and all they said was, 'Do you want to read this? Take it and go in the next room. Let us know what you think.'

This was 1980 and, at the time, both were very taken with these new cassette players that came with their own speakers. When I came into the meeting, they were lying on the floor playing with one, so we were all down on the floor going, 'Wow. How do you get this amount of sound out of this little machine?' We all thought it was wonderful! It was almost an afterthought really, reading the script.

I went in the next room and wasn't particularly knocked out, but as soon as I read the joke about the date flying in the air and the dead monkey, I thought, 'This is going to be a fun script to do!'

At the time, I'd just met my wife, who had just come from doing [The] *Dogs of War* [1980] in Belize, and I was rather more concerned with her than thinking about making a film with Steven and George. Remember that Steven's film, immediately before *Raiders*, had been *1941* [1979], and that hadn't been a great success, but they were okay about it and said, 'If you like the script, let us know!' I said, 'Yes,' and a week later, they rang me and I had the job!

You play Belloq as a very charming man, and not just a one-dimensional Nazi stooge. How did you make that decision, or was it all in the script?

There's never any interest in playing anything one-dimensionally. You must look for what makes it interesting, what's going to keep your interest going during the shoot… and that was a three-month shoot! You've also got to see what's going to [be] interesting from the point of view of the story.

That's the problem with playing villains, they tend not to write a backstory. It was more interesting to see him as an archaeologist who'd gone over to the dark side, than just a villainous figure in a suit.

Here was this extraordinary historical artefact, and he had his hands on it. I think for an historian, that would be the draw, rather than money. I don't think there was any suggestion in the script that he was doing it for money. I think it was all about history, hence that exchange at the end about how we're passing through history. 'This is history!' Similarly, as Indiana is an archeologist, he can't destroy an historical artifact. That's how important it is. He knows it's more important than his life.

Are you aware that while you are talking with Harrison in that scene, you appear to eat a fly that crawls into your mouth?

Well, I'm not only aware of it, I'm asked about it every single occasion anyone mentions the film!

Siding with the Nazis is about to end badly for Belloq in *Raiders of the Lost Ark* (1981). Photo courtesy of Lucasfilm.

I can only apologize.

[laughs] If you look very carefully, if you slow the frames down, you can see there's a frame missing where the fly must have flown off. I got a wonderful review from Pauline Kael, who was a great film critic in *The New Yorker* at the time, about my devotion to duty as an actor because of that fly!

That scene was filmed in Tunisia, and it was during that part of the shoot that a lot of the crew fell ill. Did you succumb as well?

Everyone got ill apart from Steven. Harrison got ill because, famously, there is film of him rehearsing the fight with the very large stunt man, Terry Richards, who played the Arab swordsman. Harrison had come down with a dysentery and he couldn't do it. He said, 'Well, why don't I just shoot the fucker?' Of course, that's one of the best laughs in the picture, but there were a few other lines that were improvised by Harrison at that time.

Were you surprised at the critical and positive reaction to the film when it came out, because it went on to be one of the biggest films of all time?

I suppose because of Steven and George's history, I wasn't surprised by its success. I'm continually surprised that it has carried on, and am delighted that its following grows and grows and it's still regarded as a classic.

After *Raiders of the Lost Ark*, you were naturally offered a lot of villainous roles by the Hollywood studios such as *A World Apart* (1988), *Without a Clue* (1988), and *Shanghai Surprise* (1986). As an actor, were you thrilled to suddenly have so many roles offered to you or did you feel limited because everyone wanted you as their villain?

I got offered a lot of Nazi villains after the film came out. I think there was one year when I played commandants of German concentration camps in two TV movies. Afterwards, I thought, 'I'm bored with this. I'm not going to do this anymore,' because it was just becoming a way of life. I was even auditioning to play Hitler! So, I stopped doing that until I did a TV series called *Falcon Crest*. I was then offered the part of a German called Gustav Reibman, and I only did it because the producers persuaded me he was a good German! There was also some ridiculous film I did with Joan Collins that is best forgotten!

Did you ever think that, because your German accent was so good, people just thought you were actually German and that's why you kept getting offered all these Nazi roles?

I think it might be, but they also offered me a lot of money, so what could I do?

Speaking of roles where you played Nazis, *Aces: Iron Eagle III* is a film I remember seeing as a child. That film was critically mauled but that franchise still has a cult following to this day.

Does it? I don't really remember very much about the film, but it was fairly pedestrian filmmaking. John Glen was the director and he was an amusing man, but, maybe because he'd come off making a couple of the Bond movies before, he was only interested in action. He wasn't interested in the story or anything.

When I first met him, I wasn't bothered about doing the film as it seemed like another German villain. I suggested all sorts of variations to the script, which he was happy to go along with. But when we came to shoot it, he hadn't altered the script at all! We just went along and did it as it was. John was an interesting man, because he was not very invested in story, but more by special effects. He was a very laid-back filmmaker.

Obviously, you have a stage background, performing with the Royal Shakespeare Company. Do you find that the theatre is where you have the opportunity to play more well-rounded characters as you have more time to flesh them out?

I think, when it comes to Shakespeare, whatever he does is well-rounded! No matter how big or small, whether the characters are good or bad. If Shakespeare is writing it, there will be some interesting words to say, and the interesting aspect of human nature to view.

In movies, it's a different case, and that's why villains' parts are often not so interesting. There's no time for backstory, and they don't tell you where they came from, or where they're going to. Nor very often do they get the women, either! Although *Raiders* is an exception.

When you work with directors such as Edgar Wright on *Hot Fuzz* and Neil Marshall on *Centurion*, these are obviously filmmakers who have grown up watching you in the likes of *Raiders of the Lost Ark*. Do you find that, in terms of fans, they are among the most passionate – as it's films like this that got them into filmmaking?

In fact, I'm always a little surprised that they are not very intrigued by the detailed stories about the shoots. It's usually just my presence, that I worked with Spielberg in this classic and something of that might rub off. It's not the sense that it might improve their work, but in the sense that there's a continuity. Very often, especially with Neil Marshall's cases, it was one of the films that got him into filmmaking in the first place.

Hot Fuzz has just celebrated its tenth anniversary. When you were making the film, you were working with icons of the British acting industry, like Jim Broadbent and Timothy Dalton. I imagine that shoot was great fun to work on?

It was great fun to make because all those actors were in my peer group, and we grew up and often worked together. Jim Broadbent was an assistant stage manager in Liverpool Playhouse, when I was working there in the early seventies. Similarly, Kenneth Cranham (James Reaper in *Hot*

A villain for a whole new generation as Ivan Ooze in *Mighty Morphin Power Rangers: The Movie* (1995). Photo courtesy of 20th Century Fox.

Fuzz) is one of my oldest friends, so it was just delightful to be together with them all the time, and working with Edgar Wright, Simon Pegg, and Nick Frost.

I'm guessing that it's not often during your career that you get to say, 'Oh, fuck off grasshopper,' before shooting someone in the chest?

[laughs] No, but these days, it's often thrown back at me.

There are a couple of films that I'm fascinated by your involvement in. One of them is *Mighty Morphin Power Rangers: The Movie*, where you were cast as Ivan Ooze. How did that project land on your desk?

That was completely out of the blue. I'd had a period of being out of work and, at that time, I had a wonderful house in Essex that I'd had to let go and move back into London. Then, this film came up offering quite a good deal out in Australia. I never met anyone for it, I just filmed an audition tape in London and was given carte blanche to do whatever I wanted.

It was a completely zany script, nothing like the script that we filmed. In the original script, Ivan Ooze was a shapeshifter and, at one point, he turned into a Black man, and at another point, into a woman. During the audition, I gave them bits and pieces of these various characters, and that's how I got the role. The extraordinary thing about *Power Rangers* is, while we were doing it, I thought the film would disappear without a trace, but in fact, of all the films I've made, it's the one that keeps coming back, and I'm now continually asked to do conventions and signings with the Power Rangers.

It was a surprisingly massive hit at the time and, like you said, there's a devoted fanbase who have now grown up and are introducing their own children to it.

That's exactly what they're doing. I keep meeting these families when I do these comic cons who say, 'We brought our children up watching *Power Rangers*.' I think it's a form of child abuse! I wouldn't have recommended it to my own children! [laughs]

Then there was a lot of criticism at the time about Power Rangers, because they all did kickboxing, and there were lots of articles in the press that it was encouraging children to be violent.

There was the same hysteria when I was younger, but against Teenage Mutant Ninja Turtles, so this sort of press outrage is always cyclical.

The great thing is, I've reconnected with all the *Power Ranger* actors. My wife and I run a charity for orphan children in Uganda, and all the Power Rangers have expressed an interest in coming out to the school we run later this year. I'm hoping we're going to get the Power Rangers to Africa, which will be fun! It's all come about because of this resurgence of interest in Power Rangers. I didn't hear anything for twenty years, and then, suddenly, people started requesting Power Rangers pictures!

I've got to ask about the film *Double Team,* where you starred as Alex Goldsmythe. That film is fascinating because it stars Jean-Claude Van Damme and North Korea's closest western ally, Dennis Rodman. It was directed by Tsui Hark who is one of Hong Kong's best filmmakers, but on set stories seem to revolve around the egos of the two stars. What was the entire experience like for you?

[laughs] I don't know about two. There was also Mickey Rourke.

Of course, Mickey Rourke!

The whole film was a car crash. It bears no relation to the original script. It was obvious from day one it would be a disaster. Van Damme, Dennis Rodman, and Mickey Rourke all refused to turn up for rehearsals, which were done in Rome. I turned up with some people who were playing the smaller parts and none of the principals were there!

Tsui Hark was a very nice man who had a vision for the film. He had a script, but defying all the odds, the final film bears no relation to what he thought he was working towards. I never got to speak to him about this, but I would imagine he was disgusted by the final thing. Rodman couldn't move and say a line at the same time. God knows what Mickey Rourke was going for, but he was having helicopters take him to Lourdes during the shoot.

Wow.

It really is the most bizarre film I've ever worked on. I started keeping a journal, but after three days, my writing is sloping off the page. I was either really drunk or really bored, I can't remember which. Probably a mixture of both! In many ways, it was a wonderful shoot because we had a month in Rome, a month in Holland, a month in Greece – so you can't complain about that!

You should probably try and dig that journal out and see how upbeat you are on the first day, and how quickly it all goes wrong.

[laughs] I'm sure that went in the dustbin a long time ago.

A publicity headshot of Paul Freeman. Photo courtesy of Paul Freeman.

I was just thinking, you have had several spectacular death scenes during your career – getting impaled by punji sticks, your head exploding due to the power of the Ark of the Covenant – are there any that stick out in your mind as the most memorable or the most fun to shoot?

I think it must be *Raiders*, of course, because simply, it's a classic.

Ronny Cox

"Hello, buddy boy. Dick Jones here. I guess you're on your knees right about now, begging for your life. Pathetic. You don't feel so cocky now, do ya, Bob? You know what the tragedy is here, Bob? We could have been friends... but life goes on, it's an old story, the fight for love and glory, huh, Bob? It helps if you think of it as a game, Bob. Every game has a winner and a loser. I'm cashing you out, Bob."

— Dick Jones, *RoboCop* (1987).

Select Filmography

- *Deliverance* (1972) – Drew
- *The Onion Field* (1979) – Det. Sgt. Pierce R. Brooks
- *Taps* (1981) – Colonel Kerby
- *Beverly Hills Cop* (1984) – Lt. Bogomil
- *Beverly Hills Cop II* (1987) – Andrew Bogomil
- *RoboCop* (1987) – Dick Jones
- *Total Recall* (1990) – Vilos Cohaagen
- *Captain America* (1990) – President Tom Kimball
- *Murder At 1600* (1997) – President Jack Neil

Dick Jones has a problem and that problem's name is RoboCop. After his law enforcement prototype, ED 209, malfunctions with lethal consequences, his company rival, Bob Morton, swoops in with the back-up RoboCop program. With ED 209 shelved, Bob Morton rising through the company ranks, and RoboCop cleaning up the streets, Jones hires Clarence Boddicker to take his rival out. Permanently.

Ronny Cox as Dick Jones (Ronny Cox) in *RoboCop* (1987).
Photo courtesy of Orion Pictures.

THERE WAS A TIME IN ACTION CINEMA when Ronny Cox symbol-
ized the epitome of American capitalism. Under the direction of Paul
Verhoeven, he played not one, but two, ruthless capitalist CEOs (Dick
Jones in *RoboCop*, and Vilos Cohaagen in *Total Recall*) who would do
whatever they could to hold onto power and profit.

However, in real life, Ronny Cox couldn't be further from the villains
he plays on screen. In fact, these days, acting isn't where his true passion
lies, it's folk music. When I spoke to the screen legend, he'd just returned
from a music tour in Ireland. That's right, the man who famously tried
to suffocate the population of Mars onscreen prefers to travel the world,
singing folk classics and playing his guitar.

In many ways, that's serendipitous as, for many people, their introduction to Ronny Cox was as the ill-fated Drew in *Deliverance*, who was
famously in the film's 'Dueling Banjos' scene. Of course, when I pointed
that out to Ronny, I made a musical faux pas.

**Despite you appearing in *Deliverance* playing a banjo, I had no idea
that you were such an avid music lover.**

I wasn't playing the banjo in *Deliverance*, I was playing the guitar.

There we go. Right away, my music knowledge has failed me.

[laughs] If you think I'm the one playing the banjo, we got problems! I just got back from my ninth tour in Ireland and I love it over there. I've always been a musician, and I got the role in *Deliverance* because I could play. I grew up playing music and put myself through college with a band. All the years I was struggling as an actor, I was struggling as a folk musician, too. Music has been a complete part of my life. These days, I spend most of my time playing music, although I've been lucky with my acting career. However, today, I turn down about 90% of the acting jobs I'm offered because I love to play music so much more. Don't get me wrong, I love acting, but I don't love it quite as much as the music, and I can tell you why.

Please do.

With acting, no matter what you're doing – movies, television, plays – there is, and must be, that imaginary fourth wall between you and the audience. You can't step through the lens and talk directly to the people, and you can't talk to the audience from the stage. With the show I do, because I'm also a storyteller, as well as a songwriter and a musician, there is the possibility of a profound one-on-one sharing that takes place. Nothing cuts through to the heart like music does.

It's amazing that you have such a passion for music, and yet you pursued an acting career for so long. Was there ever an opportunity where you tried to be a musician full time and do the acting part time, rather than vice versa?

I made that decision about eight or ten years ago. When I started out, my second big film was *Bound for Glory* (1976), and I played music in that, and in my first television series [was] called *Apple's Way* (1974). On that show, I picked and sang a song every week. Early in my career, I knew I was this actor that also played music. Then, I did a television series in the early nineties that was a miserable failure here, but it was a big hit apparently in the UK, called *Cop Rock* (1990), and Randy Newman did all the music for it. Those of us who worked on it loved it, but it was twenty years ahead of its time.

Again, I'm sure you know the show in England [I don't – Ed.]. They show *Cop Rock* marathons because they love it so much [They do? – Ed.]

and a lot of people think it's America's finest show [Who?! – Ed.] That show convinced me, or showed me, how much I missed music. From that point on, I've gone back and forth. I still act, and just did a movie in Bulgaria, and another with Willie Nelson down in Nashville. I'm even involved in the video game industry doing the mo-cap stuff.

For an old guy, I still work a lot! I've had a great career, but the thing that gives me the most pleasure is playing the music. That's what I do. I'm not rich, but I've got enough money that I can go and do what turns me on the most. If you're sitting and watching me and I'm saying to you how much money I'm making, if I'm holding my arms as wide as I can, that's how much money I would make doing movies. If I hold my fingers half an inch apart, that's how much money I make playing music, but it's not about making money.

It's about doing what you love. Coincidentally, I spoke to one of your *Cop Rock* and *RoboCop* co-stars for this book, Paul McCrane.

Paul's great. Paul's fabulous. Recently, we all appeared in a big, wonderful film called, *RoboDoc,* which is the definitive documentary on the making of *RoboCop.* They've got us all in there. Be on the lookout for it!

That sounds like it would be right up my street. A few years ago, there was the fortieth anniversary of *Deliverance* and you, Burt, Jon Voight, and Ned Beatty got together. Do you see each other often?

No. Ned and Burt are having some health problems. Jon Voight is having some psychological problems with his political love affair with Trump, but we won't go into that! [laughs]

You've played a couple of presidents yourself, in *Captain America (1990)* and *Stargate SG-1 (1997).*

And in *Murder at 1600*!

Of course. When I think of you as an actor, there's two camps that you fall into: there's your more villainous roles, such as in Paul Verhoeven's films, and then there's the straight-laced characters, such as your presidential roles, or police officer roles like Lieutenant Bogomil. Was it, *Taps* or *The Onion Field,* that secured those latter roles for you? Be-

cause you don't seem to be the by-the-book type, you seem to be more of a carefree artist.

Here's the thing: for about a decade after I played Drew in *Deliverance*, I was cast as the 'sensitive good guy' because Drew was the sensitive good guy. In Hollywood, especially in those days, if you played a character with any sensitivity, that somehow got equated with weak. I loved that I could play sensitive characters, but if there was a role had any balls, I never got it because I was known as 'a soft actor'.

It was frustrating, because I'm a former marathon runner and a tennis player, and I've been an athlete my whole life. For me not to get a lot of roles that I wanted to get was frustrating . . . in many ways, *RoboCop* was as big a boom to my career as *Deliverance* was at the beginning, because suddenly, I got offered every role there was. I played bad guys, I played good guys, you name it.

I recently saw some survey where Dick Jones was voted the number one villain in movies! I love playing bad guys because it's about ninety-nine times more fun than playing the good guys. You know exactly what the good guys are going to do, and that they are always going to make the right choice. Bad guys always get to make the most interesting choices, and they're always the most fascinating to watch, and the most fascinating to play. Also, I have zero interest in playing a persona. There's a lot of guys that trade on who they are as their characters, and that doesn't interest me at all. I want to be as far away from me as I can get! I've seen some actors talking about their characters, and they talk about their characters as 'me'. I would never refer to one of my characters as 'me'. My character is, 'that guy'.

If, up until that time, you were getting cast in, as you say, sensitive roles, or as hard-nosed authority figures like Lieutenant Bogomil in *Beverly Hills Cop*, do you know what Paul Verhoeven saw in you that made him want to cast you as a power-hungry CEO - not once, but twice?

Paul and I hit it off right from the get-go, and we saw that we were both on the same page about where to go with this character. I heard, after the fact, that he recognized in me this residual goodwill that had been built up through the years, so, when people see my character, there's this comfort zone. So, when that guy turned out to be bad, he's worse than anybody you've ever seen!

Ronny Cox in *Robocop* (1987) in one of two power-hungry CEO roles he'd play for Paul Verhoeven. Photo courtesy of Orion Pictures.

Paul was deliberately playing on the fact that people knew you from films like *Beverly Hills Cop*?

And from all those other roles. Someone once said to me, 'Ronny, having you play Dick Jones is like having an astronaut that's gone bad!'

Because I saw *RoboCop* quite early on, I've always thought of you as that antagonistic villain type, especially when you have those scenes with the late Miguel Ferrer in the men's bathroom.

That's one of my favorite scenes in the movie. I don't know if I'm telling a story out of school, but *RoboCop* was a very low budget film for what it was at that time. During production, we were going right up against the edge of the budget, and the money people were thinking of pulling the plug on the film. The story I heard, was that on two separate occasions, the money people said, 'Cut together a couple of your best scenes so we are assured.' The scene that they cut together was the bathroom scene with me and Miguel.

It's a fantastic scene.

It saved the film.

Everyone knows the film, now, as a satirical look at violence in media and corporate greed, but, on paper, the title *RoboCop* could easily be viewed as something cheap and cheesy, and easily dismissed.

It was! I'll tell the absolute truth, and I'm not putting down Ed Neumeier who wrote the script, but when my agents first sent me it and said, 'They're making this film called *RoboCop*', I thought it was a joke because, on paper, it just wasn't there.

Frankly, I wasn't interested in playing it until I met with Paul Verhoeven and he gave me a chance to break out of those Mr. Nice Guy roles I'd previously done. Paul showed me all his plans for the film, and again, I don't mean to put down Ed Neumeier at all, but everything that is fabulous and magic and incredible about that film, can be directly attributable [sic] to Paul Verhoeven. He saw the possibility of the humor in the film, and the social satire within that. He's the one that made us care about this robot, and he pulled off all those things that were not on the page.

I've read that a lot of those satirical adverts and news clips that Verhoeven puts into his films come from his time growing up in Nazi-occupied Holland. The level of propaganda that he puts into many of his films, like *Total Recall* and *Starship Troopers* (1997), is something that he views as a legitimate societal concern.

Exactly. We also had real problems getting the film down to an R-rating, so Paul had to go back and re-edit it time after time because of the violence. I don't particularly like gory violence, but I think that, in many ways, the censoring board did the film a big disservice.

Paul grew up in war-torn Europe and saw real violence. He wanted that violence to be over-the-top from the get-go, so that you got that this was a cartoon of violence. He wanted to make it a bloodbath from the beginning, so that the audience, after that initial shock, said, 'I get it, this is a joke.' By the censors getting him to keep cutting the violence back, pretty soon, it got reduced to a normal level of violence. In many ways, the violence was more disturbing once they made him cut it back to that.

What were your initial thoughts on the violence? Because obviously you were in the infamous ED 209 scene where the young employee gets blown apart by machine gunfire, and your character is also repeatedly shot at the end.

[laughs] We all knew that it was meant to be over the top! When they shot me out the window – do you know about squibs and blood packs?

Yes! What was that like? I've always wondered what it's like to be squibbed.

For me, and this is the truth, they put double squibs on the front, double squibs on the back and, when they set them off, it literally took me to my knees. They had to take me to the bathroom. I threw up and I couldn't work for another hour or two! It made me physically ill.

In *Deliverance*, we did our own stunts. All that canoeing, that's all us going down the rapids. [laughs] There's no stunt guys in there, anywhere. I've never had anything put me to my knees quite like those squibs in *RoboCop*.

You'd have thought they would have roped in a stunt man for that scene! With the level of success that *Beverly Hills Cop* and *RoboCop* had at the box office, what was it like to suddenly have that level of recognition that late into your career, after, like you said, being ignored by casting agents except for 'sensitive' roles.

For almost ten years, I was in every movie made. [laughs] I'm not trying to brag too much, although, I saw on the Internet that, from the mid-eighties to the mid-nineties, of the top 100 actors in the world whose movies made the most money, I was at number forty-nine!

I had a run that was almost unheard of out here. Without a television series, I once went five years without a single day that I didn't have a job. Now, I'm not saying that I worked all that time, all I'm saying is that if I finished a film on one day, I might have two weeks off and then I'd be on another film. I wasn't looking for the next project. I had five years where the work came to me.

Beverley Hills Cop **must have been an enormous career boost for you because, at the time, and for almost a decade, it was the most successful R-rated film ever.**

Because I hate sequels, I didn't want to be in *Beverly Hills Cop II.*

Well, you were barely in the sequel. You're in hospital for most of it.

I was the reason for Eddie's character to come back. They wanted me for *Beverly Hills Cop III,* and I read the script and said, 'No thanks.' They keep talking about doing *Beverly Hills Cop IV*, but again, 'No thanks.' Burt Reynolds, for years, wanted to do a sequel to *Deliverance.*

Really?

His idea was that Drew had a twin brother. I said I wasn't interested.

That would have been ridiculous.

RoboCop 2 [1990] sucks too.

Have you seen the remakes of *RoboCop* and *Total Recall*?

I refuse to. I've seen some stuff, and Colin Farrell is a friend of mine, but no thanks.

To be honest, you're not missing out on much.

RoboCop is really a good film, so to me, those remakes are like putting on a wet bathing suit.

***Total Recall* and *Robocop* are very distinct films, especially for that period, so when you try and remake them, and you don't have someone with Paul Verhoeven's vision, you get a very saturated, safe version of the story that's missing a lot. Especially with the *Total Recall* remake.**

You just have the prerequisite shit you have to put out there and then, who cares?

In both films, you have a wonderful actor playing your right-hand man. In *RoboCop,* it's Kurtwood Smith, and in *Total Recall,* you have Michael Ironside. What was it like acting with those two wonderful actors?

Turing Arnold Schwarzenegger's world upside-down in *Total Recall* (1990).
Photo courtesy of TriStar Pictures.

The fun of acting is reacting. All you have to do when you're with great actors like Michael and Kurtwood is just be there. Show up!

I once did a movie, which shall remain nameless, but I didn't like the script. I wasn't knocked out by the director and I wasn't knocked out by my part, but every one of my scenes was with Gene Hackman. For me to get to act with Gene Hackman – it was a no-brainer to say, 'Yes.' I have always been really selective about what roles I want to do. That's not to say that I don't do crap, I just don't do crap on purpose!

You said, when you made *RoboCop*, it was a relatively low budget film, but when you reunited with Verhoeven for *Total Recall*, the film was, at the time, the most expensive film ever made!

I don't know if you know this or not, but *Total Recall* had already shot for three of four weeks in Australia with Ridley Scott directing and Patrick Swayze playing Arnold Schwarzenegger's role, but they pulled the plug. We ended up shooting in Mexico City. We took over all the studios down there and it was, at that time, far and away the most expensive film in the history of the world, but, in many ways, it felt like the lowest budget film you've ever seen. They were still trying to cut corners because they'd put most of the budget into the sets and other things. It didn't feel like working on a big budget film. Not like working on *Beverly Hills Cop,* where you know you're working on a big film. It wasn't like that at all.

Oddly enough, I was shooting *Total Recall* at the same time I was shooting *Captain America* in Yugoslavia. I was flying back and forth from Mexico City to Yugoslavia. In *Captain America,* I was playing the sweetest, nicest, President of [the] United States you've ever seen. In Mexico City, I was playing the villain of the universe. [laughs] That was really fun for me going back and forth playing those two characters.

That must have also been quite a production contrast because *Captain America* was financed by Cannon Films and the studio heads, Menachem Golan and Yoram Globus, were renowned for doing things on the cheap. How did you find working with them compared to working on the most expensive production ever?

No difference. Like I said, *Total Recall,* you felt like you were working on the cheapest film you've ever been in!

[laughs] In *Captain America,* you also acted with J.D. Salinger's son, Matt Salinger, and reunited with your *Deliverance* co-star Ned Beatty.

Let me tell you something about *Captain America*: I'm not sure it ever got a real theatrical release, I think it took it two years to go to video.

It went straight to video, here in the UK.

It took two years to get there and I'll tell you the truth: on paper, it's the finest script I've ever read.

REALLY?!

Really. Michael Tolkin wrote the script and it was a brilliant screenplay. He captured the whole essence of the superhero comic book. To this day, I have never read a script that I thought was as good. I'm going to try not to cast too many aspersions, but Albert Pyun, who directed the film, didn't have the vaguest idea [of] what he was doing.

He's apparently a brilliant editor, and was discovered by Kurosawa, and he was fascinated with the Red Skull, but he didn't have the vaguest idea of what the comic book hero was all about. You had a brilliant cast with Ned Beatty, Darren McGavin, Melinda Dillon, and all those people, and you have a brilliant script and, at that time, it was a fairly decent budget. We shot in Yugoslavia, Italy, Alaska, Los Angeles – we shot all over the place. They really spent some money on that film, but it was just awful.

It has quite a cult following though.

But if you'd seen what could have been possible. Like I said, to this day - I've been in this business for forty-five years – and I've never read a script that I thought was better.

I still can't believe you were flying between Mexico and Yugoslavia between two productions. The time difference must have wrecked you.

[laughs] That was amazing, and I would have to look down to see what I was wearing to remind me which film I was in!

Verhoeven was obviously very happy with you, to let you go between two films!

You know, at the end of the film, when Arnold and I are on the surface of Mars and our eyes are bulging? Well, [special effects maestro] Rob Bottin was making those masks for us. They made a whole bunch of masks where they put air pockets in them to distort the faces and do all kinds of stuff. For them to make those masks, I had to go in, and they slicked back my hair in order to take a picture of my face. All of a sudden, I realized that that really was what Cohaagen should look like.

I got that picture and I took it to Paul and I said, 'Paul, you're going to be pissed with me, but look at this.' He looked at that picture and then he threw his clipboard down and said, 'Do you know why I'm mad at you?' I said, 'No.' He said, 'Because I'm going to have to re-shoot all your scenes.' He got it immediately. They re-shot the day or two that I had done with my regular hair to accommodate that.

It just shows how collaborative Verhoeven is as a director, because he must have been under a lot of pressure at the time.

It was the most expensive film, and they had already had the plug pulled once on a production, so for them to go back and re-shoot, you can imagine what it cost. It's going to cost at least $30,000 to go back, and they'd already shot some stuff in Australia with Patrick Swayze.

I'm just imagining you going up against Patrick Swayze. That would have been a completely different film.

It would have, and they were shooting in Australia!

How did you get on with Arnold during the filming, because he was at the peak of his career in 1990?

We got along fine, but Arnold is a bit of a bully. If he can push people around, he will, but if you push back, then he gets it. I figured that out the first day or two. He and I had a wonderful working relationship. He pushed at me, I pushed back and he accepted that, and then, from then on, we got along famously.

I want to ask you about the character you played in *Star Trek: The Next Generation* – Captain Edward Jellico. Again, on paper, he's the straight-laced, by-the-book type of character that you've played before. He clashes with the crew, but a lot of *Star Trek* fans love the character. Do you ever get people asking you about that guest role?

Absolutely, a lot of people love *Star Trek*, and there are people who think that Jellico is a villain, too. There was this wonderful article recently about how Jellico saved their asses and was the best thing that ever happened to the USS Enterprise!

Here's the thing about Jellico. He came in and did his job. Don't get me wrong, Patrick Stewart and Jonathan Frakes were fabulous in those two episodes, too, but having Jellico come in and shake up that whole situation was, in many ways, cathartic. Gene Roddenberry didn't particularly like conflict between the characters, and this gave them a chance to right that. Also, I don't know if you know this or not, but Patrick Stewart always hated those fish in his Ready Room.

Really?

Captain Jellico (Ronny Cox) butting heads with Commander Riker (Jonathan Frakes) in *Star Trek: The Next Generation* (1987-1994). Photo courtesy of Paramount Pictures.

Patrick's point was, 'Look, we're doing a series about the dignity of all creatures in the universe, and we have captured fish in the Ready Room? Why are they in there?' From the get-go, Patrick always hated those fish in there, so when I came in, as a nod to Patrick, they had my character take those fish out. When Patrick came in and saw it, he cheered! Obviously, the production people were not going to let the fish leave forever, but at least for those two episodes, the fish were gone from the Ready Room.

On a similar note, I can't tell you how much terrible fan mail I've received for kicking over the damn fish bowl in *Total Recall*!

You clearly have something against fish. That's what it is.

Exactly.

Speaking of fish, this may seem like a very strange question, but you're in the 'giant shark' film *Deep Blue Sea* (1999), and you share a scene with Samuel L. Jackson. But you just sit behind a desk, and you don't say anything for the entire duration of your time in the film. I feel that you obviously had a bigger role in that film, so can you shed some light on what exactly you were doing there?

[laughs] Let me tell you about that. That was one of the weirdest jobs I've ever had in my life. They were doing this film, and they were about halfway through the film and they realized they needed more weight. Also, no one really knew what the scientists were doing there, so they felt like they needed some exposition. They wrote three scenes for me, paid me a shitload of money, and I flew down to Mexico to shoot them in these big sets they'd built for my office.

Now, somewhere between shooting those three scenes, and cutting together the movie, my lines got cut out, but I think they hurt the film more by leaving me in, than by cutting me out entirely. I guess because they paid me, they decided to leave some shots of me in, but they would have been better off if they had completely excised those scenes. They keep cutting to my character in this big close-up, and as an audience, you say, 'Holy shit. This guy's going to do something.' All the way through the film, it's in the back of your mind, thinking, 'This guy's going to show up again,' and he never does. It hurts the film so badly.

Exactly! You're Ronny Cox from *RoboCop* and *Total Recall*. Clearly, you're the evil mastermind behind these giant sharks, and then you never say anything and you never come back. It's really weird. With so many famous films in your career, what character are you most recognized for? Do you get people coming up to you going, 'Give them the air, Cohaagen,' or are you relatively anonymous on the streets?

Here's a thing about me, and I talk about this in my show a lot, but it's true: even though I've been in a thousand, million movies and television shows, people almost never recognize me as an actor.

Everybody just thinks they know me. I've had this conversation a thousand times. When someone comes up and says, 'You're so and so's doctor aren't you?' I say, 'No, I'm an actor. You see me in movies.' Literally, I've had this conversation a thousand times.

These days, Ronny tours the world performing folk music as well as doing the occasional piece of acting. Photo courtesy of Ronny Cox.

For a lot of the characters that I've played, it's not like I'm disguising myself, but I work from the inside out. I don't try to become the character. I don't believe in that. I don't think you have to be a drug addict to play a drug addict. As an actor, sometimes you have to know things about the character that the character doesn't know. For instance, Oedipus doesn't need to know he has a Mommy problem, but the actor playing him does. Therefore, the fun for me is playing the character, and that's why I spend my time finding out everything I know about this character and just letting things come out from that.

William Sadler

"You were warned not to try to restore your systems. You've wasted lives and precious time on a futile and obvious target. Now you're gonna pay the penalty."
         – Colonel Stuart, *Die Hard 2* (1990).

Select Filmography

- *Project X* (1987) – Dr. Carroll
- *Hard to Kill* (1990) – Senator Vernon Trent
- *Die Hard 2* (1990) – Colonel Stuart
- *Bill and Ted's Bogus Journey* (1991) – The Grim Reaper
- *The Shawshank Redemption* (1994) – Heywood
- *The Green Mile* (1999) – Klaus Detterick

How can the same shit happen to the same guy twice? Once again, it's Christmas Eve and John McClane is faced with terrorists ruining his holiday plans. When a team of former Special Ops commandos-turned-mercenaries, led by Colonel Stuart (William Sadler), seize Dulles International Airport, John must figure out how to return control of the airport back to the authorities before planes start falling out of the sky. If that wasn't a big enough problem, his wife Holly is on one of the planes.

WITH INTENSE EYES that seem to burn directly into your soul, William Sadler was seemingly born to play villains. Whether they're cold and un-

After taking over Dulles International Airport, Colonel Stuart (William Sadler) decides to punish the authorities and John McClane (Bruce Willis) for trying to interrupt his plans in *Die Hard 2* (1990). Photo courtesy of 20th Century Fox.

compromising, like in *Die Hard 2*, or cowardly weasels like in *Hard to Kill*, Sadler can simultaneously have audiences wanting to see his characters meet their comeuppance, while also wishing they had more screen time.

Sadler could have easily fallen into the trap of playing bad guys in every Hollywood movie in the 1990s, but, thanks to some canny choices and being showcased by regular collaborator Frank Darabont in several roles (*The Shawshank Redemption*, *The Green Mile* and *The Mist*, 2007), he has shown he is one of the industry's most chameleonic, and arguably under-rated, stars.

He is constantly working and, when we spoke, he had just finished filming the TV series *Power* (2017). We had a wonderful conversation about everything from his being cast as a bad guy in his very first film (*Project X*), going from action to comedic roles, getting slapped around by Steven Seagal, and doing naked Tai chi for *Die Hard 2*.

Early in your career, you were a proficient stage actor, so how did you make the transition to screen acting?

The very first film that I did was *Project X*, with Matthew Broderick and Helen Hunt, and I was the villain in that. I played the Air Force doctor who set up this program that trained the chimps to fly simulators, and then killed them. It's based on true events. Apparently, the Air Force was worried that they had all of these bombers that could retaliate and fly to Russia if we were bombed, but, if the pilots were radiated, they weren't sure how long they'd be able to fly. That was my first real film role, so I was a villain right out of the box, I guess!

It's a strange role in a strange film. How did you get cast? Did they know you from your work on the stage or was it something you auditioned for?

I had just spent a year and a half on Broadway in *Biloxi Blues* [1984-1985] and Matthew Broderick was in the original cast. I'm guessing the director must have seen the play. I don't remember having to audition for this role, so they must have decided I was seemingly evil!

After the kind of success that film had, did you find that similar roles were offered to you? You didn't really do many roles immediately after *Project X*, until about 1990, so were you dividing your time between the stage and screen?

After *Project X*, my wife and I moved back to New York. We owned an apartment in the East Village, and I wasn't really interested in moving to Los Angeles, although I loved working on the movie. There's a learning curve to working for a camera if you've spent that much time on stage.

I was cast in a TV show called *Private Eye* [1987-1988] as a regular, and that brought me back out to Los Angeles. Once I was out there in the land of films and television, I was cast opposite Steven Seagal in *Hard to Kill* and Dennis Hopper in *The Hot Spot* [1990] - both pretty evil dudes!

It's around that time when you started getting all the prominent villain roles like Senator Trent in *Hard to Kill*. When you get cast as a corrupt senator, do you do any research into that, or do you embrace the out-and-out villainy of being the bad guy in a Steven Seagal film?

You just watch as many Republicans as you can! I'm joking, of course, but the way I approach villains is the way I approach just about anybody.

No one who does bad things thinks what they're doing is bad. They don't set out to do bad things. They have their own justification and what they think is their own moral compass. Very often, people, like Colonel Stuart in *Die Hard 2,* have all the qualities of a hero, except he is playing for the wrong team. He's brave, he's smart, he has a sense of humor and he's a good leader. I always find the more interesting antagonists are where there is room for them to be seen as human, as I think that makes them more dangerous. The more believably human they are, the more awful whatever it is that they are doing.

I think the worst crime for an actor is to say, 'Ah, this is a bad guy,' and then do nothing but twirl your mustache and leer at people. Alan Rickman, in the first *Die Hard,* set the bar pretty high. His performance showed a fascinating human and I loved it. It never bothered me that I played so many bad guys because you can't have a James Bond without a really good villain.

And often the villains are more memorable than the heroes.

You really need somebody to create a gigantic sense of evil or else it doesn't look like your hero is conquering anything.

If we could talk about making *Hard to Kill,* from everything that I've read, it was quite a difficult shoot, because Steven Seagal and director Bruce Malmuth didn't get on at all. How did you find the whole experience?

[laughs] Well, Bruce and I got along very well. Steven was respectful, and we were professional with one another. I didn't really hang out and socialize with either one of them. I remember that we had to shoot a different ending. There was an ending where my character, Vernon Trent, takes a swing at Seagal's character with a fireplace poker, and he grabs me and throws me into a fireplace and holds me down while I burn to death.

Wow.

They shot it and then decided that a hero can't do that, and so we all got back together again to shoot a different ending, starting with that swing of the fireplace poker. When we got to the set, Bruce decided it was going to be a fight scene that ends with me being arrested.

He and Seagal got into this big argument. Seagal was saying, 'Well, I should grab him by the neck and pull his tongue and kick him in the balls and smash his head against the floor!' The two of them went back and forth and, all the while, I'm standing there in a white bathrobe wondering how this is going to end. Finally, Seagal got angry and left the set. He went to this trailer and then I remember I had this idea: Seagal's character has a sawed-off shotgun and I thought, 'What if he puts that under my chin and drops it out of sight?' The audience can tell by my expression, and my begging, that he's got it aimed at my genitals, and then you hear it go off and Seagal can say something like, 'I don't know how I missed. It must be smaller than I thought.'

I told the producers and Malmuth, and they said, 'That's great. Who's going to tell Steven? If it comes from us, he's going to hate it.' So, they asked me to go tell him! I went to his trailer, told him my idea and he said, 'Great, let's shoot it.'

It seems he was open to the idea if it made him look good.

Yes, [laughs] and it seemed like a better idea than having my head smashed against the floor, having my tongue pulled out, and my neck being broken.

William Sadler has appeared in several episodes of *Tales from the Crypt* (1989-1994) including the film *Tales from the Crypt: Demon Knight* (1995). Photo courtesy of Universal Pictures.

Do you get many people coming up to you and quoting your line from that film? Saying that they're going to 'take it to the bank'?

[laughs] I do hear that quite often. 'You can take that to the bank.' I had no idea that was going to be such a catchphrase. I half expect to hear it out of the mouths of politicians these days.

After the kind of success of *Hard to Kill*, I'm going to assume you got offered the role of Colonel Stuart in *Die Hard 2*. Were you wary of accepting it after what Alan Rickman did in the first film?

I was apprehensive about playing the villain in the second *Die Hard,* but I was excited by the prospect of it. Like I said, I was a big fan of what Alan had done in the first *Die Hard* movie, and they were not small shoes to fill. Between *Hard to Kill* and *Die Hard 2,* I did the movie *The Hot Spot* with Dennis Hopper, where I played another evil guy.

I think what led to *Die Hard 2* was that I'd done an episode of *Tales from the Crypt.* It was the very first episode of *Tales from the Crypt* that Walter Hill directed called, The Man Who Was Death. I was an executioner who gets laid off from the prison when they abolish the death penalty. He goes and hangs out in courtrooms and sees people getting off on technicalities, so he arranges for them to have accidents. Just as he's caught by the police, they reinstate the death penalty and he goes to the electric chair!

It was a great break for me that they let me play that part. It was a terrific, funny, and tongue-in-cheek role, but the producers on the show were Joel Silver, Richard Donner, Robert Zemeckis, and Walter Hill. I've worked with every single one of them since!

I think when Joel Silver was getting ready to do *Die Hard 2,* he saw that episode, and I think that may have influenced him. It was a really, really fun role. Colonel Stuart is a different kind of guy, but they wanted that evil presence, I guess.

Colonel Stuart was famously based on Colonel Oliver North, who was responsible for the Iran-Contra scandal during Reagan's term, but he was in nowhere near the kind of physical shape you got into for the role.

I had been working out for a few years, but I was nowhere near that kind of shape. Also, when I agreed to the script, there wasn't a nude scene in it!

Ah yes, your famous naked Tai chi scene.

Yes, my naked Tai chi scene! I found out about that during costume fitting, because there wasn't any costume for that scene! Renny Harlin, the director, was there with the costumer and I said, 'So, what's [Stuart] wearing in the hotel room scene?' There was this awkward pause and Renny looked at the costumer, and he looked at me, and he said [puts on Finnish accent], 'Well, Bill, actually, I was thinking you would be nude.' I said, 'Oh.' After another long pause, I said, 'Well, I tell you what. You push that scene off to the end of the shoot and get me a trainer. I'll see what I can do.' And that's what we did!

It worked out well because, frankly, nothing motivates you like knowing your bare ass is going to be hanging out in the summer blockbuster sequel to *Die Hard!*

I bet that's very motivational, knowing that millions of people will be staring at your buttocks.

It scared the crap out of me. You'd be surprised how many sit-ups it makes you want to do!

You also just demonstrated something else that you do in that film, which is your ability to put on an accent. When you crash the plane in *Die Hard 2*, you put on a Southern accent, and it's something that you appear to be very adept at. Is there a particular accent that directors or studios want you to lean towards when you're playing certain villainous roles?

I don't know that it's so much at their request, but it often seems appropriate to me. It seemed like it would make it more horrifying for the pilot that he hears this friendly American voice. I've always had a facility with accents and it seemed appropriate to me. It was an instinctive thing to do.

You also do it in a very calm and detached way, which makes it all the more terrifying, and you crash poor Colm Meaney into the ground, who you would later star with in *Star Trek: Deep Space Nine*! [*Sadler would have a recurring guest role on DS9 as Luthor Sloan, the mysterious head of Section 31*]

A publicity photo from *Bill and Ted's Bogus Journey* where William Sadler appeared as The Grim Reaper. Photo courtesy of Orion Pictures.

Yeah, I hate it when I have to do that!

In *Die Hard 2*, you're surrounded by a whole bunch of other character actors like John Leguizamo, Robert Patrick, and Franco Nero. Did you become close with your evil 'Band of Brothers'?

[laughs] I love my evil 'Band of Brothers'. We've kept in touch more or less since then and it's been fun watching everybody's careers move along. In a lot of ways, the villain in *Die Hard 2* set the tone for lots of films to come for me. If you demonstrate that you're good at portraying that one kind of character, [studios] are more than happy to probably bring you in again and again for that same thing because there's no risk. Everybody knows you can pull that off.

If you're doing a romantic comedy, you have to convince a lot of folks to risk the money they're spending on the movie that you can also be funny, which I have to do from time to time as well.

While I think of you primarily as playing villains, I've always been impressed that you've never been typecast by that and you always seem to find roles that people wouldn't associate you with, such as The Grim

Reaper in *Bill & Ted's Bogus Journey*. Was that a deliberate move on your part to shake it up and to keep it fresh and not let studios pigeon-hole you in that manner?

It was a deliberate move on my part. With The Grim Reaper, what was really fun about that role was that he starts off being the scariest thing you can imagine. He starts out being a scary monster of a figure, and then, when the boys beat him at all the board games, he falls apart. Then the real Reaper, who is this insecure character, emerges. He's not such a toughie after all. That was fun to play.

Can you still remember the rap? 'You may be a king or a little street sweeper . . . .'

I wrote that.

You wrote it?!

I wrote that little rap. There was a place in the script where they had written what they called a rap, but it didn't rhyme and I just couldn't make it sound good. I asked them if I could take a shot at it and I came up with, 'You might be a king or a little street sweeper, but sooner or later, you'll dance with the reaper!'

That's amazing. I had no idea that you wrote that.

Again, it's one of my favorite things to do in the business. Every once in a while, if I have an instinct about something, I love to be able to put it out there and let them see my idea. If it works, it works. If it doesn't, that's fine too. I love to feel part of the creative process, especially with a character like that. Once I was in the skin of The Grim Reaper, with the accent and the makeup, I was riffing all over the place. The character could read the phonebook and it would come out sounding funny.

Would I be right in assuming that's the role that you're most recognized for, despite the amount of makeup and everything?

[laughs] I don't know whether it's the most recognizable. It's memorable. I keep hoping they get it together to make a *Bill & Ted 3*.

They've been saying that for years. Have they talked to you about it?

They have. They said, 'We have a script.' I guess they have to get financing for it, but they better hurry up! I had such a good time playing that guy. I would love to do it again. Like I said, I don't get a chance to be funny all that often, and I have a silly streak in me. (Ed. – Eight months after this interview, Bill and Ted: Face The Music was officially green-lit).

One director who lets you play with that silly streak seems to be Frank Darabont as, in *The Shawshank Redemption,* your character [Heywood] is more the comic relief of the group, but then, Frank also turned you into a religious zealot by the end of *The Mist*. He clearly recognizes that you can do pretty much anything. What's it like working with Frank, with a director who seems to let you really experiment?

Frank is an extraordinary director in my opinion, because he writes these pieces as well. He expects more from himself and from his actors than other directors. He knows these people so intimately that he gives you license to go for it. Frank Darabont has a company of actors just like Orson Welles had – a group of people that he has worked with again and again because there is chemistry between these talented people. It's like a baseball team. It can take a while to get to know everybody's rhythms.

Frank was actually a writer on *Tales from the Crypt*. That's how we met. He came up to me on set and said, 'I'm going to do this film called *Rita Hayworth and The Shawshank Redemption* and I'd love you to be in it.' He gave me a copy of the Stephen King novella and I must confess that when he said that, I didn't believe him!

The thing is that my character, Heywood, as he's written in the script, is not really funny. He's not a funny person. It's not clear that he's the comical lead or that there's a human side to him. He makes the bet that gets Fat Ass killed and wins all the cigarettes, and then, when Andy [Dufrene] says, 'What was his name?', he says, 'What do you care what his fucking name is? He's dead.' You could read that and say, 'He's a cold-ass motherfucker,' and let it lay right there, and I didn't want to do that. I gave him a slight stutter to soften and humanize him. I imagine that I have a dial where I can turn my character's IQ up or down. I turned his IQ way down. The further down I turned it, the more I liked him. He's always just one step behind what's going on around him. They are just colors that, if you add them to the mix, make for a more believable human, and not simply a hard-ass. I find human beings are much more complicated than that.

These days, you're offered a wide variety of roles. You were Chesty Puller in *The Pacific* (2010), you're the President of the United States in the Marvel Cinematic Universe, you're currently working on several TV series - how do you think the industry sees you today?

I think over the years, the business's view of me has evolved. I think, at first, I really was pigeonholed, as it was easy to see me as just the senator from *Hard to Kill* or Colonel Stuart. I did go from one evil bastard to another, but I think over the years, people's impression of me has expanded. Today, I play a lot of fathers, but they're not always nice people! [laughs]

We've evolved from bad guys to bad fathers?

A fair number of bad fathers, yes! But, I get a chance to add more color to my roles these days.

I want to end with a quote that I found in an interview you did a few years ago. You said, 'I get asked to play a lot of badass evil people and I really don't mind that.' Is that something that you still agree with?

William Sadler (second from right) as Heywood in *The Shawshank Redemption* (1994). Photo courtesy of Columbia Pictures.

I'm happy to play the main heavy in the story. If you can't be James Bond, then be Dr. No! Villains are challenging because they don't have to abide by the same rules that heroes do. There's a freedom to playing somebody truly evil. They don't have to be honest and they don't have to be trustworthy. Anthony Hopkins is the best in *The Silence of the Lambs* [1991] because, within this soft-spoken gentleman, is the most frightening monster you can imagine. It's made all more frightening by the fact that he's so sweet and soft-spoken and polite. It's always a challenge, but it's a wonderful challenge to play these kinds of people.

Julian Glover

"Hitler can have the world, but he can't take it with him. I'm going to be drinking my own health after he's gone the way of the dodo."

– Walter Donovan, *Indiana Jones and
the Last Crusade* (1989).

Select Filmography

- *Quatermass and the Pit* (*Five Million Years to Earth*, 1967) – Colonel Breen
- *Star Wars: Episode V – The Empire Strikes Back* (1980) – General Veers
- *For Your Eyes Only* (1981) – Kristatos
- *The Fourth Protocol* (1987) – Brian Harcourt-Smith
- *Cry Freedom* (1987) – Don Card
- *Indiana Jones and the Last Crusade* (1989) – Walter Donovan
- *Harry Potters and the Chamber of Secrets* (2002) – Aragog
- *Troy* (2004) – Triopas
- *Game of Thrones* (2011-2016) – Grand Maester Pycelle

Indiana Jones has been searching the world for his father, Henry Jones Snr., after he went missing searching for the Holy Grail. Despite being warned by his father's benefactor, Walter Donovan, to "not trust anybody", the Jones boys and their friends, Marcus Brody and Sallah, have found themselves captured by Nazis at the final resting place of the cup of Christ. Determined to get the prized artifice for

355

Walter Donovan (Julian Glover) hunts for The Holy Grail in *Indiana Jones and the Last Crusade* (1989). Photo courtesy of LucasFilm.

himself, as well as the promise of eternal life, Donovan, who is working for the Nazis, shoots Henry in the stomach, telling Indiana that only the healing power of the Grail can save his father's life.

EXUDING SOPHISTICATION, CHARM, and a distinct air of authority, Julian Glover has played villains in some of the biggest franchises of all time; *James Bond, Indiana Jones, Doctor Who, Star Wars, Harry Potter* – he's been in them all. First gaining recognition in popular sixties TV shows like *The Saint* [1964-1968] and *The Avengers* [1965-1969], Glover is still earning the loyalty of new fans today, thanks to his role as the scheming Grand Maester Pycelle in *Game of Thrones.*

Despite growing up watching all the films that Glover is best known for, it took years for me to realise that Greek smuggler Kristatos in *For Your Eyes Only* and General Veers from *The Empire Strikes Back* were played by the same actor. With his (RSC) training and an ability to master even the hardest accents, Glover disappears into his roles, surprising many. He's been hiding in plain sight in so many infamous films.

When I spoke to Julian Glover, he was about to start rehearsals for *Julius Caesar* at the Bristol Old Vic (2017), and he was keen to explain how Shakespeare has shaped much of his career.

On your IMDb page, it says that your 'talent for accents and cold expressions has always made you ideal for playing refined villains.' Would you say you have a particularly good cold expression?

[laughs] I suppose it must be a reason, but I didn't know I had that. It's something which I would say I use. I have a coldness in the eye, which I can turn on quite quickly.

A great deal of my career has been spent playing villains, as you know, and I always try to find the man underneath the character. I've never played a villain who was a magic person or who has a hat that he can throw and chop somebody's head off, or a hook on the end of their arm. I always try to find a reason for why my character does what he does.

Do you think your time with the Royal Shakespeare Company prepared you for a lifetime of playing villains both on the small and big screen?

Shakespeare is the cornerstone of my theatrical life. In those days, it was called the Shakespeare Memorial Theatre and young aspiring actors like myself applied to do things that young actors would never do now – apply to be a supernumerary. I went to Stratford just to be on the same stage as these fantastic actors and to see if I could build my way up to getting better parts.

I went to Stratford in 1957 and stayed for three seasons. I met my first wife, Dame Eileen Atkins, and all the great masters of Shakespeare were working there. Not all of them, of course, became Knights and Dames and Lords, but I was on the same stage at the same time as them. That was the most extraordinary kick-off to a career.

Do you find that playing villains is more fun as an actor?

People always enjoy villains. In quite a lot of films people remember the villain, but they don't always remember the hero. I've played so many villain parts, and some have been really dreadful and very one-dimensional. It's very difficult to find some sort of real human life in them, but when they're well-written, they're great to play.

As I've gotten much older, I'm playing more nice people and I find those very gratifying too. I love finding the good sides of people's characters, which offsets the bad side. For instance, in *Indiana Jones and the Last Crusade*, I ask, 'What would you do for the secret of eternal life?' I throw that back at the audience, because I think people would do a great deal for that.

In *For Your Eyes Only*, [Kristatos] is a really nice chap and a successful businessman. He's paying for this girl to go to the Olympics, but the trouble is, he wants more money, so he goes to the Russians and that makes him a villain. He knows it's treacherous, but that's the reason for it. That's how I've always tried to play my villains. We're all two-faced, so I try to portray that. Sometimes I succeed and sometimes I don't, but then some bank managers succeed and sometimes they don't!

One of your most famous early roles is that of Colonel Breen in *Qua-termass and the Pit***. A lot of your characters seem to have a bit of a**

A publicity card of General Veers (Julian Glover) in *The Empire Strikes Back* (1981). Photo courtesy of LucasFilm.

military air about them. Did you have any military training in your youth?

I became an officer when I did National Service, so I got to know quite a lot about the army and military training. Actually, I've only done – there was one episode of *The Avengers* where I was a military person, and yes, Colonel Breen. Can you think of any others?

Well, General Veers in *The Empire Strikes Back.*

Yes, of course! I'm good at military people because I learned how to stand up straight! [laughs] I could do a very good drill in the army, and I learned about obeying orders and all that shit. It's such rubbish, but I had to do it in the army. There was another role in *Two Men Went to War*, a lovely little film I did with Kenneth Cranham. I suppose I have played quite a lot of military people and I don't mind that!

At the National Theatre, I was in with Arnold Wesker's play, *Chips with Everything* [1997]. I played the grimy officer on that, who was not a very pleasant man! [laughs] Another in my long line of horrible people.

The role of Colonel Breen in *Quatermass and The Pit* is an interesting one because he's not an evil man, he's just very entrenched in his beliefs and unwilling to change them.

I liked the part for all the reasons that you mentioned because he wasn't a villain, he just knew what he knew. However, he was intransigent and immovable, which is a great human fault. It's like politics, I've always voted Labour, so I'm always going to vote Labour whatever happens!

I also enjoyed making the film because of the wonderful cast. Andrew Keir is sadly lamented as he was one of my favourite people in the whole world as a human being. He was such a lovely actor. Barbara Shelley was such a sweet woman and easy to work with. James Donald was a superb film actor and it was very exciting to work with him. I got on very well with the director, Roy Baker, who is known for being quite difficult, but he liked me for some reason!

You also had one of your first, but not your last, gruesome death scenes.

Roger Moore and Julian Glover in *For Your Eyes Only* (1981).
Photo courtesy of MGM Pictures.

Oh, yes. Not as gruesome as in *Indiana Jones*, but it was pretty gruesome, wasn't it? [laughs] The makeup took a long time to perfect, because it's a difficult thing to create a fatally burnt face, but one that is still recognisable. Also, you had to be able to see the uniform, so it couldn't be completely burnt off, which of course, in those instances, it would have been, as that will go faster than your whole face!

It was a difficult piece of technical work which took us a long time. We shot it in about three hours and in one go, because we knew it was going to be unpleasant. It was very uncomfortable because I had all sort of bits and pieces all over my face, such as parts of canvas and a chewing gum-like substance that was all painted on to be peeling skin. It was uncomfortable, but that's what I was being paid for, wasn't it? [laughs]

Obviously, your film career took off in the 1980s when you were cast as the Bond villain Kristatos in *For Your Eyes Only*. Is it true that you auditioned to be James Bond in the early seventies after Sean Connery retired from the role?

Well, I tested along with some other people, but I was not terribly hopeful. It was an enormous thing to do, but we knew pretty well from when we started testing that Roger Moore was going to do it. He was such an obvious takeover, having played *The Saint* [1969] as a dashing English hero who can do anything. He was an obvious replacement and wasn't he good?

He was fantastic. You obviously made an impact on [Bond producer] Cubby Broccoli for him to later cast you in *For Your Eyes Only*. Were you called in for that, or did you have to audition for the part?

I was called in, but I think I'd already got it, unless I screwed up the interview. Cubby Broccoli and his wife has seen me playing the part of Alexander Dubcek of Czechoslovakia in a drama documentary on television called *Invasion* [1980]. Dubcek was one of the nicest, most sensible men of the 20th century and, apparently, Mrs. Broccoli turned to Cubby and said, 'That's the sort of guy we need. Someone who's absolutely plausible. Someone the audience won't guess is the villain until we tell them.'

I was making a film out in Greece at the time and I'd had a very difficult weekend flying out there. I think I took five aeroplanes all together for the return flight. I met him on a Sunday morning with everybody else and got the role, which was absolutely tremendous. I was going through a very poor phase financially and career-wise at that point and that absolutely lifted me out of it. I flew straight from where I was filming in Greece to Corfu. It was a big change in my professional life, but then I had to wait for three days while they sent back the rushes of the first day because I still could have been sacked on the spot! That's what Cubby could do!

At the time you couldn't get bigger than being in a Bond film, but hadn't you previously worked with Roger Moore before on several British TV shows?

I did two episodes of *The Saint*, I think, so I'd known Roger for a very long time, so it was a delight to work with him again.

Often being cast in a Bond film as a villain makes some actors get typecast into those types of roles for the rest of their career. Did you ever have any reservations about taking the part?

Yes, but I'd done so many villains before that it got to the point where I'd say to the directors, 'Don't hire me, because everybody will know that I did it!'

I'd done so many of those types of roles that *For Your Eyes Only* was a natural progression in the end. That was the reason I got the role, because I was trying to be terribly reasonable and nice, until it turned out that I wasn't!

Your role as Kristatos sees you portraying a Greek smuggler, so what was it like working on the accent for the role?

I was determined to get the accent right. I know I eventually did because a lot of Greek people and experts in language said I did! [laughter]

It was the same with *Indiana Jones and the Last Crusade*. I obviously worked very hard on that accent too. We had just done a big scene in the desert and we were all hot and sweaty. It was the end of the day and Steven Spielberg came over to me and said, 'Julian, your American accent is so good you'll never stop making America films after this!' Well, I've never made one since. [laughs]

I read that you were quite self-critical of your accent?

I was very critical with myself. I insisted on having a chap with me all the time to make sure I got it absolutely right. He was called Julian Shagra and he's a very well-known expert in dialects. He was on set the whole time and, after every single take, I'd talk with him and he would correct little nuances of the dialect. He was a very fine coach.

As the character of Walter Donovan is American, why do you think you were offered the role over an American actor?

Because I'm such a good actor! I'd also done *Star Wars*, so I came out of the same stable as several other actors in the film! The producers first asked me to go up for the role of the Nazi sergeant.

Vogel? [played by Michael Byrne in the film]

He was a very nasty piece of work. I auditioned for that and didn't get it and wasn't arguably disappointed, but I didn't realize at that time what a great film it was going to be. I knew it was going to be good, of course, I just didn't know how great.

Anyway, two days later they asked me to play Donovan and I simply couldn't believe it. I went along as I had to do an interview for it. I did it with a rudimentary American accent, and they hired me! So, I worked very hard on it, as any actor would do, and got the best role I've ever had in any film! Those actors! That director! The locations! And knowing I was playing a really good part that they couldn't cut! [laughs]

Then you have that infamous death where you 'chose poorly' . . . .

It took two and a half days to film that sixteen-second sequence. We didn't do it with CGI, we did in the old-fashioned way. Lots of cutting as the face changed and degenerated and then we sped the whole thing up. It was a really quick shot, but it was worth it.

I noticed in the film, you even got your wife a part playing Donovan's wife.

[laughs] I bet you haven't seen the billing at the end?

No.

She wanted to be in it because she wanted to be in a film which was directed by Steven Spielberg!

Don't we all?

[laughs] She [said] that one line and wasn't particularly anxious to be known for doing that tiny little part, so Steven came up with the billing at the end. As the titles come up, it says Walter Donovan played by Julian Glover, Mrs. Donovan played by Mrs. Glover! The next time you see it, watch out for that. [laughs]

Sean Connery was apparently treated like royalty on set by Steven Spielberg and George Lucas. I assumed you knew Sean from your theatre days?

I've known Sean since he was in his early twenties. There was a series on television early on, where young actors, like Judi Dench, were invited to play specific parts, There was one character called Hotspur and they got in Sean Connery for the role. Of course, he was brilliant as this hot-headed young Scotsman. He played it wonderfully.

Since then, I've met him on many occasions and worked with him four times. When I came to work with him on *Indiana Jones*, he called me Mr. National Theatre. He comes to see me whenever I'm in the West End theatre. He never misses that and he's quite a chum.

We're going to have to talk about *The Empire Strikes Back*, because for *Star Wars* fans, you're famous as the unshakeable General Veers. I imagine for you it was just two day's filming where they shook the set a lot?

It was a very boring shoot. We were there for five days and I think I was paid £400 for the week. Of course, I've since managed to make up that up quite nicely with all the conventions I go to!

Although it was a small part, Veers had two very important things to do: I had that scene with Darth Vader and I drove that fighting giraffe thing. Those two things made him into quite an important character in the film. Of course, not a leading character, but important enough for me.

I've got my own figure and all that stuff, an invented biography, and so it's a very valuable credit particularly when I go to these conventions. *Star Wars* is a franchise which will go on and on and on. It just goes from generation to generation. When I go to these conventions, there are kids of six and seven-years-old who are very familiar with *Star Wars* and, interestingly, are mostly impressed with the first three. I was in the second one, which I still think is the best. Nothing to do with me being in it! And it's all still going on, isn't it? In these spin-off *Star Wars* films?

Maybe we'll see General Veers return like Peter Cushing's Moff Tarkin did in *Rogue One*? After all, he's that rare thing in the *Star Wars* universe – a competent Imperial officer who gets the job done.

Yes, he does. We also don't know if he's killed at the end? I know everything was blown up, but there was talk of me coming back in the next film.

You were going to be in *Return of the Jedi*?

Unfortunately, I was doing something else and so I wasn't even available for consideration, so I didn't come back. [laughs]

Julian Glover as Grand Maester Pycelle in *Game of Thrones* (2011).
Photo courtesy of HBO.

I believe your son Jamie has reprised the role of General Veers in some Star Wars computer games?

That was an extraordinary coincidence as he was asked to do it and when he went in, he said, 'You know my father played him in the film?' They had no idea of the connection between the two of us! They knew I played Veers in the film, but they hadn't made the connection with the name Glover. They'd cast him because of his voice, which of course is very much like mine. [laughs] It was a nice squaring of the circle as it were.

You said that, at these conventions, you're recognized by a lot of children. Are you constantly surprised at how you've got a new generation of fans thanks to *Harry Potter* and *Game of Thrones*?

I'm very lucky. Older fans know me, of course, from the sixties shows, so they want pictures from *The Avengers* and the first series of *Doctor Who* that I was in. But then I've also got the new people who recognise my *Harry Potter* voice [as giant spider Aragog in *Harry Potter and the Chamber of Secrets*], which is extraordinary. People buy photographs of the spider! It has nothing to do with me, but they like my signature on it, and now I star in *Game of Thrones* of course, where I'm much older than I am. I'm 104 in that!

How do you go about getting cast as the voice for a giant spider?

I went up to the Harry Potter studios with several other people and, of course, they had no idea what a spider would sound like. [laughs] They'd written the lines, but they had no idea, so I did something with my voice and suddenly they went, 'Ah, yes that's it. That's what we want.'

It wasn't as if we were auditioning for *Hamlet*, where people know what they want. They didn't know what the character was meant to sound like, but they found it in me. I got a standard recording fee, but we had to re-record it three times because they kept re-writing it! Of course, I won a little tiny royalty for the film, so it's done me well!

Were you surprised at the success of *Game of Thrones*? I can't imagine you dreamed it would be the global phenomenon it's become when you were first cast.

I was tremendously lucky to get a part like that. I'm eighty-two now and I'm still working, but to get any part at all at such an advanced age is lucky. For *Game of Thrones*, I had to go and audition for three parts on three separate occasions as they couldn't place me! It wasn't until one actor got terribly ill and had to drop out that they asked me to play the role of Grand Maester Pycelle. I felt a bit guilty because I thought the actor was going to snuff it, but he didn't, thank God. He came back and played another small part in *Game of Thrones*, so I felt okay about it then!

With most of these jobs, the pleasure or not, is determined by who you work with. *Game of Thrones* is full of such great, particularly British actors that it was a joy to do, even with that bloody beard! [laughs]

You've worked with so many famous directors like Steven Spielberg, Richard Attenborough, and Wolfgang Petersen. Is there anyone who's impressed you over the course of your career?

Irvin Kershner [director of *The Empire Strikes Back*]. He was wonderful.

A publicity headshot of Julian Glover. Photo courtesy of Rory Lewis.

With such a large number of characters under your belt, which role would you say you're most frequently recognized for?

I would hope that it's *Indiana Jones,* but I get a lot of recognition for *Star Wars* in the streets or restaurants. Those two are the main ones that I'm recognised for, but I get a lot of recognition for a TV series I did early on called *Spy Trap* [1972]. It was on just after the news, which was a very popular time, and a lot of people watched that.

I also get recognised for the one-off things that I've done on television, like a fantastic series called *An Age of Kings* [1960], which was a remarkable piece of television, which was so brave in those days. That was a time when the BBC would allow inspirational film directors to pick their cast and just get on with it and not interfere. That was the 'good old days' of television. Now, of course you know you have to go through so many hoops before anything is decided.

I've never been a star, so I've never been pestered in the streets or in restaurants or anything like that, like so many of my acquaintances. I've earned a comfortable living and I've manged to keep body and soul together. I have a lovely wife and son who both work, and a lovely semi-detached house in South London. I've managed to keep a very nice, regular life together without being a star, and that encapsulates what my whole career has been, and I am very grateful to the Lord Almighty, or whoever it is, that I'm in that position.

Steven Berkoff

Select Filmography

- *A Clockwork Orange* (1971) – Det. Const. Tom
- *Barry Lyndon* (1975) – Lord Ludd
- *Outland* (1981) – Sagan
- *Octopussy* (1983) – Orlov
- *Beverly Hills Cop* (1984) – Victor Maitland
- *Rambo: First Blood Part II* (1985) – Lt. Col. Podovsky
- *The Krays* (1990) – George Cornell
- *Legionnaire* (1998) – Sgt. Steinkampf
- *The Girl with The Dragon Tattoo* (2011) – Frode

Sent behind enemy lines to see if there is any truth to the rumor that American soldiers are still being held by the Vietnamese, years after the end of the war, John Rambo (Sylvester Stallone) soon finds himself captured, strung up, and tortured. Eager to embarrass the Americans, the Soviet Union, represented by the sadistic Lieutenant Colonel Podovsky (Steven Berkoff), are eager to get a confession out of the expendable asset, but Rambo isn't having any of it.

IT'S AN UNDERSTATEMENT TO SAY that Steven Berkoff is a force of nature. The acclaimed British actor has not only starred in some of the

Lt. Col. Podovsky (Steven Berkoff) oversees the torture of John Rambo (Sylvester Stallone) in *Rambo: First Blood Part II* (1985). Photo courtesy of TriStar Pictures.

biggest action films of the eighties, but, as a renowned author, playwright, and director, he is constantly working and performing all around the world, both on and off stage.

Of course, cinema audiences are well aware of Berkoff's roles in Stanley Kubrick's films *A Clockwork Orange* and *Barry Lyndon*, but the British actor reached a new level of fame when, after appearing in the James Bond film, *Octopussy*, in 1983, as the traitorous Russian general Orlov, he was courted by Hollywood. There, he appeared in big-budget actioners like *Beverly Hills Cop* as the nefarious art dealer Victor Maitland, and as the evil Russian colonel Podovsky in *Rambo: First Blood Part II*.

On stage, his legendarily intense performances have led to some critics citing his dramatic style as "in your face theatre", underlined by the fact that several of his productions are one-man shows. As well as writing original plays such as *Decadence* (1981), *West* (1983), and *Sink the Belgrano!* (1986), Berkoff is also steeped in Shakespeare, performing not only in the likes of *Hamlet*, *Macbeth*, and *Coriolanus*, but also writing and starring in the one-man show *Shakespeare's Villains*. There, Berkoff expertly breaks down The Bard's most villainous characters and explores the situations that led to them to committing their evil deeds.

After months of trying to get an interview with the ever-busy actor, I finally managed to get him on the phone and, over the following half hour, whilst desperately trying to hide how nervous and terrified I was, we talked Shakespeare, Stallone, and the trappings of Hollywood. Berkoff was everything I expected him to be: no-nonsense, extremely knowledgeable, and of a singular vision when it comes to the arts.

You've written extensively on the dynamic between heroes and villains in Shakespeare's plays. In your mind, what makes the best villain and the likes of Iago, Macbeth, and Richard III so appealing for an actor?

I think the best villain goes very deep into a person's psyche. They really delve much further than any other emotions because they deal with flaws in the human spirit. A great writer enables people to identify with these characters, as everybody has that touch of villainy in them. We all have that touch of malevolence. Sometimes when we see somebody doing something quite horrid, if there's a sense of bravado to it, it can touch us in our deepest souls. That's why people love villains in the cinema.

Now, the hero also does that. If you hear a great speech from a hero, like Henry V, it inspires the act of playing. There's a dichotomy between the two characters. Some villains, like Richard III, Iago, or Macbeth, touch everybody. With Richard III, it can inspire, because he's clever with his villainy. What a villain does for people who are inclined, or have that inside them, is to feel as if they have been singled out and have been allowed to breathe. It allows them to express their villainy, because it's so beautifully detailed.

When you're writing, or even playing villains, what sort of motivation do you find is most terrifying, both to play and for the audience? Greed? Changes to their circumstances that drive them down that path? Or a character who is inherently evil?

I think the characters who are evil at their core. I think that's the most terrifying. Characters who have no empathy and who have no feeling. They are dead souls, and they only relish extinguishing life. Macbeth is a killer, but he has regrets. He feels let down and he commits murder reluctantly. Others do it with great pleasure. Iago is an out-and-out disgusting villain. There is no sense of empathy in him whatsoever, and he relishes the crime.

Steven Berkoff performing Shakespeare's Villains.
Photo courtesy of StevenBerkoff.com

Richard III is probably the worst, because he easily kills the two young princes in the tower and has no reluctance, no concern nor guilt. He is the is the worst because he justifies his villainy. There is nothing that he will not do. As Richard says, 'To make an envious mountain on my back, where sits deformity to mock my body; to shape my legs of an unequal size; to disproportion me in every part, like to a chaos, or an unlick'd bear-whelp.' He is justifying his villainy, none of Shakespeare's other villains do that as they are mostly frustrated losers. Iago is disgusting, frustrated, and ambitious, but who could never find the right level of charm that Othello has. Macbeth is frustrated because he wants to be the king, but neither of those characters use those excuses. It's extensively the malfeasance done by people to justify it. They are the worst kind of followers.

You've played real-life monsters such as Hitler and Saddam Hussein. Do you take a different approach when playing people who existed and committed atrocities in real life?

Absolutely. In some ways, it's no difference whether the character is fictional or factual, as most villains are based on real characters and crimes. If you play Iago, you play him as if he had existed, even if he's fictional. He may be even more interesting to play because he is a creation of the writer's imagination, but you can refine and plan it. With Hitler, we know he is a terrifying, evil monster, but as somebody said, 'When you play them, as an actor, you are obliged to support the villain.' You must like the villain. You must admire them, even love them a little and, of course, get laughs for them. The more villainous you are, the more the public will laugh, because you're touching them, but with someone who's real, there are no laughs. All you can do is play it quietly, while still feeling some kind of identification with the villain. You must switch your internal computer to villainy and enjoy it. You can't play an evil villain disliking him. You must play him like he is the best man in the world.

Is that how you approach all of your roles? Do you play them with that level of truth even when they're more outlandish and cartoonish, like a Bond villain?

Even with those small movie villains, you must play them as if their lives depended on you. You are their spokesman. You have to justify them and, sometimes, as you play them, you begin to support what they do. The funniest thing in the human brain is that, as you identify with somebody, they start to permeate your imagination and you somehow become wedded to them and start to support them. As an actor, that's more or less the only way you can make it work.

You've said in the past that you took on many Hollywood roles simply to finance your theatre work, and you appeared in certain productions that lacked artistic merit. Is it not the case that when you have a hit like *Beverly Hills Cop*, it gives you more freedom to pick and choose your projects?

The more you're known in movies, the more the public sees you, judges you, and values you. Appearing in certain films may have helped me because I was able to get more of an audience and a bit more financial support. I don't look down my nose at some of the roles I've done, I just don't feel that they touched me.

In your memoir, *Tough Acts*, you write about how, when you were filming *Beverly Hills Cop*, you were very aware of the unreality of Hollywood. Do you still feel that way about the American movie industry? When you appear in a big Hollywood film, does it still feel like a different world?

Oh, yes. It is another world and I still feel that. There's still the excitement, because it's the major producer of movies in the whole world and has made some of the greatest cinematic artworks that anyone has ever seen. However, once you get in the studio, you become incredibly bored. It's nice when you get out on set in the morning when it's still wonderful and exciting, but if you're just playing Joe Bloggs and you're sitting in a trailer, it can become very tedious.

Steven Berkoff is his first major Hollywood role as Victor Maitland in *Beverly Hills Cop* (1984). Photo courtesy of Paramount Pictures.

I read that you wrote your play *Kvetch* while you were sat in your *Beverly Hills Cop* trailer.

That's absolutely right, yes. I enjoyed it. I do a lot of writing in trailers. I later did another action film called *Legionnaire* with Jean-Claude Van Damme. Not very well directed, unfortunately. There was a lot of waiting in my trailer, so I rewrote *Oedipus* and eventually put that play on. It's always useful to take a notepad when you're in your trailer. You can write massively because you're confined in a small space and that's absolutely brilliant.

How did you end up getting cast in *Beverly Hills Cop* as Victor Maitland? Weren't you cast early on when Sylvester Stallone was attached to the project.

Yes, I met him for it and he wanted me for the role. I was in it from the beginning and enjoyed doing it. When Eddie Murphy was cast, I think he respected me because he thought that as I was a theatre actor, I could keep up with his improvisations. We got on very well.

You allegedly turned down *RoboCop* and *Invasion U.S.A.* (1985) because of the violence. Are there any factors that influence the roles that you take or turn down?

I never turned down *Roboop*, that's a mistake. I don't recall what *Invasion U.S.A.* was?

It was a Chuck Norris movie.

Yeah, I probably turned that down. It all depends. If I turn down something, it probably has something in it which I find absolutely repellent.

I turned down a film [once] and half of me regrets doing it. I mentioned to the director the parts that I didn't like, and he made a note of it. In the end, he recast it. The new actor didn't do any of the things that I was meant to do! If that was the case, I would have done it!

What was the film?

I can't say, but there were scenes where the character was grabbing a woman's breasts and I thought, 'I can't do this.' At the time, I was working in the theatre directing and I didn't want the actors that I was directing, who looked up to me, to see me on screen groveling around. In the theatre, you are closer to expressing the most fundamental parts of mankind. To go from that to a film where I'd be behaving it that manner spoiled it for me. I'd been corrupted by my own kind of sense of purity.

I think it's good to have standards when you are taking on certain villainous roles, because some of them can be very gratuitous.

Steven Berkoff in the James Bond film *Octopussy* (1983) as General Orlov.
Photo courtesy of MGM Pictures.

Absolutely, yes. It was gratuitous, that's why I didn't like [it]. When I was cast in *Octopussy*, I took the role because I was at the beginning of my career, because I was a late starter, and I thought it would be exciting and stimulating to be in a Bond film. They have a good reputation, and they usually have good villains, so I had no qualms about taking on that project. The cast and crew on a James Bond film are very professional and calm and you're treated with respect. Usually, with British films, it's a much better experience than with an American production, but it can vary.

After you played General Orlov in *Octopussy*, you played a Russian general in *Rambo: First Blood Part II*. Do you find that once you've played a Bond villain, or appeared in a blockbuster smash, that Hollywood typecasts you into those kinds of roles?

The studios don't pigeonhole you, the casting people do. They have a lot of work where they're casting dozens of films and looking at hundreds of actors, so they usually go for the easiest option. 'Oh yes, Berkoff does a good Russian,' or 'He's good at playing weirdoes!' That's, unfortunately, the cost that you pay to be in the movies because you are typecast from roles that casting agents have seen you do. I'm never going to be cast as a nice, loving father. That's just the nature of that terrible business.

Did you ever get frustrated?

Yes, because I can do comedy. I'm a comedian and I can do so many other things so it's always frustrating. However, when I cast myself in my plays, I can do whatever I want!

I do love how you take your experiences and make your own projects from them. For example, you wrote your docudrama *Acapulco* while you were filming *Rambo: First Blood Part II*. On making that film, you said, 'I felt like a creature from another planet. In the bar area, everyone talked about discos, food, and the day's work, and sex, and everything was based on primal basic needs and emotions.' Did you use *Acapulco* as an outlet of your frustration, or did you find the entire experience fascinating?

Yes, it was an escape and it was fascinating. All these guys around me were wonderful people, who were imaginative, thoughtful, sensitive, and stu-

A publicity headshot of Steven Berkoff. Photo courtesy of StevenBerkoff.com

pid as well! Everyone was having a bit of excitement in *Acapulco* with the modest per diem that we were getting. Every day was a bit of an adventure, because many were doing nothing in the film. Every night, the cast and crew would come to the bar and talk about the birds they've screwed or what the director had done, and I thought it would be a wonderful play. I even played the villain in it! I cast myself as the actor 'Steve'! It didn't run that well, but I thought it was a very interesting piece.

After not working with Stallone on *Beverly Hills Cop*, what was it like to finally collaborate in *Rambo: First Blood Part II*?

We worked well together. He's a charming man. He's very friendly, easy to get on with, and a good worker.

I heard that you suggested he tackle Shakespeare at some point in his career?

He would be an ideal Coriolanus! I would like to see a lot of American actors tackle The Bard, but many think it's out of their field. I bet they could do it. I think it would be fantastic.

You once said, 'In our movies, the villains tend to be the better actors, so I'm flattered when I'm asked to play a villain.' Do you still feel that way about your career?

I'm always looking for new challenges, but it's an accepted truth that the villains are played by the best actors. They're binary characters; they have two sides. They have to show their good side while carrying out their nefarious side. They're playing two roles.

As Richard III says, 'I can smile, and murder as I smile.' We can see that the actor has to be a little bit more astute than the guy who is playing the same two or three notes. The villain has to [have] more tricks and sides to him. Therefore, we must convince, but the hero doesn't. He just has to be the good guy.

There are some heroes who are phenomenal, and the great heroes are greater than any villain could ever be, if you get those parts. A role where the hero is the greatest, most fascinating man is *Cyrano de Bergerac* [1990], which I saw many years ago with Jose Ferrer. I thought, 'No villain is as magnificent as that!' Also, Shakespeare's *Henry V*, the excitement, the passion of those lines is wonderful, but there seem to be fewer of those great roles compared to the villains.

Joaquim de Almeida

"Now you drive around town. You see someone you don't know, you shoot them. How hard is that?"
                                        – Bucho, *Desperado* (1995).

Select Filmography

- *Clear and Present Danger (1994) – Col. Felix Cortez*
- *Desperado (1995) – Bucho*
- *Behind Enemy Lines (2001) – Piquet*
- *24 (2003-2004) – Ramon Salazar*
- *Fast Five (2011) – Reyes*
- *Diablo (2015) – Arturo*
- *The Hitman's Bodyguard (2017) – Jean Foucher*

El Mariachi (Antonio Banderas) is out for revenge. After his lover was shot and killed, he is hunting the drug lord who was responsible: Bucho (Joaquim de Almeida). After reports of several of his men being killed by the gun-toting mariachi, Bucho is getting nervous, and is ordering all strangers in town to be shot on sight.

HOLLYWOOD OFTEN REFLECTS what is happening in the headlines and, in the late eighties and early nineties, the War on Drugs dominated newspapers and cable news. Pablo Escobar, Columbia, the Iran-Contra scandal – all of this led to an increase in films where America's military,

381

Bucho (Joaquim de Almeida) schools his men on how to identify potential threats to his organization in *Desperado* (1995). Photo courtesy of Columbia Pictures.

or assorted mercenaries, took the fight to the cartels and films like *Licence to Kill (1989)*, *Delta Force 2: The Colombian Connection* (1990), *Fire Birds* (1990), and even *Predator 2* (1990), made cocaine-dealing warlords the villain de jour.

For actor Joaquim de Almeida, it was a busy time. After appearing in Paolo and Vittorio Taviani's *Good Morning Babilonia* in 1987, Hollywood quickly came calling and found Joaquim's fluency in six languages perfect for international villain roles they were looking to fill. It wasn't long before he was cast in big-budget thrillers like *Clear and Present Danger* and *Desperado*, which made him a familiar face to audiences around the world.

Today, Joaquim is still working, appearing in blockbusters like *Fast Five* and *The Hitman's Bodyguard*, but Hollywood still casts him, primarily, as South American villains. Considering the actor is originally from Portugal, I was curious to know if Hollywood's fluidity when it comes to ethnic casting had ever been frustrating for him, or if it was a welcome source of work.

When we spoke, Joaquim was sunning himself in his beach house in Los Angeles and was happy to talk about his famous roles, being a romantic lead in Europe, and why working on a *Fast and Furious* film can be pretty dull.

Your first film role was in the action film *The Soldier* (1982) where you played a member of an elite international anti-terror force. How did you go from theatre work in Portugal to appearing in American action films?

I had appeared in a small Italian film in America beforehand, but my first big role was in *The Soldier*, and I didn't have much to do in that film! I had come from Portugal to study and had got married in Vienna to a classical pianist from Hungary. She had a scholarship to the Julliard School, so we both moved to America. I wanted to study with Strasbourg and so I took English classes and got involved with local plays, because I couldn't work as I didn't have any papers. I was doing a play and a casting director from Paramount Studios, who was a friend of a friend, saw me and sent me out to some agents.

The first two times I was sent out to an audition, I got the jobs! One of them was for *The Soldier* and the other one was for a commercial. I then got cast in *The Honorary Consul* [1983], with Michael Caine and Richard Gere, and then I got signed. That's how it all started.

A publicity still from *The Solder* (1982) with Joaquim de Almeida (far right) in one of his first film roles. Photo courtesy of Embassy Pictures.

I kept doing plays for a while, but I used the theatre to get into the movies because that's what I wanted to do. I didn't even want to do television at the time, though, today, all the best scripts are on television! That's what the best money is!

Do you find you get offered different roles depending on what country you're working in? Obviously, in America, you're cast primarily as a villain, but in Portuguese films, you're a romantic lead.

I do more films in Spain than in Portugal. I think I've done about fifteen Portuguese films and twenty Spanish. My first two movies were made in Spain and I was cut because I couldn't speak Spanish without an accent, so I couldn't be a real Spaniard!

Then I did a movie called *The Dumbfounded King* [1991]. When they first offered me a role, I noticed in the script there was a character called Almeida, meaning he was Portuguese, so I said, 'Why don't I play that?' Once I played that, and the film was a success, I started getting cast as a Portuguese and it didn't matter if I had an accent! In Spain and Portugal, I star in a lot of romantic comedies, and in France, too. I did a French film where I played a seventeenth century painter and I had to work with someone to make sure I got the accent right. After that, I've had several roles in French films.

However, it's the American films from which I'm recognized the most. People recognize me on street all the time because American movies go all over the world; you see them everywhere. I have so many films playing at the same time on cable TV because of re-runs! Those are the films that people recognize me for, and yes, I'm always recognized as the villain!

As you get so many varied roles in other countries, I don't suppose you find it frustrating that you're always cast as the villain in American movies?

In Europe, I rarely play a villain, but when I started doing studio films playing villains and they were successful, then, suddenly, people saw me as a villain. There was a period in my life that I decided I wasn't going to play any more villains as I wasn't reaching the big studio films. Then more and more offers came in and [I] decided to do them, but I was going to have fun with them!

People love the villains and I've always tried to put some humanity into my villains, because playing them is not very fun. Villains are humans, but with less or different sentiments, so you just can't play them as simplistic characters, but they're the roles I'm most recognised for.

I see it when I'm on a plane. Someone will be looking at me trying to figure out where they know me from. I can sense them. Sometimes they're a little scared, and then finally they go, 'Excuse me, I know you, but I can't place you! I [know] you are a villain from a film though!' It's always great fun!

What film do people primarily recognize you from?

Desperado, Clear and Present Danger, and, lately, *Fast Five*. Also, the film *Our Brand is Crisis* [2015], because it has been playing on HBO forever! I'm also recognized a lot from *Only You* [1994], which is a comedy with Bonnie Hunt that was shot in Italy. Apparently, a lot of people do the trip that [the] girls do in the film. They also recognise me as the charming guy who is driving a Ferrari.

There are other independent films that people recognize me from. In those films, I'm rarely asked to be a villain. Unfortunately, in the big bud-

Felix Cortez (Joaquim de Almeida) covers his tracks in *Clear and Present Danger* (1994). Photo courtesy of Paramount Pictures.

get films, they always offer me the villain part, but I've had a good living playing villains, so I can't complain!

You have a deep voice and, when you're playing nefarious roles like in *Clear and Present Danger,* you speak very softly, which is incredibly effective and threatening. Do you think your voice is a key asset in why big studios hire you for those roles?

I have a raspy voice, but there's nothing I can do about it! I always try to play my characters coolly – doing things slowly, and I talk slower to make sure that the speech sounds better. I'm not sure, but I know people recognise my voice as I've had people say, 'When I saw you I knew I recognised you from somewhere, but when you spoke, I knew immediately who you were!' [laughs] The voice is a characteristic of mine and there was a period when I did a lot of voiceovers too. However, I don't smoke anymore, so it may not be as deep and raspy as it used to be! [laughs]

Your big break was *Clear and Present Danger,* where you play Felix Cortez, opposite Harrison Ford. What was it like moving from relatively low budget European films to a big budget Hollywood movie?

It's a big difference, and I did *Clear and Present Danger* and *Desperado* in the same year. There's a big difference going from *Desperado*, which was a $7 million film to *Clear and Present Danger*, which I think was an $80 million film! Today, the budget for films like *Fast Five* are ridiculous. It goes into the hundreds of millions of dollars.

It's all the steamed chicken that The Rock eats.

[laughs] Yes, I know. In *Fast Five*, we filmed in Puerto Rico and we took over the place! It's amazing because, with those movies, it's like the circus has come to town! There are so many trailers and, depending on your part, the trailers get bigger and bigger!

The big difference in doing big budget action films is you need so much money to do them. The French do some, but nothing like the Americans do or the British do with the James Bond films. I remember in *Clear and Present Danger*, when Harrison Ford's convoy gets attacked, that took ten days to shoot the whole sequence, and it's just a three-minute sequence on film!

That entire street location was built on a soccer field! They copied a street in Bogota and re-made it on a soccer field. That's where the money goes! And, of course, we have better hotel rooms and trailers! There's always a production assistant following you on big budget films because they want to know where you are at all times in case they need you!

One smaller movies, the cast all talk to each other and you feel like you are part of the film. On big budget films, you just do your part and that's it. There are also so many fucking producers! And the rewrites never end! On independent films, you have dinner with the director and producer and you talk and decide what is best for the film. On a big budget film, you're more alienated from everything.

I'm sure that's the case with a mega-franchise like *The Fast and the Furious*. Was that the case on *Clear and Present Danger*? Did you get to know the rest of the cast at all?

When we started the film, my role wasn't that big. We started shooting, and when we got to Mexico, Harrison Ford's assistant came to me and said that he wanted to have lunch with me. I brought my wife and son and, over lunch, he started being kind of rude and I got really got upset.

I said, 'Listen, I don't care if you're Harrison Ford, you don't talk to me like that,' and he started laughing! He said, 'Okay, that's what I wanted to know! I just wanted to see how you'd react because I've watched you and we're going to change the end of the film so that you're the guy that I'm there to get!' Suddenly, my role was rewritten, and it became a bigger part of the film. I had more of a say and I would meet with Harrison and the director Phillip Noyce to make my character the bigger threat.

Clear and Present Danger was a big hit, but when it comes to ethnic actors, Hollywood tends to stereotype. Did you find that you were just offered similar roles as a drug lord after Clear and Present Danger came out?

There's nothing you can do about it as they don't give you a chance to play a different role. It's frustrating, but then I would go to Europe and do independent films. Yes, I would love to get anything in a big studio movie, because not everybody gets to do them, but if they would offer me a different type of role, I would be happy.

Joaquim de Almeida as Bucho in *Desperado* (1995).
Photo courtesy of Columbia Pictures.

Unfortunately, these days, it has gotten harder and harder to get funding for both big budget and independent films. For us actors, the future is television because there are 400+ channels, and they all need to have their own products, so there's a ton of work out there! I was almost cast in *Narcos* [2015-], but the Brazilian producer thought it was better to have faces that weren't immediately recognizable. Pedro Pascal has done very well from it and is now in big, big films.

You worked with Robert Rodriguez on *Desperado*, and he is famously independent when it comes to his productions. How did you find that after the big budget extravaganza of *Clear and Present Danger*?

I met with Robert Rodriguez, but Columbia Pictures wanted Raul Julia for the role of Bucho. Even though he wanted to do the role, Raul was very sick, so I got a call when I was in Portugal asking if I could be in Texas in four days to start shooting! There's a lot of dialogue and my character has several monologues, so I asked them to send me the script. I still wasn't sure, so I flew to Texas and, when I got to the set, they were already into their fourth week. My scenes were going to be the last two weeks.

I met Robert and he said, 'Stay around and watch a bit,' and he was shooting the scene where Antonio [Banderas] and Salma [Hayek] both jump from the roof. Robert said, 'I want to show you one of the scenes, so you have a feeling about what the film is about.' When you read the script off the page, it was very weird and seemed terribly violent. You didn't get the humor. So, Robert showed me the opening bar scene and I got it!

I remember I asked for a suite, because I like to walk while I'm learning lines and can't be in a hotel room. There were limited hotels in the town where they were filming, so they ended up making a door between two rooms to make me a suite! [laughs] I had four days to memorize the whole thing! I just remember the four days in that room memorizing those speeches! It was a great experience, but it was still a good budget! $7 million in Europe is a massive budget.

You were set to reunite with Antonio Banderas in *The Mask of Zorro* (1997) where you were cast as General Santa Anna, but then all your scenes were cut out! What happened there?

Let me explain! I said I didn't want to have a credit on that film, because they just wanted me for the last scene of the film. Antonio asked me to do it, so we agreed on a very good sum of money, for what was going to be the very last scene.

I came to set, got all dressed up and the scene was to be me with my troops meeting Antonio as he leads all the slaves out of the mines. I asked if we were going to film it in the studio and they said it would be out in the desert. Then there was a delay because, when they did the scene of the mine exploding, two guys got killed. Something went really wrong. I got sent back to Los Angeles and asked to come back in two weeks. I had already been paid and they said they'd pay me again for when I came back!

So, they did the explosion scene again, but the whole set fell down, so they had to do it again, so for a day's work I was being paid three times! When we got to filming in the desert, it was forty-five degrees Celsius! We were all dressed up and we were about to shoot the scene when they yelled, 'Cut!' I looked back, and ten guys had fallen off their horses because of the heat. This kept happening repeatedly, because the heat was amazing. We finally finished the scene and then someone told me they were going to shoot a different ending to show the baby at the end to set up the sequel. That's why they cut the scene because they wanted to have the baby in it!

That's amazing. Still, you can't be too bitter if you got paid three times! You seem to work mostly in Europe these days, but every now and then, you return to Hollywood to appear in a blockbuster. Is there anything you look for when accepting these roles, or is it purely for the money?

I used to live in New York, but when I got cast in *24*, a friend of mine suggested I rent a place on the beach in Los Angeles. I never liked Los Angeles, but I fell in love with living on the beach. I sold my New York loft and bought an apartment on the beach. I live half of the year in Los Angeles and the other half, if I'm not working, I spend in Portugal.

Diversity is obviously a big issue in Hollywood. As a Portuguese actor, who generally plays South American or Central American characters. Do you ever feel you're taking roles away from Latino actors, or is it a constant fight to get good roles?

When I started in the film business, Hollywood wanted real accents. They didn't want Americans playing with fake accents anymore. There weren't that many foreign actors around and, once I had done one of those big movies, they kept coming to me because, if they're spending the money, they want to invest in people they know. I think, in a way, it was easier for me because there was less competition, but on the other hand, there wasn't as much work. Today, I feel there are so many more foreign actors in Hollywood. The diversity of accents and people from all over the world is greater than it was when I started and there is this great variety of talent.

You've also done a lot of voice work, such as playing Bane in the *Batman* series. Is there a trick to acting bad on screen and acting bad as a voice actor?

I wish I played more of those voice parts because they pay very well! I think an association with me is my raspy voice, and I'm hired by young writers and directors who know me from watching re-runs of *Desperado* and *Clear and Present Danger.*

I think one of the reasons I don't get asked to play good guys is because of this raspy voice. I remember Paul Walker was being interviewed for *Fast Five* by a Portuguese television show and they said, 'It's the second time you've worked with Joaquim de Almeida. What do you think of him?', and he said, 'He has to be a great villain with that voice. How can you not be a great villain?' [laughs]

Image Credits

Front cover illustration: Ben Turner

Sven-Ole Thorsen

First and second image: 20th Century Fox/John Milius/Dino De Laurentiis Corporation
Third image: TriStar Pictures/Paul Michael Glazer/Braveworld Productions
Fourth image: TriStar Pictures/Walter Hill/Carolco Pictures
Fifth image: Universal Studios/Ridley Scott/Scott Free Productions
Sixth image: Universal Pictures/John Woo/Alphaville Films
Seventh image: Warner Brothers/Steven Seagal/Nasso Productions

Benny Urquidez

First image: Golden Harvest/Sammo Hung/Raymond Chow
Second image: www.bennythejet.com

Third image: Golden Harvest/Sammo Hung/Corey Yuen/Raymond
Chow
Fourth image: Buena Vista Pictures/George Armitage/Hollywood
Pictures

Vernon Wells

First image: 20th Century Fox/Mark L. Lester/Joel Silver
All remaining images from Vernon Well's personal collection

Derrick O'Connor

First image: Warner Brothers/Richard Donner/Joel Silver
Second image: Warner Brothers
Third image: Buena Vista Pictures/Stephen Sommers/Hollywood
Pictures

Bob Wall

All images from Bob Wall's personal collection

Paul McCrane

First to fourth images: MGM Pictures/Paul Verhoeven/Orion
Pictures
Fifth image: 20th Century Fox

Gus Rethwisch

First and third images: TriStar Pictures/Paul Michael Glaser/
Braveworld Productions
Second image: Ethan Wiley/New World Pictures

Bill Duke

First to third images: 20th Century Fox/Mark L. Lester/Joel Silver
Fourth image: 20th Century Fox/John McTiernan/Joel Silver
Fifth image: Warner Brothers/Craig R. Baxley/Joel Silver

Matthias Hues

First and fourth images: Vision International/Craig R. Baxley/Epic
    Productions
Second and third images: Ron Derhacopian

Martin Kove

All images: MartinKoveOnline.com

Superman II

First to third, fifth and sixth images: Warner Brothers/Richard
    Donner/Pierre Spengler
Fourth image: Jack O'Halloran
Seventh image: Universal Pictures/Richard Fleischer/Raffaella
    De Laurentiis

Die Hard

All images: 20th Century Fox/John McTiernan/Joel Silver

Andreas Wisniewski

First image: 20th Century Fox/John McTiernan/Joel Silver
Second image: MGM/UA/John Glen/Albert R. Broccoli
Third image: 2015 Kristjan Czako/Visual Impact

Clarence Gilyard Jr.

First and third images: 20ᵗʰ Century Fox/John McTiernan/Joel Silver

Second image: Paramount Pictures/Tony Scott/Jerry Bruckheimer
Fourth image: CBS Studios

Dennis Hayden

All photos from Dennis Hayden's personal collection

Al Leong

First image: Warner Brothers/Richard Donner/Joel Silver
All remaining photos from Al Leong's personal collection

David Patrick Kelly

First to third images: Paramount Pictures/Walter Hill/Laurence Gordon
Fourth image: 20ᵗʰ Century Fox/Mark L. Lester/Joel Silver
Fifth image: 20ᵗʰ Century Fox/Joseph Ruben/Chuck Russell

Andrew Robinson

First and second images: Warner Brothers/Don Siegel
Third image: Warner Brothers
Fourth image: Paramount Pictures

Jeremy Bulloch

First and second images: LucasFilm/Irvin Kershner/George Lucas
Third image: MGM Pictures/Lewis Gilbert/Albert R. Broccoli
Fourth image: David Wellbeloved

William Atherton

First and second images: Columbia Pictures/Ivan Reitman
Third and fourth images: 20th Century Fox/John McTiernan/Joel
Silver

Billy Drago

First image: Paramount Pictures/Brian de Palma/Art Linson
Second image: Warner Brothers/Clint Eastwood/The Malpaso
Company
Third image: Rapi Films/Ackyl Anwari

David Warner

First image: Buena Vista Distribution/Steven Lisberger/Donald
Kushner
Second image: Avco Embassy Pictures/Terry Gilliam
Third image: Paramount Pictures/William Shatner/Harve Bennett
Fourth image: 20th Century Fox/James Cameron
Fifth image: Lisa Bowerman

Paul Freeman

First and second image: Paramount Pictures/Steven Spielberg/
LucasFilm
Third image: 20th Century Fox/Bryan Spicer/Haim Saban
Fourth image: Paul Freeman

Ronny Cox

First and second images: MGM Pictures/Paul Verhoeven/Orion Pictures
Third image: TriStar Pictures/Paul Verhoeven/Ronald Shusett
Fourth image: Paramount Pictures
Fifth image: Ronny Cox

William Sadler

First image: 20th Century Fox/John McTiernan/Joel Silver
Second image: Universal Pictures/Ernest Dickerson/Gilbert Adler
Third image: Orion Pictures/Pete Hewitt/Scott Kroopf
Fourth image: Columbia Pictures/Frank Darabont/Niki Marvin

Julian Glover

First image: Paramount Pictures/Steven Spielberg/LucasFilm
Second image: MGM Pictures/John Glen/Albert R. Broccoli
Third image: 20th Century Fox/Irvin Kershner/LucasFilm
Fourth image: HBO
Fifth image: Rory Lewis

Steven Berkoff

First image: TriStar Pictures/George P. Cosmatos/Buzz Feitshans
Second and fifth image: StevenBerkoff.com
Third image: Paramount Pictures/Martin Brest/Jerry Bruckheimer
Fourth image: MGM Pictures/John Glen/Albert R. Broccoli

Joaquim de Almeida

First and fourth image: Columbia Pictures/Robert Rodriguez
Second image: Embassy Pictures
Third image: Paramount Pictures/Phillip Noyce/Robert Rehme

About the Author

TIMON SINGH has previously written for a number of film websites and magazines including Den of Geek. He also runs the Bristol Bad Film Club in the UK that screens cult genre films to raise money for local charities. This is his first book.

Twitter: @TimonSingh

Acknowledgements

THERE ARE MANY PEOPLE I'd like to thank for their help in putting this book together, both for their advice and inspiration.

Huge thank you to the following people for all their help in writing this book, providing suggestions and convincing me that it wasn't a terrible idea: my wife Helen Harfield, Tara Judah, Peter Walsh, Dave Taylor-Matthews, Pete Sutton, Thomas Parker, Tom Vincent, Mike Fury, David J. Moore, the crew at 20th Century Flicks and Ben Ohmart and everyone at BearManor Media who supported this project!

Also, a special thanks to Owen Williams for allowing me to use his interview with Billy Drago for the book and to Ben Turner, whose skill as an artist is unsurpassed and who is responsible for this book's amazing cover art.

I must also give credit to the following people who, through their own creative projects, be they books or podcasts, provided me with the creative inspiration to actually sit down and write my own book: Rob Hill, Ben Johnson, Andrew Glester, Matt Gourley, Paul Scheer, Matt Mira, Kevin Smith, and Marc Bernardin.

Big shout-out to my old school friends Michael Shapland and Leo Vincent who introduced me to a world of violent movies that I shouldn't have been seeing at such an impressionable age. You guys shaped me ways you can't even possibly imagine.

I am also incredibly humbled by legendary action screenwriter Steven E. de Souza agreeing to write the foreword for this book. Thank you once again and for giving us *Die Hard*! *DIE HARD*!

Most of all, thanks to all the actors that agreed to speak to me for this book, their agents and managers for making it happen, and the scriptwriters and directors that gave us some of the greatest action movies of all time.

Index

Numbers in **bold** indicate photographs

24 89, 90, 91, 97-98, **98**, 227, 381, 390
48 Hrs. 241, 248-249, 250

A-Team, The 223, 224
Abraxas: Guardian of the Universe 20, 21
Aces: Iron Eagle III 315, 321
Ackland, Joss 61, **62**, 62, 299
Action Jackson 113, 117, 119, **120**, 207, 208, 209-211, 215, 223, 224
Adventures of Ford Fairlane, The 256
Affleck, Ben 9, 68, 287
Age of Kings, An 368
American Gigolo 113, 115, 118
Anastasia, Albert 151, 153, 156-157
Angel of Fury **297**
Another 48 Hrs. 207, 215-216, 349
Art of Loving, The 186
Aspen, Max 49
Atherton, William 61, 179, 279-287, **280**, **282**, **285**, **286**
Auberjonois, René 265
Avengers, The 356, 359, 365
Avildsen, John G. 137, 138, 139, 140
Aykroyd, Dan 164, 282, 283

Baby Face Nelson 145
Baker, Joe Don **186**
Baker, Roy 359
Banderas, Antonio 381, 389
Barbato, Nancy 157
Barrett, Martine 250

Bass, Bobby 224
Baxley, Craig R. 131, 208, 210, 217, 218, 223, 224
Baywatch 24, 102
Baywatch Nights 24
Beattie, Jim 153
Beatty, Ned 330, 337, 338
Berkoff, Steven 2, 299, 369-379, **370**, **372**, **374**, **376**, **378**
Beverly Hills Cop 2, 327, 331, 332, 334, 337, 369, 370, 373-374, **374**, 375, 378
Beverly Hills Cop II 327, 335
Beverly Hills Cop III 219, 335
Biao, Yuen 27, 34-35, 84
Big Trouble in Little China 219, 224
Bill and Ted: Face the Music 352
Bill and Ted's Bogus Journey 62, 343, **350**
Bill and Ted's Excellent Adventure 219, 228
Biloxi Blues 345
Birch, Jackie 211
Bisset, Jacqueline 236
Black Belt Jones 71, 86
Blair, Linda 105
Blood and Bone 71, 87
Bloodsport 29, 31-32
Bloom, Jake 133
Bonn, Gerald 234
Boston and Killbride 103, 104
Bottin, Rob 94, **96**, 338

Brandauer, Klaus Maria 142
Brando, Marlon 149, 159, 175, 176
Broadbent, Jim 322
Broccoli, Cubby 188, 361
Broderick, Matthew 345
Brown, Clancy 99, 260, **264**
Buhringer, Hans 234-237
Bulloch, Jeremy 267-277, **268**, **272**, **276**
Busey, Gary 219, **220**, 225

Caccialanza, Lorenzo 233
Cagney & Lacey 135, 138, 139, 142
Caine, Michael **23**, 110, 383
Cameron, James 312
Capone 145
Capri, Ahna 82
Captain America 327, 330, 337
Car Wash 115, 117
Carpenter, John 224, **225**, 229
Carson, Johnny 156-157
Cassar, John 227
Castle, William 295
Centrepoint 67
Chan, Jackie 1, 27, **28**, 28, 32-34, **34**, 38, 72, 84, 87, 227
Child's Play 3 263, 266
Chips with Everything 359
Chong, Rae Dawn 113, 251, 252
Clear and Present Danger 381, 382, 385, **385**, 386-387, 389, 391
Cleese, John 68
Cleveland Show, The 217
Clouse, Robert 32, 82, 83, 84
Cobb, Tex 110
Cobra 227, 259, 266
Code R 142
Coffin, Frederick 260, **264**
Cohn, Harry 157
Collins, Joan 321
Commando 1, 2, 10, 13, 41, **42**, 42, **50**, 51-55, **53**, **54**, 57, 113, **114**, 117, 117-118, **118**, 119, 241, 250-252, **251**, 254
Conan the Barbarian 7-8, **8**, 10-13, **11**, 20, 105, 171

Conan the Destroyer 7, 10, 12, 105, 167, **174**, 175-176
Concorde . . . Airport '79, The 101, 103-104
Connery, Sean 289, 294, 360, 363-364
Contract, The 38
Cop Rock 91, 329-330
Corman, Roger 134, 145, 246
Costner, Kevin **143**, 290
Cover Up 235
Cox, Ronny 2, 89, 91, 327-342, **328**, **332**, **336**, **340**, **342**
Cresnick, Johan 185
Crocodile 2: Death Swamp 135, 144-145, **144**
Crouching Tiger, Hidden Dragon 87
Crow, The 2, 241, 253
Crowe, Russell 8, **17**, 18-20
Cruise, Tom 193-195
Cusack, John 28, 35, 36-38, **37**
Cyborg 133

Dalton, Timothy 184, 186, 188, 322
Daly, John 133
Dano, Royal 106
Dante, Joe 55-56
Darabont, Frank 99, 344, 352
Dark Angel 123, **124**, 124, 129, 130-132, **131**, 133
De Almeida, Joaquim 381-391, **382**, **383**, **385**, **388**
De Laurentis, Dino 104
De Palma, Brian 293
De Souza, Steven E. xiii-xiv, 36, 179, 200, 215, 252, 401
Death Race 2000 142
Death Warrant 220, 229-230
Deep Blue Sea 341
Deep Rising 61, **68**, 69
Deliverance 252, 327, 328-329, 330-331, 334, 335, 337
Dench, Judi 303, 363
Dennehy, Brian 38
Desperado 381, **382**, 382, 385, 386, **388**, 389, 391
DiCaprio, Leonardo 19, 312

Dickey, Christopher 252
Die Hard 6, 177-181, **178**, **179**, **180**,
        183-184, **184**, 185, 191, 192,
        197-204, **198**, **201**, 207-208, **208**,
        211, 212, **213**, 213, 215, **216**,
        217, 219, 220, 224, 226, 233-237,
        279, 280, 282, 284-285, **285**, 287,
        316, 346, 348
Die Hard 2 279, 284, 343-344, **344**, 346,
        348, 349, 350
Dirty Harry 259-263, **260**, **262**, 264, 265
Divoff, Andrew 215
Dobbins, Bennie E. 16, 251
Donald, James 359
Donner, Richard 21, 63, 147, 148-149,
        151, 158, 160-161, 163-164, 169,
        208, 348
Double Team 315, 317, 324-325
Douglas, Sarah 148, **158**, 161, 167-176,
        168, **170**, **174**
Doyon, Bruno 233
Dragnet (1987) 164
Drago, Billy 289-298, **290**, **292**, **297**
Dragon Blade 38
Dragons Forever 27, 28, 34-35, **34**
Dreamscape 241, 249, 255, **255**, 256
Duke, Bill 14, 113-121, **114**, **116**, **118**,
        119, **120**, 208
Dumbfounded King, The 384
Dumont, Margaret 282
Dux, Frank 31-32

Eastwood, Clint 259, 261, **262**, 273,
        275, 290, 292-293
El Muerto, The Dead One 298
Elliot, Sam 36
Empire Strikes Back, The 267, **268**, 268,
        271, **272**, 274-275, 355
End of Days 61, 62, 67-68
Enter the Dragon 32, 71, **72**, 72-73, 80-
        86, **81**, 87
ER 89, 90, 91, 97
Exorcist, The 104-105

Fabulous Baker Boys, The 173
Falcon Crest 171, 176, 315, 320-321

Fame 89, 91, 92, 96, 97
Farewell, My Lovely 153, 156
Fast Five 381, 382, 385, 386, 391
Ferrer, Miguel 332
Ferrigno, Lou 17, 103, 124
Fisher, Carrie 269
Fist Fighter 101, 110, 123, 130
Flight 222 180, 184
Fonda, Jane 125, 233
For Your Eyes Only 267, 355, 356, 358,
        360, 360-361, 362
Force: Five 27, 32
Ford, Harrison 269, 272, **316**, 319, 320,
        386, 387
Four Musketeers, The 149, 159-160
Frakes, Johnathan 339, **340**
Francis, Fred 285
Freeman, Morgan 38
Freeman, Paul 315-326, **316**, **319**, **322**,
        325
From Here to Eternity 157
Fromm, Erick 186

Game of Thrones 121, 355, 356, **365**,
        365-366
Garber, Victor 312
Ghostbusters 256, 279-281, **280**, 282,
        282, 283-284, 287
Giancana, Sam 157
Gibson, Mel 43, 47, 63, 66, 224-225,
        231
Gilliam, Terry 68, 302, 306
Gilyard Jr., Clarence 197-206, **198**, **199**,
        201, **205**, 207, 233
Gladiator 7, 8, 17, **17**, 18, 20
Glazer, Paul Michael 108
Glen, John 321
Globus, Yoram 337
Glover, Danny 65, 226,
Glover, Julian 355-368, **356**, **358**, **360**,
        365, **367**
Godfather, The 157
Goins, Jesse 90, 94
Golan, Menachem 337
Gore, Sandy 46
Gothic 183, 188, 194

Great White Hope, The 153
Grey, The 43
Griffith, Thomas Ian 140, 141
Grosse Point Blank 27, **37**, 37-38
Gudunov, Alexander **180**, 180, 184,
        207, 216, 226
Gunton, Bob 99

Hackman, Gene 19, 147, 149, 160, 161,
        162, 336
Hanks, Tom 164, 180
Hannah, Daryl 171-172
Hard Target 7, 16, **20**, 23-24
Hard to Kill 343, 344, 345, 346-347,
        348, 353
Hark, Tsui 324
Harryhausen, Ray 1, 255
Hasselhoff, David 24
Hawk the Slayer 61, 63
Hayden, Dennis 207-218, **208**, **209**,
        213, **216**, 233, 236
Hellraiser 259, 260, 261
Herek, Stephen 228
Hexum, Jon-Erik 235
Highway to Hell 133
Hill, Walter 215, 242, 244-245, 246,
        247, 248, 249, 348
Hills Have Eyes, The 289, 295-297
Hogan, Hulk 133
Holocaust, The 304, 306
Hopkins, Anthony 142, 354
Hosanna 46
Hot Fuzz 315, 317, 322-323
Hot Spot, The 345, 348
House II: The Second Story 101, 105, **107**
Hudson, Rock 111
Hues, Matthias 110, 123-134, **124**, **126**,
        129, **131**
Hughes, John 49, 51
Hung, Sammo 27, 32, 84, 85
Hunt for Red October, The 7, 8, 14, 15,
        62

Imada, Jeff 224, 229
Indiana Jones and the Last Crusade 355,
        356, 358, 362

Innerspace 41, 43, 55-56, 57
Invasion 361
Invasion U.S.A. 71, 86, 289, 290, 375
Ironside, Michael 335-336

Jackson, Samuel L. 341
Jagger, Mick 304
Johnson, Ted 139
Jones, Gary 144
Jones, Grace 175-176, 296
Jones, James Earl **8**, 11-12, 153
Julia, Raul 389

Kael, Pauline 247, 320
Karate Kid Part III, The 135, 137, 140
Karate Kid, The 135-138, **136**, **138**,
        142
Keir, Andrew 359
Kelly, David Patrick 2, **118**, 241-257,
        242, **245**, **247**, **251**, **255**
Kelly, Jim 84-85
Kershner, Irvin 272, 275, 366
Kidder, Margot **158**, **168**, 169
Kiel, Richard 5, 110, 164
Kove, Martin 135-146, **136**, **138**, **141**,
        143, **144**
Krabbé, Jeroen **186**, 189
Kray, Reggie 155

Last Action Hero 7, 219, 231
Last Man Standing 41, 241, 248
LeBell, Gene 74, 75, 87
LeBrock, Kelly 22
Lee, Brandon 85, 228, 229, **230**, 231,
        253-254
Lee, Bruce 1, 9, 32, 71-73, **72**, 77-79,
        80-86, 87
Lee, Christopher 305
Lee, Damian 21
Lee, Shannon 38
Legionnaire 369, 375
Leong, Al 207, 208, 211, 219-231, **220**,
        221, **225**, **230**, 233
Lester, Mark L. 51
Lester, Richard 149, 158, 159, 161, 163-
        164, 169

Lethal Weapon 1, 6, 7, 8, 13, 65, 208, 219, **220**, 220, 224-225, 226
Lethal Weapon 2 61, **62**, 62, 63, **64**, 65-66, 67
Lethal Weapon 4 219, 226
Lew, James 224
Lewis, Huey 217
Lewis, Joe 32, 73, 76, 78
Li, Jet 226, 227
Living Daylights, The 183, 184, 185-186, **186**, 189, 191
Llewelyn, Desmond 277
Lucas, George 268, 269, 271, 272, 274, 275, 316, 318, 320, 363
Lundgren, Dolph 106, 123, 124, 125, 127, 128, 130, **131**, 132, 133, 167, 231
Lustig, Branko 18
Lynch, David 256

Mabe, Joni 256
Macchio, Ralph 135, **136**, 137, **138**, 141, 142
Mad Max 46
Mad Max 2: The Road Warrior 2, 41, 42, **44**, 44-49, **48**, 56, 57
Mad Max: Fury Road 46-47, 49
Magnum P.I. 103, 109
Mallrats 7, 16-17
Malmuth, Bruce 346-347
Man with Two Brains, The 301, 307
Mankiewicz, Tom 164
Maris, Peter 297
Marshall, Neil 322
Masada 306
MASH 292
Mask of Zorro, The 389-390
Masters of the Universe 167
Masur, Richard 260, **264**
Matlock 197, 198, 204
McCambridge, Mercedes 104-105
McClure, Marc 163
McCrane, Paul 89-99, **90**, **92**, **95**, **96**, **98**, 330
McDowell, Malcolm 304-305
McGinley, John C. **23**

McKinney, Kurt 128
McQueen, Steve 76, 81, 146, 152
McTiernan, John 14-15, 21, 193, 199, 200, 202, 203, 214, 226, 235
Meaney, Colm 349
Menace II Society 113, 120
Mercury, Freddy 42, 52
Meshack, Charles **118**
Meyer, Nicholas 304, 305
Mighty Morphin Power Rangers: The Movie 315, **322**, 323-324
Miike, Takashi 291
Milano, Alyssa 41, **54**, 251
Milius, John 10, 13, 21
Miller, George 46-47, 48, 49
Mission: Impossible – Ghost Protocol 193-194, 195
Mist, The 344, 352
Mitchum, Robert 153, 157, 308
Moonlighting 191, 192
Moore, Roger 277, **360**, 361
Morita, Pat 136, **138**, 139
Moving McAllister 298
Mr. T 172
Mullins, Skipper 76, 78
Murphy, Eddie 249, 375
Murray, Bill 279, 282, **282**, 283
Mutiny on the Bounty 159

Narcos 388
Neeson, Liam 43, 134
Neumeier, Ed 333
Newman, Randy 329
Nightfall 175
Nightmare on Elm Street, A 3, 307
No Retreat, No Surrender 32
No Retreat, No Surrender 2: Raging Thunder 123, 124, 127, 128-130
Nolte, Nick 215-216, 248, 249
Norris, Chuck 73-74, 76, 77-80, 82, 86, 87, 88, 204-205, **205**, 290, 375
North, Colonel Oliver 348
Norton, Richard 32
Noyce, Phillip 387

O'Connor, Derrick 61-69, **62**, **68**

O'Halloran, Jack 148, 151-165, **152**, **154**, **158**, 167
Octopussy 267, 277, 370, **376**, 377
Omen, The 301, 302, 312-313
On Deadly Ground 7, 22-23, **23**
Only You 385
Our Brand is Crisis 385
Over the Top 130

Pale Rider 289, 290, 291-292, **292**, 293
Palmerstown, U.S.A 121
Peck, Gregory 312-313
People That Time Forgot, The 175
Pfeiffer, Michelle 173
Pinter, Harold 202
Plewa, Joey 234
Plummer, Christopher 132, 164
Point Break 233
Poitier, Sidney 117, 260, 264
Power Rangers Time Force **58**
Predator 7, 8, 13-14, 113, 114, 117, 118, **119**, 119, 177, 208, 210, 211
Presley, Elvis 81
Project X 343, 344, 345
Prowse, David 162
Pryce, Jonathan 304
Puck, Wolfgang 237
Pyun, Albert 337-338

Quatermass and the Pit 355, 358, 359
Quick and the Dead, The 7, 19-20

Radner, Gilda 282
Raiders of the Lost Ark 5, 177, 315-320, **316**, **319**, 321, 322, 326
Rambo III 21, 130, 226
Rambo: First Blood Part II 2, 135, 137, **141**, 142, 369, **370**, 370, 377, 379-379
Rapid Fire 219, 228, 229, **230**
Real Genius 279, 282, 284
Red Heat 5, 7, 15, **16**
Redgrave, Vanessa 193-194
Reed, Oliver 149, 159-160
Reeve, Christopher 147, 160, 162-163, 169, 176

Reeves, Keanu 133, 228, **350**
Reitman, Ivan 281
Remar, James 248, 249
Replacement Killers, The 219, 227
Rethwisch, Gus 101-111, **102**, **104**, **107**
Return of the Jedi 267, 269, 275, 364
Reynolds, Burt 330, 335
Richard, Tony 194
Richards, Terry 320
Rickman, Alan xi, 177, 178, 179, **179**, 180, 181, 192-193, 202-203, 216, 226, 235, 236, 299, 346, 348
Road House 27, 35-36, 216, 234
Roberts, Gary 233
Robin Hood: Prince of Thieves 178
Robinson, Andrew 259-266, **260**, **262**, **264**, **266**
RoboCop 2, 89-91, **90**, 92-97, **92**, **95**, **96**, 327, **328**, 328, 330, 331, **332**, 332-334, 335, 336, 341, 375
RoboDoc 330
Rock, The 109, 231, 386
Rocky 125, 136, 137, 142, 210
Roddenberry, Gene 339
Rodman, Dennis 324
Rodriguez, Robert 389
Rothrock, Cynthia 124, 128-129
Rourke, Mickey 324
Running Man, The 7, 8, **14**, 101, **102**, 102-103, **104**, 105, 106, 107-109, 111
Russell, John **292**, 293
Russell, Ken 188
Russell, Kurt 28, 38

Sadler, William 343-354, **344**, **347**, **350**, **353**
Saint, The 356, 361
Salinger, Matt 337
Salkind, Alexander and Ilya 148-149, 158-159, 160, 161
Saturday Night Live 281-282
Savage, Milo 74
Saxon, John 82
Say Anything... 36

Schwarzenegger, Arnold 1, 2, 7, 8, 9, 10, 12, 13-14, **14**, 15-16, **16**, 21-22, 42, **42**, 51, 52-53, **53**, 54, 55, 67-68, 73-74, 101-102, **102**, 103, 105, 106, 107-108, 109, 113, 114, 117, **118**, **119**, 124, 127, 133, 140, 175-176, 231, 242, 251, 252, **336**, 338, 339
Scorpion King, The 101, 109
Scott, Ridley 8, 18, 19, 336
Seagal, Steven 22-23, 86-87, 127, 128, 231, 344, 345, 346-347
Selleck, Tom 103
Shawshank Redemption, The 89, 97, 98-99, 343, 344, 352-353, **353**
Shelley, Barbara 359
Shoot to Kill 259, 260, 264, **264**
Siegel, Don 262
Silence of the Lambs, The 354
Silver Streak 165
Silver, Joel 10, 12, 13, 49, 51, 54, 63, 117-118, 208, 210, 211, 214, 216, 223, 224, 226, 235, 244, 250, 252, 348
Sinatra, Frank 151, 157
Smith, Charles 251
Smith, Kevin 16, 167, 401
Smith, Kurtwood 89, **92**, 94, 335-336
Sniper 2 207, 217
Soldier, The 383
Spengler, Pierre 160
Spielberg, Steven 1, 55, 56-57, 316, 317, 318, 320, 322, 362, 363, 366
Splash 171-172
Spy Trap 367
Spy Who Loved Me, The 5, 164, 267, 276-277
Stahelski, Chad 253
Stallone, Sylvester 1, 2, 21-22, 38, 127, 133, **141**, 142, 226, 227, 266, 369, **370**, 371, 375, 378-379
Stamp, Terrence 148, 161, 167
Star Trek V: The Final Frontier 301, **309**, 309
Star Trek VI: The Undiscovered Country 123, 132, 301, 309

Star Trek: Deep Space Nine 259-260, 265, **266**, 349
Star Trek: The Next Generation 309-310, 339-340, **340**
Star Wars: Episode II - Attack of the Clones 269 Empire
Stewart, Patrick 309-310, 339-340
Stone, Mike 76, 78
Street Fighter 27, 36
Strunholtz, Cuno 142
Sum of All Fears, The 9, 15
Superman 121, 147, 148, 149, 151, 158, 160, 161, 162, 163, 164, 167, 168, 169-170, 171, 172, 173, 175, 176
Superman II 147-149 **148**, 151, **152**, 158-164, 167-170, **168**, **170**
Superman II: The Donner Cut 149, 160, 163, 164, 167-170 176
Swayze, Patrick 35-36, 216, 336, 339

Tales from the Crypt 348, 352
Tales from the Crypt: Demon Knight **347**
Teenage Mutant Ninja Turtles II 301, 314
Thatcher, Margaret 67
Thorsen, Sven-Ole 7-25, **8**, **11**, **14**, **16**, **17**, **20**, **23**, 109
Three Musketeers, The 149, 159-160
Time After Time 301, 304-305, 306
Time Bandits 61, 63, 68, 301, 302-303, 304, **305**, 306, 308
Titanic 301, 303, 304, 311-312, **311**, 314
Tolkin, Michael 337
Top Gun 197, 198, 199, **199**, 204, 206
Total Recall 2, 15, 62, 327, 328, 333, 335-337, **336**, 340, 341
TRON 301-302, **302**, 304, 307, 308
Turner, Kathleen 172
Twin Peaks 241, 256-257
Twins 7, 101, 105, 109
Two Men Went to War 359

Untouchables, The 289, **290**, 290, 293-294

Urquidez, Benny "The Jet" 27-39, **28, 30, 34, 37**

Vajna, Andy 15
Vamp 290, 296-297
Van Damme, Jean-Claude 2, 23-24, 31-32, 38, 124, 127, 128, 129-130, 133, 220, 229-231, 317, 324, 375
Vanity 210-211
VelJohnson, Reginald 214
Ventura, Jesse "The Body" 14, 103, 211
Verhoeven, Paul 92, 93, 94, 97, 328, 330, 331, 332, 333, 335, 336, 338
Voight, Jon 330
Von Homburg, Wilhelm 234

Walker Texas Ranger 86, 197, 198, 204, **205**, 290
Walker, Paul 391
Wall, Robert 71-88, **72, 77, 81**
Warner, David 299, 301-314, **302, 305, 309, 311, 313**
Warriors, The 2, 223, 241, **242**, 242, 244-249, **245, 247**, 250, 254
Way of the Dragon, The 71, 72, 73, 78-80
Wayne, John 110, 208
Weathers, Carl 1, 14, **120**, 208-210, 211
Weintraub, Fred 84, 86
Weintraub, Jerry 137, 139
Weiss, Joel 248
Welch, Raquel 159-160
Weller, Peter 89, 90, **92**, 97
Wells, Vernon 2, 41-59, **42, 44, 48, 50, 53, 54, 58**
Western, Bill 187
Wheels on Meals 27, **28**, 28, 32-34, 35
White, Michael Jai 87
Wild Bill 216
Williams, Owen 290
Willis, Bruce 1, 2, 133, 179, 180, 184, **184**, 191-192, 200, 214, 215, 231, 284, 285
Wilson, Don "The Dragon" 36, 124, 134
Winter, Alex 228, **350**

Wise, Ray 89, 90, 94, 97
Wisniewski, Andreas 183-195, **184, 186, 190**, 215, 233, 236
Wong, Douglas 222
Wright, Edgar 322, 323
Wyatt Earp 135, **143**, 143, 145

Yamasaki, Kiyo 12
Yeung, Bolo 84
York, Susannah 149, 159
Yuen, Corey 128
Yun-Fat, Chow 227

Zabka, William 135, 136, 137
Zimmerman, Herman 111
Zombie Hunter 297